THE COMMON LIFE

AMBIGUITY, AGREEMENT, AND THE STRUCTURE OF MORALS

THE COMMON LIFE

AMBIGUITY, AGREEMENT,
AND THE
STRUCTURE OF MORALS

BURTON ZWIEBACH

TEMPLE UNIVERSITY PRESS • PHILADELPHIA

Temple University Press, Philadelphia 19122
Copyright © 1988 by Burton Zwiebach.   All rights reserved
Published 1988
Printed in the United States of America

The paper used in this publication meets the minimum requirements of American National Standard for Information Sciences—Permanence of Paper for Printed Library Materials, ANSI Z39.48-1984

Library of Congress Cataloguing-in-Publication Data

Zwiebach, Burton
  The common life : ambiguity, agreement, and the structure of morals / Burton Zwiebach.
    p.   cm.
  Includes index.
  ISBN 0-87722-530-3 (alk. paper) :
  1. Ethics.   I. Title.
BJ1012.Z84   1988
170—dc19
                                                87-20151
                                                  CIP

Designed by Adrianne Onderdonk Dudden

TO MICHAEL AND PETER

CONTENTS

Preface ix

PART ONE
RATIONALITY

1 *The Limits of Rationality* 3
2 *Morality as a Temper* 23

PART TWO
THE CONSTRUCTION OF MORALITY

3 *The Use and Abuse of Community* 57
4 *Moral Rules* 85
5 *Structuring Principles* 105

PART THREE
THE STRUCTURING PRINCIPLES IN PRACTICE

6 *Freedom* 129
7 *Equality* 157
8 *Civility* 177

Notes 207
Index 213

PREFACE

Titles that inform can also mislead. I want to take special care that that is not the case with this book. For this is not a book about community in the ordinary sense of that word. The life referred to in the title is our moral life: what I seek to do is explore the common basis of that life.

We can cope with the ambiguity and uncertainty that characterize moral life only through common action. That, at any rate, is what I shall argue. Morality is necessarily a common enterprise. But while this is one of the most important things to say about morality, it is not the only thing. Nor does the concept of a common enterprise require us to think of agreement as the sole, or even definitive, means of determining the content of moral principles. The common life is a more complex, more subtle conception. It speaks to a way of life built on common action, but common action structured in a particular way. Indeed, one crucial argument of this book is that structuring (and therefore constraining) common action is not merely consistent with the idea of a common life, but virtually demanded by it.

If that is so, it would be foolhardy to assume that the concept of the common life has clear social or institutional implications—that, for instance, it is reducible to particular institutional forms, such as small democratic communities, or to particular moral practices, such as civic republicanism or collectivism. It is, of course, tempting to anticipate the sorts of arguments that one may expect from a moral theory that refers to a common life. But a reader who does attempt to anticipate them will probably be wrong. My initial conclusion about community is a minimal one: at the outset, community stands for nothing more profound than a model of the practices needed to justify a moral theory. If one wishes to anticipate possible arguments, this might be a safe place to start. Let the book take over from there.

At the risk of seeming arch, I want to explain why I have omitted much of the panoply of scholarly argument that frequently characterizes works of philosophy and political theory. There are, in this book, only a few intensive discussions of other philosophers. Missing are discussions of Oakeshott, MacIntyre, Habermas, and Walzer, to mention only a few obvious examples. Some readers may be troubled by these omissions. They find it helpful to see how an author reacts to cognate works, or distinguishes his ideas from those of others. The reason I do not do this has nothing to do with a general rejection of the practice itself; and it certainly has nothing to do with the worth of the books I ignore. On the contrary, many of them are books I greatly admire, or that have influenced the course of contemporary moral and political thinking.

But the point is that this is not a book about contemporary moral and political thinking. It is a book about morals and politics, an attempt to come to terms with particular aspects of human action. And the two projects are not at all the same. While consideration of the former may certainly cast light on the latter, it usually does so in specific circumstances. One must decide whether it is in or out of place in each specific work. In this case, much of that discussion seems to me out of place, irrelevant to my purposes. I discuss the works of others—such as Rawls and Nozick—where the discussion advances the argument, or is necessary to clarify it, and refrain from discussion where it does not. For example, it must be clear that my conceptions of agreement and convention differ enormously from Walzer's (in *Spheres of Justice*). But, as I am unable to see how my argument would be enhanced or clarified by setting these differences out (except, perhaps, to show that there *are* differences), I have refrained from doing it. Similarly,

I do not see that my rejection of discursive models of agreement would gain in strength or clarity from a critique of Habermas; our differences are on too basic a level. And I assume that readers to whom these differences matter will be familiar enough with Habermas' work, as with Walzer's, to see them without my having to point them out.

There are undoubtedly some who see scholarly discussion as a legitimizer of inquiry. I profoundly disagree with that view. I believe that the most economical construction of an argument is the best, and that we should strive to avoid the loss of clarity and narrative direction that often accompanies extended discussion of others' works. But I do not think that this is the place to argue that point. Probably nothing I could say would anyway dissuade advocates of scholarly discussion from condemning, or at least resenting, my practice. They may be right. Perhaps it is simply that my tastes run to a different style of analysis. And speaking of tastes, I must add that economy of analysis and style suggests to me one other practice: the limiting of footnotes. I have footnoted where I thought it was necessary and refrained (as the reader will already have noticed) where at all possible, on the (I hope) sensible ground that footnotes distract readers and distractions are the last thing that readers need.

A number of people have stimulated my thinking about morals and politics. Peter Manicas of the Queens College Philosophy Department has been a close and encouraging reader and critic of much that I have written. Irving Leonard Markovitz and Henry Morton of Political Science, and Charles W. Smith of Sociology have been, sometimes unwittingly, sounding boards for some of the ideas that found their way into this work. Equally important, I have been helped by, and have learned a great deal about philosophy and politics from, all of them. Finally, I owe a debt of thanks to Christian Bay for his help on this work in particular and for aid and encouragement over the years.

I owe a debt also to a most peculiar academic institution. Scholars speak passionately of the importance of collegiality; but collegiality has become a casualty of the academic marketplace, a rare phenomenon in an increasingly alienating environment. So I am particularly pleased to mention an extraordinary exception to this pattern—a group of about thirty Queens College professors (mostly social scientists) who meet each Monday for lunch and discussion. For about a decade, this Monday Lunch Group has provided its members and its many guest speakers with opportunities to test ideas and present on-going research, and to have them subjected to serious analysis and criticism. The range of presentations and discussions has provided us with an unparalleled education in all areas of social theory and practice.

I have also learned much from my fellow members of the Columbia University Seminar on Content and Methods in the Social Sciences, before whom I presented the substance of the first chapter of this book. I have benefited enormously from the variety of their interests and the consistently high quality of their papers and discussions.

Since a book is rarely the product of a single mind, it is a pleasure to acknowledge the efforts of those who contributed to the creation of this one.

PART ONE

RATIONALITY

1
THE LIMITS OF RATIONALITY

CHARACTERIZING ACTIONS

The subject of morality is action—human behavior informed by purpose and intention. Action reflects our existence as moral beings who choose, evaluate, hope, fear, judge, sin. Now I shall argue that action is ambiguous and that this ambiguity compromises our attempts to make rational moral judgments—judgments that claim to be analytically valid or right. I shall not argue that the irrational and ambiguous nature of human action prevents us from framing rational propositions about it. This is a position that is both trite and fallacious. I shall argue instead that we cannot characterize action in a way that is sufficient to yield categorical judgments.

The ambiguity of action is partly the result of complexities in the concept of intention. In dealing with the concept of action, philosophers sometimes separate intention from motivation and ask only whether the act is the result of an actor's conscious mental processes. In simple cases, this sort of approach (however incomplete or naive it may seem to the psychologist) presents no problem to the moral philosopher. If A points a gun at B, pulls the trigger, and shoots him, and if A is not drugged, mad, etcetera, it is not confusing to say that he intended to shoot B. In other cases, however, the separation of intention from motivation creates misleading pictures of human action. A human action is an attempt to bring about an end, and it is this end that is the object of the actor's intention. But suppose the end is something more than a discrete and identifiable act. Suppose it is something like manifesting feelings of love for another, or enlisting in the Communist Party, or leaving one's family to join a circus. Such actions involve complex sequences of interrelated behaviors, thoughts, and choices. Can we consider independently the several actions that these complex actions are composed of, rather than take the entire complex sequence to be the action? Furthermore, in describing the intentions behind these sequences, we are bound to ask whether a simple rational characterization of intention will do. Will it not obscure the extent to which such actions are accompanied by feelings of ambivalence, confusion, anxiety, guilt, and so on? And if it does obscure this, will it not affect the philosopher's account of the moral choices involved, and so render his recommendations trivial or irrelevant? Put another way, the feelings of ambivalence, confusion, and so on affect the actor's intentions and his conception of his ends. Where his intentions exist in a state of tension, action is the attempt to resolve that tension. Often, that is, we discover or create our intention through action. The process of action often reveals to us the nature of our dilemmas or doubts and helps us to define our intentions; and the characterization of action is often a record of incomplete resolution of tension. In this sense, the characterization of action is the characterization, not of intentions in any clear sense, but of ambiguities and contradictions, or of intentions whose identity even may vary from action to action.

If being in love partly satisfies a desire to possess the beloved (as Robert Briffault somewhere suggests), are the acts involved in manifesting one's love to be understood in terms of simply rendered conscious mental processes? What role does anxiety or guilt play in the concept of intention? What does the word "intention" mean in the case of a person whose actions reflect divided or conflicting allegiances? Is the separate characterization of related actions sufficient to satisfy the moral philosopher if the actions reflect contradiction or ambiguity?

The supposition that it is (like the belief that the preceding questions are irrelevant) can be defended if the moral philosopher

5   *The Limits of Rationality*

is content not to prescribe or recommend, evaluate or judge. But if he wants to do these things, if he wants to advance views of right or good that can exist in the world he writes about (that is, the world of action), then he cannot ignore the extent to which human action is enmeshed in a context of ambiguity and contradiction.

Ignoring that context need not, of course, destroy the logical coherence or elegance of the theory. Powerful arguments can be made for analytical conceptions of morality that dispense with appeals to the tensions and anxieties that surround human action. No one can deny, for example, the architectonic power of categorical morality, derived as it is from the awesome arguments of Kant. At the same time, we may be impressed with the old complaint that categorical morality ignores the confusions and uncertainties that characterize moral action and, in doing so, trivializes the enterprise of morality. For moral decisions are attempts to resolve moral dilemmas. Moral actions are often *explorations of intentions*—the means by which we try to understand ourselves in tension. And dilemmas exist precisely because we cannot rid ourselves of doubt, confusion, guilt, uncertainty, anxiety, ambivalence. If we ignore this context, we make things easy for ourselves and thus falsify the most obvious—and the most crucial—element of human moral experience.

The first question we need to address is not the subtle and difficult one of how to analyze action or intention, or how to deal with complexity and ambiguity. The first question is much more elemental: how can a moral philosopher characterize action? The moral philosopher must, at some point, force himself to ignore complexity and ambiguity; at some point he must take an action in some stated form and ask how it is related to moral rules or values. This is ordinarily done by trying to *characterize* action—by giving an action a name that stands for its character and that the philosopher may then employ in determining its relation to rules and values. Thus, if we say it is wrong to kill, it is because we have some idea of what killing means—of the actions comprehended by the word.

Now, suppose I live in a dictatorship where attendance at certain meetings is proscribed. I am asked by the police whether my friend, Jones, was at such a meeting, and I know that he was. Nevertheless, I answer that he was not. How may my act be characterized? Clearly, it may be characterized as a lie. But that is to take the words I use to answer the police to be the entire action, rather than a part of the action. For, in truth, my action may be much more complex, depending on my intentions. Suppose my first concern, the focus of my intentions, was to protect my friend from the police. Or suppose I saw my words as having two different effects: conveying information to the police or signifying the extent of my devotion to my friend. My act may be characterized not merely as a lie but also as an act of support for, or devotion to, a friend. It may also, depending on the circumstances, be a conscientious act of disobedience of authority, a refusal to cooperate with a tyrannical regime, an expression of courage. Each of these characterizations speaks to a different aspect of my intentions.[1]

To characterize my action so that it is uniquely related to a moral rule is to decide that one of these aspects is of predominant importance. How do I show this? The contention that one aspect of my intentions is predominant may be supported by considering my subjective motivation, by getting a disinterested person's opinion of my intentions, by trying to weigh the consequences of my action, and so forth. But can this question be merely methodological? If the purpose of characterizing an action is to be able to relate it to a moral value or rule, the mode of characterizing actions must be one that yields characterizations that fit the conceptual framework of the theory that justifies the value or rule. In characterizing actions, a Kantian cannot weigh consequences nor a utilitarian motives without introducing radical incoherence into his moral philosophy at the outset.

Nor does adopting a particular moral philosophy necessarily resolve the difficulty of characterizing an action. For example, it might seem that a Kantian could allow an individual to characterize his own action, so long as its maxim could be made into a universal law. But as soon as we attempt to create that universal law, we can see that this argument does not work. I may agree with Kant that lying is wrong because the very concept of a moral order requires that we be able to rely on other people's affirmations. On the other hand, a moral order involves, by definition, voluntary submission to standards. And such voluntary submission cannot take place except where people recognize the need for some mutuality of concern for each other.[2] Indeed, a moral order may be defined in

7   The Limits of Rationality

terms of mutuality of concern, without which morality cannot begin to deal with the problem of the good will or, indeed, advance beyond a primitive Hobbesian condition. If this is so, both lying *and* abandoning this mutuality of concern fail a Kantian test. Now this means—returning to my example of the police inquiry into Jones's activities—that Kant requires me to tell the police both that Jones was present at the meeting (thereby not lying) and that he was not present (thereby not rejecting my commitment to mutuality of concern).

To be able to create a categorical law, one must be able to characterize an action in such a way as to exclude all other characterizations—or, in a looser version, to exclude all other characterizations whose implications are inconsistent with the one chosen. That means that the characterization of the action *cannot* be a product of subjective judgment, but must be a unique rational inference drawn from the behavior itself. We might ask what intention we may ascribe to an ideal rational actor. But then everything would turn on the attributes we assign to that actor, and it is by no means certain that we would all agree on what these attributes were, or that the concept of rationality is so circumscribed that it admits of only a single consistent set of attributes. What is required to characterize action so that it can be uniquely related to moral rules or values is not merely agreement on a moral philosophy but agreement on, or demonstration of, a single and exclusive concept of rationality as well. In the absence of such an agreement or demonstration, the characterization of action remains problematical. Even with such an agreement or demonstration, there is no guarantee that characterization will be free from dispute: agreement or demonstration may merely reduce the range of disputed characterizations. If this is so, morality remains enmeshed in a context of doubt, ambivalence, confusion, disagreement. There are, of course, other sources of doubt in morality, but the ambiguity of human action is certainly one of the most critical. It allows us to understand why many people who have reflected seriously on the problem of moral choice see those choices as attempts, not merely to do the right or the good, but to resolve the dilemmas that characterize the enterprise of morality.

Suppose, however, I say that, while we cannot characterize, say, the action of lying, we can agree, on a common sense level, that certain acts do constitute lying and are wrong. Could we not start here and slowly build agreements on a number of actions we call lying, until a relatively comprehensive rule emerges?

The solution is undoubtedly tempting, especially to Americans, who fancy that this is the way their law develops. But what, exactly, do we expect will emerge? Surely, a comprehensive moral rule presumes—on pain of arbitrariness—some rational means to relate the different elements of behavior it comprehends. Saying that a comprehensive rule *emerges* does not relieve us of the need to show why and how the rule *is* comprehensive. And to do this, we must be able to characterize action in the appropriate way.

Perhaps we can do without a comprehensive rule and rely on common sense agreements that certain acts constitute lying. We should then come to be governed by a myriad of rules, each applying to a particular aspect of human action and—because they could not be related to each other in any way except *ad hoc*—logically discrete and the subjects of endless dispute and claims of exception. So this alternative cannot work either.

CONFLICTING CONCEPTS OF RATIONALITY

I suggested earlier that we have neither demonstrated nor agreed to an exclusively valid concept of rationality. It is now time to pursue this suggestion. To argue against an exclusively valid concept of rationality is not to reject rationality altogether. But it is to alter our understanding of it. It is to see rationality not as an objective principle, sovereign over human thinking, but, with Dewey, as the product of human thinking and invention. The concept of rationality refers to the rationality of human beings, because no other sort of rationality can be known to us. It cannot refer to the rationality of an ideal or abstract being, for we cannot know how such a being would think. And if human beings invent concepts of rationality, they necessarily invest these concepts with meanings that reflect human judgments.

These judgments can concern many things. For instance, the idea that an ultimate reality can be perceived or imagined gives rise to a concept of rationality that must leave itself open to this perception. Rationality, then, comes to be seen as the mode of perceiving reality or as a process that mirrors this mode. It can be seen in terms of logical dialectic (Plato) or historical dialectic (Hegel) and so on. But this concept of rationality will differ radically from Dewey's, which reflects his more relativist, instrumental, open-ended, and experimental conception of knowledge, or from a concept like Russell's, which reflects his concern with rigorous description of what is "out there."

Or consider the currently popular Weberian conception of rationality as taking the most appropriate means to a given end. There is a sense in which the plausibility of this view depends on our willingness to conceive of the possibility of individual ends. That is, we must be able to understand the concept "end" to be something that can be developed independently by individuals and that can be relevant to individuals alone and apart from their association with others or with a higher truth. Liberal individualist theory, which sees the terms of human association to be products of agreements between independent individuals, is especially hospitable to the Weberian conception. But the Weberian conception stands in direct contrast to other views of rationality, such as the medieval view (where ends and means are conceived in terms of a divinely ordered existence and, therefore, never free of moral connotations) or the Hegelian view (where ends and means are rational because they participate in a process of development toward the absolute). In these latter views, rationality is an attribute of the context in which action is enmeshed, whereas, in the former, rationality is an attribute of action itself.

Now, how can the choice of one particular version of rationality be justified? How can we say that one version is exclusively valid? One way is to show that the version is entailed in a conception that is richer and more extensive than the concept of rationality itself. Examples of such richer conceptions are God, reality, and nature. Now, we may use a richer conception to demonstrate the *exclusive* validity of a particular version of rationality only where that conception is in some sense ultimately true or valid. But such truth or validity can be demonstrated only by appeal to a conception, or principle, richer and more extensive than it, and so on, *ad infinitum*. Alternatively, the truth or validity of the conception may rest on an intuitive apprehension quite beyond communication. It is beyond communication because, to believers it is the *source* of standards of reliable demonstration and, to skeptics, it is the *consequence* of employing such standards, which the skeptics doubt exist. In any event, its acceptance is surely a matter essentially of faith. And this is hardly the firmest foundation for a concept of rationality, let alone one that claims to be exclusively valid.

If we reject this argument, we can try to show that a particular concept of rationality provides the best description of human action, or makes possible the development of theories that provide the best descriptions. We cannot make this argument unless we can characterize the actions that the theory describes; for, otherwise, we should not be able to show that it provides the best descriptions. But we cannot characterize these actions without an exclusively valid theory of rationality. So we have a circle: we cannot characterize action without an exclusively valid theory of rationality and we cannot create an exclusively valid theory of rationality without being able to characterize action.

We might try to escape this circularity by developing a theory of rationality unrelated to action. Such a theory would be limited to propositions or protocols concerning abstract discourse. It might, for instance, deal with the rigor or coherence of deductive arguments, or with the logical uses to which evidence may be put. One thinks of logic and mathematics as prime examples of such theories. But there still is no way to prove the exclusive validity of such a theory without appealing to a richer and more extensive concept, thus setting the stage for infinite regress. That such theories, when appropriately used, may be immensely useful and enormously powerful is beyond question. But they cannot be shown to be exclusively valid theories. And because of this, they cannot be used to characterize action.

Rationality, therefore, cannot be thought of as the sovereign form of thinking or as a uniquely valid or objectively true form. There are, as I shall shortly argue, ways to limit indeterminacy and to give rationality a claim to power in moral theory. But that power can never be as absolute as the attribution of exclusive validity implies.

So on two counts the characterization of action is mired in ambiguity. First, it is often a record of the incomplete resolution of the psychological tensions involved in action and points to confused, ambiguous, or contradictory intentions. Second, it requires a single and exclusively valid theory of rationality that cannot be demonstrated. And all of this difficulty is compounded by the fact that characterization is something we learn to do. Our conceptions of intention and action reflect—although they are obviously not wholly determined by—the impressions and perceptions, the habits of thought and expectations, we acquire in the process of acculturation.

LEARNING MORAL CONCEPTS

Philosophers who understand the enormous impact of language on action sometimes ignore the impact of action on language, and hence on moral concepts. Now since the general proposition that action influences language may be too commonplace to need argument, I shall pursue only a particular aspect of it. In doing this, I shall assume the validity of the empirical claims involved in the argument. I do this to avoid extraneous discussion, but I think the assumptions justified in any case.

Before we learn and employ moral rules, we need to develop and understand a repertory of moral concepts. Now we do not encounter moral concepts (such as loving, lying, work, responsibility, and so on) in the abstract or in a logical universe. We encounter them in action—in the context of particular dilemmas and situations. It is in these contexts that we tacitly develop understandings of their meanings. Our attention is focused, not on a universe of possible meanings, but on particular forms of actions, practices, and situations. In the particular case, these shape our sense of the scope and applicability of the moral concept and so tacitly help to structure—although not determine—our understanding of it. This is not, of course, a once-for-all learning process. Our understandings change and grow more complex as we gain more and different experiences. The comprehension of moral concepts is an on-going process of developing tacit understandings.

I shall, with some trepidation, call these actions, practices, and situations the *referents* of a moral concept because, when we use a concept, we unconsciously refer to them, or tacitly incorporate them into our understandings. In a developed culture, there undoubtedly exists a body of related activities and practices that constitute, in effect, a store of referents. But this cannot lead to the belief that culture makes a universal understanding of moral concepts possible. We certainly become progressively familiar with the culture's store of referents and, as we develop such a familiarity, we begin to comprehend common usages of moral symbols and concepts. But this gives us only additional contexts that we may incorporate into our understandings. For we comprehend common usages in contexts of action and so on, and since these contexts may be expected to vary, we may expect that our understandings even of common usages will vary as well. So our common usages may be multiple, ambiguous, even conflicting. The existence of a developed culture, with its store of referents, certainly narrows the range of possible understandings. But this is far from saying that it produces a set of universal understandings.

Referents are mostly learned by absorbing certain practices or by internalizing certain norms without consciously or reflectively knowing so. We internalize a way of seeing or perceiving certain things or actions, and every time we seek to use these things in conscious thought, we use them in the sense in which we have internalized them. That is, we think of them in the particular way in which we have internalized them. So when these things are reduced to language—when they are named or used in sentences—our understanding of them reflects the way they have been shaped by our subliminal experiences. The substitution of words that name things or actions for abstract symbols introduces an indeterminacy into our "rational" accounts of the world, because not all people have the same experiences. Words acquire overtones or shadings that are often not understood, but that nevertheless are incorporated into, and shape, our language usages.

But may we not say that, while we use different referents, things even out in the end so that there is a general understanding worked out in society, with a common referential sediment coming into being?

I think that such an answer abuses the concept of what is common and suggests a very misleading set of agreements. Referents do not function to vary the general meanings of words or the rules of usage so as to impose a serious degree of relativism on language. Such a conclusion would be a superficial and unwar-

13 *The Limits of Rationality*

ranted extension of my argument. I suggest only that referents affect the way we perceive and characterize concepts because we learn these concepts in the context of actions and practices and situations. Referents merely impose a degree of variability on the things that rule-bound words comprehend. So societies may "agree" about the formal meaning of words and establish rules concerning their usage. It is not possible for societies to agree on the referents incorporated into those words by its members for the simple reason that this incorporation is tacit and the members are unaware of the differences in referents or are unable to specify them with anything resembling clarity and precision. If we tacitly understand a word in the context of particular referents, then we must acknowledge that, absent identical experiences, we are likely to understand it differently than others. This difference in understanding will undoubtedly not extend to all aspects of a concept and will undoubtedly not affect our characterizations in many circumstances. Still, it will affect some aspects or characterizations, and we cannot say which. And if everyone's understanding is affected in this way, then we cannot conflate what *we ascribe* to a word with what *is ascribed* to it, or state the range of actions it is *generally* understood to refer to. This suggests a shared experience that does not exist. It is also misleading to speak of a common referential sediment, for the word "common" would have to stand for the outcome of a practice that has never taken place.

It might be clearer, at this point, to adopt the view that a word is a structure. It is composed of rules regarding meanings, rules regarding usage, and rules (if we can call them rules) that determine the actions, the parcels of experience, the segments of the world that that word relates to or incorporates. These latter rules are affected by referents that modify—sometimes slightly, sometimes greatly—the actions, practices, and situations comprehended by the word. Hence, referents impose a degree of indeterminacy on the senses, if not the agreed-upon meanings, of words. Our conception of a word is affected by subliminally absorbed experiences and perceptions. In the absence of an ability to make this subliminal absorption wholly conscious and to describe a typical pattern of experiences that subliminally shapes our understanding of the word and that corresponds to an objectively determinable shaping pattern, we cannot escape this indeterminacy.

We may take a word like "love" to refer to intentions or actions associated with care and concern. A strict parent may be said by his child to act out of love for her, and this may confuse another child who has been raised to believe that concern entails encouraging her participation in decisions that affect her. The issue is not who is right, but whether the children understand the word "love" in a way that allows them to characterize actions similarly. Or consider how the meaning and usage of a concept like "work" are affected by our sense of what makes work fulfilling or alienating.

This should not be taken to mean that our ability to entertain any particular concept depends on our having had the relevant concrete experiences. It is clearly possible to grasp a concept by the use of reason. Of course, some referents will have been incorporated into the structure of the word and our usage will reflect that incorporation, whether we realize it or not. As we continue to use it, however, we tacitly expand, contract, or modify the referents incorporated in it, until the word begins to reflect our own experiences. At this point, we may find ourselves applying the concept differently.

In short, referents do not prevent us from rethinking the meanings of abstract moral terms or from creating new and radical moral propositions. But they do affect the way we perceive and understand moral concepts and, therefore, moral action; and they influence the way we relate moral concepts to action or develop their implications. And, clearly, they affect our perception and evaluation of dilemmas and situations. In doing these things, they tacitly modify the abstract nature of moral discourse and convert abstract categories into concrete practical ones.

The impact of referents raises two objections to the use of the concept of universality in moral theory. One of these objections is strong and the other weak. Let me consider the strong objection first. Every substantive moral proposition must be read in conjunction with referents that influence our understanding of moral action and the way we relate moral concepts to action. This tacitly structures our perception of the scope of action relevant to the proposition, and thus structures our understanding of the proposition itself. The universality of the proposition is limited in the sense that the actions comprehended by the proposition are themselves limited by referents. Put another way, a proposition may be

15   The Limits of Rationality

universal in form, but our understanding of it is limited by our understanding of the actions comprehended by it. By imposing restrictions on the actions that are, so to speak, incorporated into the proposition as we understand it, referents impose restrictions on its universality as well.

Next, consider the weak objection. Once we move from the use of abstract symbols to moral words, we can never know the extent to which our understanding of moral language is restricted by referents. Indeed, we cannot even isolate, in a rigorous way, the referents that might have influenced us. But because we cannot know what influence referents have on our moral language, we can never be certain that the universal terms of a proposition are in fact universal.

The limits of universality in action compromise moral theories—such as categorical theories—that decisively depend upon it. For example, a social contract theory such as John Rawls's cannot work if the actions comprehended by its values cannot be given a unique and definitive meaning. But if the characterization of actions and the understanding of moral concepts reflects the limits imposed by the impact of referents, then how would we decide which characterizations and meanings are appropriate to the original position? The role played by referents suggests at least the probability that such factors as the experience of political association would lead to changes in our understanding of the symbols and practices associated with any particular moral value. In that case, we cannot assume that, having experienced association, we would understand that value as it was understood in the original position. For example, our understanding of equality might be one that emphasizes a sense of community. It does so because we have come to understand that this sense is indispensable to that mutual respect of each other's worth as human beings that is a crucial basis of self-respect. Such a view might plausibly imply that the value of equality transcends the more immediate benefits available under the difference principle; and this might lead us to reject inequalities altogether. Or if, as Bernard Williams suggests, some of the force of equality comes from the belief that it affirms a pre-existing natural equality,[3] the perception of limited natural equality might lead to a more restricted notion of equality than Rawls proposes. The medieval conception of equality was radically affected by the understanding that inequality reflected the divine ordering. The widespread commitment to inequality in the nineteenth century reflected, in some part, the conclusions of nineteenth-century science, however, inadequate that science may seem to us. It would be hard to imagine a thirteenth- or a nineteenth-century version of the original position yielding the difference principle.

IMAGINATION AND REASON

It is easy to jump to the conclusion that, as social practices influence our moral conceptions and our characterizations of action, any attempt to escape from relativism is vain: what you can't say, you can't say, and you can't whistle it either. But that jump is not justified. For if we cannot escape from the influence of social practice, we are not entirely prisoners of it either. There are various ways to modify the restraints imposed on us by referents.

For example, art is a process of constant reconsideration of referents and action. The artist can explore action and perception, as well as the language in which they are expressed. Of course, she may become obscure as she gropes about in the unexplored territory of action or language. Indeed, we often hear an artist say that she does not understand something she has written or painted. But she has an intuitive belief that a particular reaction of a character, or a particular extension of a line, is right or appropriate; and she may strive to figure out *why* it is so. Or an artist may become abstract as she tries to understand the elements of her artistic language. While people have objected to abstraction and obscurity, that objection is less often heard today. We have come to accept these things, perhaps because we recognize the crucial role they play in advancing our understanding of ourselves and our sense, or perception, of our world. The social role of art is to examine critically the scope and texture of human action and perception—to make us see, as Conrad put it. But, as we can be made to see in unusual as well as in conventional ways, art may fulfil its social role when it forces us to *experience* language, form, sound, color, and so forth outside of any traditional (or, indeed, comprehensible) context.

In the framework of moral action art can, by creating, imaginative contexts and dwelling on internal conflicts, help us to break free of the limits imposed by existing referents. For this reason, it has a crucial role to play, not merely with respect to philosophy, but with respect to social science as well. The social scientist, according to conventional theory, must be able to relate the concepts she uses to a deductively derived model. Even where social science allows considerable latitude for development within that model, the model's power ordinarily restricts the range of usable concepts to those relevant to it. So only in the rarest of circumstances, and after the most rigorous of arguments, can radically different understandings of concepts be legitimated and accepted. No such limit is placed on the artist. Her principal constraints range from a mere need for plausibility to the need for some kind of consistency of vision. Freed from the constraints on language and conceptualization imposed by models, she is able to entertain possibilities that the social scientist is not. Artists, then, can expand the understanding of social scientists and, in doing so, add greatly to the power of social theories. (It should be unnecessary to add that I do not intend the last two paragraphs to constitute a theory of art, a description of its purposes—whatever that means—or anything like that.)

Another way to modify the restraints imposed by referents is to employ history in a particular way. Certain understandings of human action or moral concepts may be unfamiliar to us. But, if these understandings have persisted for a sufficient time, it is plausible to argue that historians may come to recognize them. Once recognized, they can spark an examination of the referents behind them. We may become aware of referentially cognate understandings—that is, understandings different from our own, but nevertheless perceptibly related to the same sorts of actions. The study of these understandings can generate perceptions that allow us to transcend, somewhat, our own understandings. We can, for example, perceive characterizations of action that appear to us to be strange or exotic and, thus sensitized, strive to grasp the referents that led, or might have led, to such characterizations.

The study of history can, then, lead to a sort of *ad hoc* enlargement of our store of referents, and, as the enlarged store of one historian can be communicated to others, to a better grasp of the way moral concepts are understood. Naturally, we cannot assume that this enlarged understanding corresponds to what is needed to characterize action rationally, for we can never be certain that we have exhausted the universe of possible referents. Indeed, this assumption is not simply a logical protocol, but corresponds to our experience of the continuous appearance of different understandings. We also must recognize that the enlarged store will include referents we no longer accept (such, for example, as those associated with magic).

This poses a familiar problem. Clearly, evaluation of past understandings is constrained by the fact that this evaluation must be filtered through present understandings. There are two limited correctives for this. First, we may expect that intersubjective and critical interpretation of the past, resulting from the participation of many people in the process, will help to widen the store of present understandings. Second, the sheer persistence of certain understandings sometimes forces us to recognize them. On occasion, the persistence of a certain characterization of action may even be a reason to accept it as the most persuasive one available. In any case, in taking account of persistent characterizations, we may discover or develop understandings different from our own; or we may be able to widen our understandings so as to grasp those of the past from the point of view, so to speak, of the past. Intersubjectivity and persistence make possible a limited, but significant, escape from present understandings.

Without burdening the reader with more examples of how we may modify the restraints imposed by referents, let me suggests a common property that runs through all of them. It is the exercise of imagination, the act of creativity. I shall not deal with this point now. But I shall soon argue that imagination and creativity are essential to our understanding of moral concepts; and, if the act of moral thinking can be called rational (as I shall suggest it can), they are essential to the concept of reason as well.

I fear that I have spent too much time on referents, considering the role they play in this book. My principal purpose in introducing the concept is to reinforce the argument that it is impossible to characterize an action in an exclusively rational way and, therefore, that it is impossible to justify a categorical morality. My secondary purpose is to show that the challenge of relativism cannot easily be by-passed. For even if we show that different human experiences can be communicated and their centrifugal implications overcome, and that agreements can be reached (within broad cultural limitations), we should have to recognize that these agreements will employ concepts that we tacitly understand in different ways.

RATIONALITY AS THE RECONSTRUCTION OF ARGUMENT

Can the act of moral thinking be called rational? It would appear that my purpose has been to demonstrate the impossibility of rationality, or at least its doubtful utility. But I do not want to be understood to have said that. While I have rejected what I would think is an extravagant version of rationality, I suggest that a looser version is possible. Let me summarize it now, leaving fuller analysis to the next chapter.

What would this looser version look like? I have argued that characterizations of action are, in principle, ambiguous and that we cannot assume that the terms of moral discourse can be given universal meanings. And this leads to a third conclusion. Unless we can produce an exclusively valid definition of rationality, there is no way to know what the rational requirements of a moral order are without taking account, at least tacitly, of the way people actually reason. We have no other sources of information. Consider the problem raised by Kant's argument that it is never right to lie. How, without relying at least tacitly on experience, could Kant arrive at the crucial connection between universal mistrust of words and the negation of moral order? This connection must depend on the sense people have—or are assumed to have—of the uses of promises and affirmations. Only by knowing that we do not apprehend truth in mysterious ways, but depend on communication to get at it, and, therefore, depend on communication to structure our actions, can Kant reach this conclusion.

We may, of course, speak of the decisions of abstract rational persons. But we can create such persons only by determining that certain properties of people are uniquely related to rational action. But as we cannot identify an exclusively valid concept of rationality, we cannot determine the properties uniquely related to it.

Our construction of the abstract rational person is, therefore, always arbitrary.

If these initial observations are valid, we may begin to draw some conclusions. The most obvious conclusion is that we must give up employing the concept of entailment in discourse concerning action. (We may, of course, continue to use the word, much as Hume continued to use "prove," provided we realize the sort of restricted meaning it must have.) Now, giving up the concept of entailment does not justify the conclusion that we must abandon rigorous or controlled argument. We are still entitled to employ inference to determine whether certain propositions or arguments are consistent with each other. We must simply acknowledge that these inferences cannot create uniquely valid or categorical propositions and rules. We are also entitled to draw some conclusions with regard to action where we can show that that action has been persistently and intersubjectively understood in a certain way. This does not allow us to argue that action *must* be understood in this way, but only that it *may be* or *should be*. We may also show that our understandings of action and the inferred propositions and rules reinforce both each other and an identifiable general theory. This imposes a *coherence* on our argument.

Such arguments may be called rational. But they may be called so only if we are willing to accept a looser, less extravagant view of rationality. Rationality, in this view, is a coherent, unified, and controlled argument that claims to describe, explain, or justify an identifiable area of action, but whose claim is supported not by demonstration but by persuasiveness.

If ambiguity and doubt are inescapable in moral discourse, if moral action is partly an attempt to understand and resolve ambiguity and doubt, do we not seem to be condemned, as Sartre would say, to create our own morality? And can this process of creation be thought of as a wholly rational, even logical, process? Clearly not. We need to invent resolutions and actions, and we cannot do this unless we employ insight and intuition. But we do not create without constraints. And the delineation of these constraints seems to be the contribution of rationality.

Rationality, in this view, is not a mode of constructing theories and arguments. It is, rather, a constraint on their construction. Put another way, rationality is not a creative force in theory, but a mode of constraining what is created by other means. It functions, in this sense, retroactively, critically even, to shape existing arguments or theories. A theory cannot be built *ab initio* by rational argument. But once constructed, a theory can make a claim to rationality and, if that claim is successful, can then serve as the basis for further inferences. For this reason, we can expand the conception of rationality and call it a *reconstructive* mode of thinking. Rationality shapes and limits a theoretical construction so that it makes a claim to being coherent, consistent, persuasive. Out of this shaping may come additional inferences and insights—alterations of the original construction and developments from it.

A successful claim to rationality—that is, a claim that a theory (or explanation or justification) is coherent, consistent, and persuasive—does not make a theory uniquely valid. It does graft a degree of validity onto it. A claim to rationality excludes any theory that is clearly and directly inconsistent with it, or that is dependent on characterizations that do not match the claimed rational theory's characterizations in persistence and intersubjective acceptance, or that is based on evidence the claimed rational theory wholly rejects, and so forth. So what is excluded by a claim to rationality is clearly limited. Theories composed of different elements, some of which are opposed to, or are different from, the elements of the claimed rational theory, or theories that evaluate evidence differently, or develop different criteria of relevance, cannot be said to be excluded. One may prefer one or the other of these theories, or one element or mode of evaluation over another. But one cannot say that the competing theories are excluded by the claim to rationality, because the claim cannot be stated so rigorously. Rationality limits or confines ambiguity and doubt. It does not eliminate them.

A claim to rationality creates boundaries that allow for some alternative theories, explanations, or justifications, but that exclude others. I propose shortly to construct such a version of rationality with regard to moral action and judgment. I believe that the basic approach of this version can extend to knowledge generally. But as this extension cannot be developed automatically or by obvious implication from the arguments I make about moral theory, it would require an analysis unrelated to the immediate concerns of this book. I therefore leave its development to another time and return to moral action.

2
MORALITY AS A TEMPER

THE AMBIGUITY OF IDEALS

Morality is a field of persistent conflict. When we speak about this conflict, we usually attribute it to the ambiguity of action, our inability to generate moral truths, the faults of human nature, and similar causes. While these are hardly inconsiderable, they are not my immediate concern. In the last chapter, I argued that there were unavoidable ambiguities inherent not merely in action but in the analysis of action, that these made it impossible to claim to have presented a uniquely valid characterization of an action, and that this radically limited the claims of rational analysis. Now I want to examine a different sort of ambiguity, but one that also compromises the possibility of deductive rationalism: the ambiguity of moral ideals themselves.

I mean the word "ideal" to stand for a general notion of a moral aim or precept—to refer to the sorts of things we have in mind when we speak of ends, principles, values, goods, rights, and so forth. I emphatically do not intend it to stand, directly or indirectly, for any theory of reality or of ultimate moral worth or obligation, or for any argument about legitimate human ends. I realize that my usage may be somewhat arbitrary, but the other possible words carry with them connotations I want to avoid. For instance, the word, "value" suggests that moral judgments are comparative or that moral worth can only be determined in a process of exchange. Moral judgments may indeed have only this sort of worth, but that is a conclusion to be argued for rather than a premise to be assumed. "Principle" has the sense of reducing morality to a structure of rules, "end" to instrumentalism, "good" or "right" to consequentialism or deontology. "Ideal" seems to avoid these pitfalls; and if we remember that it carries with it no connotations of justifiability (we can speak of an unjustifiable ideal) and implies no commitment to an idealist view of reality or to a naive perfectionism, it can serve nicely as a merely inclusive term.

In dealing with the ambiguity of ideals, I am not speaking about our inability to state ideals clearly or to find an unambiguous language of moral discourse. I do not mean to dismiss these problems: the fact that they are commonplaces does not make them unimportant. But I am not concerned with the defects of language. I am concerned with the fact that the things that language refers to—the actions, states of affairs, conditions of life, and so on, that the words stand for or name or describe—are also ambiguous. So if we should discover that we could create clear and precise moral symbols, resolve all conflicts of interests, take the same general moral positions, and act in good faith, we should still be unable to end moral conflict and uncertainty. We should be unable to do this because, however we could agree on how the right or the good should be stated, we could not be clear about what precisely they involved. We may be able to know how to ask people to be good or to do right, but we could not know what it is we should ask them to be or do. This may appear to be as commonplace as the observations about language I have referred to; and perhaps it is. But there are two other points to consider. The first is that, however obvious the ambiguity of ideals may be, it is clearly contrary to the enterprise of deductive rationalism. To show that the conclusions rigorously mandated by sovereign reason are uncertain and ambiguous is to play the role of satirist, not advocate—to do the sort of thing Molière relished. Second, and more important, there are different sorts of ambiguities, and their consequences by no means lead in only one direction. So it is important to state the sort of ambiguity one has in mind and to discover just where it takes us.

Why are moral ideals ambiguous? In the last chapter, I argued that action is inevitably ambiguous, that we cannot create exclusively valid characterizations of action. I also argued that action is not simply the employment of moral ideals: it is a mode of understanding moral dilemmas. Action is the means by which we come to terms with moral dilemmas, explore the ideals that may be related to it, discover where right or good lies. Moral ideals are, therefore, creatures of action, not in the sense that abstract statements of ideals are impossible, but in the sense that the meaning and texture of ideals are shaped in action. Abstract statements of ideals may have some value, but they remain empty generalizations waiting to be filled in; and they can be filled in only through action. Ideals, therefore, reflect the ambiguities of action, and especially the ambiguities imposed by the varied forms of action in which their meanings and textures are forged.

If all actions could be plotted and categorized clearly, then moral ideals could be developed to match or cover them. For instance, suppose we want to know what exactly a maxim like "thou shalt not kill" means. It is not enough, of course, to be able to point to obvious or common sense examples of killing for, sooner or later, we would come up against an action we could not categorize easily or by common sense. We might want to know, for example, whether killing included responsibility for the death of a person we intentionally placed in immediate danger, but excluded responsibility for the death of our agent in a plane crash, even though we had to be aware of such a possibility when we sent him. To answer these questions, to know exactly what killing means or can mean, we must be able to conceive it in terms wide and rich enough to apply to future events that are both unanticipated and occur in conditions we cannot predict. This we cannot do. If a sufficiently rigorous theory of rational action could be developed, it might get around this difficulty. If, as I argued in the last chapter, this cannot be done, it is likely that the plotting and categorization of actions will remain the result of broad agreements on the use of language and, therefore, be subject to all of the traditional uncertainties of conventions. Consequently, each time we are faced with a new action, we may not be able to match or cover it with a known ideal. Instead, we should have to adapt an ideal to match it. But in adapting an ideal to an action or situation different from the one in which it is normally used, we inevitably introduce ambiguity into it.

Even if we did not have to adapt ideals to cover new sorts of actions, we would face crippling problems. Ideals are made to be applied to concrete actions and practices. In the absence of application, the ideal remains hopelessly abstract and its coherence or lack of it incapable of being shown: there is no way to deny the possibility of its being ambiguous. But applying an ideal in a concrete case introduces ambiguity into it. There is, consequently, no escaping the conclusion that ideals are ambiguous.

AMBIGUITY AND JUSTIFICATION

How does the application of an ideal to concrete action or practice introduce ambiguity into it? It does so as we use the ideal to justify action, which is, ostensibly, its fundamental purpose. To justify an action or practice, we must be able to incorporate the central terms of the description of that action or practice into the terms of the justification. If I argue that P is good (right) because J; and if the central terms of P are a, b, c; then I must be able to incorporate a, b, c into J. If I cannot, I have not made a sufficient showing that the action or practice I *am* justifying applies to the action or practice I *seek* to justify. I have not shown that that justification, however powerful or elegant it may be, is relevant to the practice in question. It is not enough to determine relevance by *ad hoc* or intuitive means, or by merely showing that the practice being justified and the practice we seek to justify generally correspond. We need to be specific. For example, if I rely on consent theory to justify an exercise of authority, I should have to show that the consent presumed by the justification is the same as the consent actually given in practice. A justification that presumes unanimous consent would not be relevant to a practice of majority rule, since it does not address a central issue of the practice, namely the coercion of the dissenting minority. In the same way, we cannot justify a large measure of corporate autonomy in a complex modern economy by using a concept of competition articulated in a simple, and therefore sanitized, exchange model.

Our inability to characterize action in exclusively valid ways and our employment of action to explore moral dilemmas guarantee the persistence of problematic elements in our descriptions of action. And as long as there are problematic elements in the descriptions of the actions and practices that we must incorporate into our justifications, and as long as these justifications merely constitute different modes of stating our ideals, we cannot avoid introducing ambiguities into our ideals.

Let me pursue this by exploring briefly the ambiguities of consent. If we can fairly agree that a fully conscious, deliberate, freely given assent constitutes consent, then it might seem that such assent, unanimously given, constitutes *unambiguous* consent. This may very well be true. As I shall shortly suggest, it may be possible to state a moral ideal unambiguously if we are content to state it in a sanitized form. By "sanitized," I mean stated in a way that resolves *by stipulation* all possible complications from action. (This, of course, proves nothing more than that we can eliminate ambiguity by mutually agreeing to respect each other's pretensions to clarity and coherence.)

We could not, however, pretend that the ideal of consent need not allow for the possibility of majoritarian consent. We could not allow a conception of unanimous consent to exhaust the entire theoretical field. Even if there were a sufficient number of people curious enough about the logic of that argument to refrain, for the moment, from laughing us out of court, we could not use the word "consent" in such a restricted way. And with the entrance of majoritarian consent, the ideal of consent becomes very complicated. There are some obvious reasons why this is so. We cannot, for example, say with any assurance just what constitutes consent (apart from conscious, deliberate, freely given, public assent), or what percentage of a population need consent. But I do not want to rely on these well-known, though effective, arguments. I want to raise other issues.

Rationally given consent—whether we mean a hypothetical consent given in a state of nature, or a coherent and consistent assent given after reflection and given consciously, or whatever— may proceed merely from our desires or will. That is, we may choose a particular vision of justice or moral worth entirely because we desire certain results that reason tells us are the fruits of certain practices. Or we may choose a version because reason suggests the superiority of a particular moral principle apart from our desires. However we choose, we must know that consent embraces both the knowledge and the justification of the possibility of coercion. That is, the possibility of majoritarian consent contemplates actions concerning dissenters, and one such possible action is coercing them. But is a consent that proceeds merely from our desires or will sufficient to justify coercing a minority? Clearly, the *fact* of consent is not enough: we need to know why and how it may justify coercing them. We may argue that the majority is always right. We must then say why it is. And the answer we give necessarily becomes a root part of the justification—a partner, if you will, of consent. That is, once we admit the need to give a *reason* to say the majority is always right, we admit the need to show *why* consent justifies coercion; and thus we admit that consent is, by itself, insufficient. But how insufficient? The reason we give bears a relation to the ideal of consent: it supports it. But what is this relation? How much does consent need this support? Can it stand on its own in the sense that, without the reason supporting coercion, its justifying power is weak, but still stronger than any competing theory?[1] More important, the reason given to justify coercion is unlikely to have implications so limited that they relate only to consent. In that case, do these other implications affect the arguments about consent? Do they, for example, impose restrictions on consent, on threat of inconsistency, or increase the scope of consent arguments? To realize that this problem is not a fanciful one, think of the range of implications that partisans of Rousseau have given his justifying reason of the general will.

We may, however, decide that we need a greater assurance of the rightness of consent than will, and seek to tie that rightness to the dictates of natural law or the conclusions of hypothetical and disinterested rational actors. In that case, we might be troubled by the question of whether we have recast, and reduced, the role of consent in the justification of political practices. If the justifiability of consent is governed by natural law or disinterested rationality, how can we avoid consenting to a practice that reflects these? I have raised this question elsewhere, with regard to Locke.[2] Briefly, except in the most exigent circumstances, it would be arbitrary to deny consent to such a practice, because the practice would satisfy a moral conclusion that was more worthy or more compelling than any competing conclusion. And it would be arbitrary to give our consent to a practice that violated these, except again in extremis. If we would conclude, as Locke did, that we could not fail to consent to a government that observed the natural law, and that our consent to a government that did not was of no effect, then what, exactly, is consent but the ratification of moral truth? This is a serious process indeed, but not what we ordinarily think of when we debate consent. What is the relation of natural law or disinterested rationality to consent? How is the ideal now to be structured? In demanding that dissenters agree to obey the law or emigrate, do we not put an additional burden on them? Where in the ideal of consent is the justification for imposing this additional burden located? Is the option of emigration justifiable only if we naively assume (as Hume charges Locke with doing) that emigration is comparatively painless? These are not insuperable problems, but answers to them are not rigorously implicated in the ideal of consent.

IDEALS AND PRACTICES

It may seem that I have put the logical cart before the horse. Am I not confusing the statement of an ideal with its use (justification) and basing my claim of ambiguity on this confusion? I suppose that, if all I cared to argue was that you cannot use an ideal where it is not relevant, the answer might be yes. But that is not what I want to argue. I want to argue that *the use shapes the ideal*, radically affecting its content, and that this is unavoidable. It is unavoidable because we cannot explore the meaning of moral language except in and through practice, and through the impact of referents. Moral ideals are, by themselves, empty and abstract words—sanitized concepts. We cannot define moral words by logical or linguistic analysis alone. If we did this, we would be exploring the meanings and usages assigned to words only by conventions already in existence. So the analyses would only be extensions of existing conventional usages and understandings of these words. But how can we know that these conventional usages and understandings are coherent, not arbitrary, defensible? That is, how can we check their logical aptness, their relation to linguistic conventions? We cannot know that conventional usages and understandings are coherent and so forth without being able to measure them against new or changed or competing usages. But these are generally products of new or changed experiences, or new or changed knowledge. So it is only through practice that we can explore the meanings of ideals. And it is through practice that we *must* do so. We have no way of *justifying* the restriction of analysis to the contours of existing conventions. Such restriction is entirely arbitrary. We need to leave ourselves open to new usages and new usages are, as I have said, ordinarily the products of new or changed experiences.

If this is so, the need to delineate ideals in practice is not merely a reflection of the demands of actuality—not merely an attempt to correct the mythology of rationalism and eliminate pretensions to divinity from the process of earthly logic—but a requirement of logic itself. Everything is what it is, said Bishop Butler, and not another thing. So far we may agree: an ideal ought not to be confused with a practice. But the content of an ideal is unknown except as it becomes entangled in practices: its meaning and contours change as we get to know more (or less) about it in the only way we can know about it.

Rawls would have it otherwise. He constructs a situation—the original position—in which hypothetical rational actors choose principles of justice behind a veil of ignorance. That is, they can know only the most general facts about social life, and are entirely ignorant of specific facts and practices. This ignorance is thought to be a theoretical strength because it allows the parties to choose the principles of justice disinterestedly. I want to show that it is actually a weakness. I believe that in charting this weakness I can illustrate how the failure to explore ideals through practices leads to arbitrary conclusions.

When Rawls tells us that the decisions of rational actors in the original position reflect knowledge of *the* principles of economics, psychology, and so forth, our first reaction might be to demur. We have good reason to doubt the possibility of definitive principles in these disciplines. On the other hand, it may be that, while *we* cannot know such principles, hypothetical rational actors may. In that case, however, how should we know what conclusions they would come to? Indeed we cannot. We can know what conclusions *we* would come to, but this is hardly sufficient. After all, our conclusions are unavoidably based, to some extent, on remembered experiences and particular knowledge. But this is knowledge that Rawls's contractors cannot have. Can we nevertheless say how they would act, what they would choose? In order to know how rational actors would act, we need to know, as Thomas Nagel put it in a different context, what it is like to *be* a rational person. We need to have some idea of what Nagel calls "the subjective character" of the rational person's experience.[3] We need to be able to grasp her sense of herself. But we cannot have this knowledge. We must instead fall back on our own subjective experience and our own sense of what rationality is. Inevitably, we create a picture of the rational actor that is an extrapolation from that sense. Is the fact that Rawls's contractors choose what it is credible for twentieth-century liberals to choose a coincidence? In describing the rationality of persons, we must refer to those mental activities that are most apt to help us identify and realize our ends, or, as Rawls calls them, our life plans. But to be able to determine what those mental activities are, we should have to refer to the mental activities of actual persons. And to the extent that we describe the mental activities of ideally rational persons in terms radically different from those of actual persons, we have no way of *knowing*—as distinct from *claiming*—what they would do.

The typical rationalist conception of the person's mental activities takes no notice of people's concrete interests, nor of their internal psychological conflicts. To do so, after all, would compromise the rationalist decision-making scheme. But not to do so falsifies it, because it attributes to people's mental activities an orderliness and coherence that is not there. And it cannot be placed there by impersonal reason, unless impersonal reason can tell us which of several conflicting perceptions it is most rational to have, or which feelings of guilt, anxiety, or confusion are more rational than the others. Such choices are literally absurd. If they are made, they are made not by impersonal reason but by the very personal reason of the philosopher himself. But then the rational person becomes a personal construct and, on the assumptions of rationalist theory itself, arbitrary.

Rawls's contractors are persons who are only interested in

maximizing their best interests and, as a consequence, do not suffer from envy.[4] Now if we are to take the original position seriously, we cannot just assume that the absence of envy in the contractors is a natural property; we need to have a reason for it. For if the absence of envy is a natural property, then the mental processes of those without envy would be different from the mental processes of those who suffer from it. Indeed, it would be hard to deny that they would be different sorts of creatures. It may be that both sorts of creatures would reason in the same way. On the other hand, it may not be; and as we have no way of knowing what these hypothetical envy-less creatures would reason like, we cannot say. But then the transfer of the ideals that the hypothetical creatures develop to the world we inhabit is simply arbitrary—an act of faith, a substitution of the entailments of something called rationality for the revelations of something called God.

So we must assume that the absence of envy is due to the unique characteristics of the original position. In that case, the rational decisions of the contractors are, at least to some extent, functions of those characteristics. Among the unique characteristics of the original position, the most relevant for our purposes is that the contractors know nothing particular about themselves or their society. They know only general social principles. And persons who know nothing of their own place in society, or their personal properties and attributes, cannot suffer from envy. But self-interest in such a context must differ from self-interest in a context where one has particular goods or courses of action to protect, or, for that matter, where one is starving. In the original position, self-interest can operate in a way that is detached from one's concrete wants precisely because one has no concrete wants. Disinterested choices can be made because no other sorts of choices are available.

But where a person *has* concrete interests, what reason can Rawls give to have her choose as she would where she had no concrete interests? He cannot argue that choosing as the person would in the original position is more rational because rational choice is, by Rawls's definition, self-interested choice; and one's conception of what "interest" means may vary with the nature of the interests or satisfactions available. In another context, Peter Singer makes an analogous argument about choice.[5] He says that a society that sees freedom in terms only of exchanges creates expectations that affect our conception of choice and our perceptions of our wants. People in such an environment are less likely to see their inability to make altruistic gifts to others as a deprivation of freedom or to recognize the impact that the exchange environment has on their wants. In a similar way, the absence of concrete interests can affect the individual's perception of what is encompassed by the concept "interest." And this, in turn, would alter our understanding of what it means to be self-interested and, therefore, rational. We certainly are given no reason to assume otherwise. Now the question is, which version of interest (and, therefore, of rationality) applies? If circumstances critically alter our conceptions of interest, and if we cannot know how hypothetical rational actors think, how can we know what would be rational in the original position? If we cannot know this, we cannot use a justification that takes rationality to mean what it means in the original position. Nor can we argue that, in social practice, the most rational course is to choose disinterestedly. So even if we could know how hypothetical rational actors would act, we could not use their actions as a model for rationality in social practice or, therefore, as a justification for actual choices.

Let me extend this argument by returning to the issue of envy. Why is it not rational to respond to the emotion of envy? It would be strange to insist on a rigid distinction between the rational and the emotional so late in the twentieth century. We are, after all, dealing with persons: the veil of ignorance assumes an absence of certain knowledge, not an ontological transformation. The contractors, like the rest of us, remain, as Hegel noted, creatures with the reason of passionate beings and the passions of rational ones. If the reason the contractors do not suffer from envy has to do with the circumstances of the original position and not with the nature of rationality or of the rational person, then it follows that, under different circumstances, we may make different and equally rational decisions while taking envy into account. Such decisions may not be as fair as those made in the original position, but they are as rational. And if it is clear that the rationality of the contractors differs from the rationality of the actual persons who are to be persuaded to accept the two principles, then some other argument than rationality must be appealed to. In a larger sense, if rationality involves maximizing one's interests, and if one knows one's concrete interests, it may be rational to maximize them. Why would it be more rational to ignore these interests in the name of fairness? Indeed, it would not be. To do so would be to subrogate rationality to fairness. This may be the *right* thing to do, but it is not the *rational* thing to do, as Rawls would have us understand rationality.

It should be obvious to everyone that I am not addressing the worth or persuasiveness of Rawls's intuitive conception of fairness. This is quite powerful, even compelling. It is his treatment of rationality that is not convincing; and, therefore, his attempt to discover what rational actors would choose in conditions of fairness adds nothing crucial to the intuitive argument. More important, it seems hardly possible to understand fairness itself in the abstract. Rawls's intuitive idea of fairness is powerful where we know what it means to be in the lowest position in society. We may know by having experienced poverty or deprivation, lived among the poor, seen poverty, even simply read about it and seen pictures of it. We may have seen the bloated stomachs of starving children, the legs that cannot support the bodies, the necks that cannot support the heads. We may have discovered that, while life is far better in the slums of affluent nations than in those of the Third World, it is a life filled with arbitrarily wrecked opportunities, with violence, frustration, grief. Hence, when someone asks us whether we would choose the same rules that govern the world if we lived in Bangladesh, or in Bedford-Stuyvesant, we can instantly see why we would not. We know what fairness means in fact precisely because we have seen the consequences of its violation. But if we had not seen this, if we were as blissfully unaware of the horrors of poverty as many Victorian worthies are thought to have been—as ignorant, as Disraeli charged, of the habits, thoughts, and feelings of the poor as we would be if they inhabited a different planet—would we be as likely to interpret fairness in the same way, or see it as implying the same things? Might we not see it merely as justifying giving people adequate, although not necessarily equal, chances to compete in the great social race? If we thought that poverty simply meant inconvenience, having less of everything, but still living an acceptably comfortable life, or that the poor, being simple, were happy, would we be moved to choose equality out of self-interest or conceive of fairness in a way that encourages such a choice? A rational person living in such ignorance might very easily give pride of place to, say, providing incentives for production, believing that the cost of such an advantageous system would be altogether minimal, even if he had to pay it himself. It is not merely the *principles* of economics that must pierce the veil of ignorance to produce the difference principle, but some vital *facts* of economic life as well—facts that are immediate and particular and graphic enough to frighten self-interested actors into accepting Rawls's version of fairness.

The dependence of the meaning of moral language on practice can be shown in other ways. A generation ago, rather than speaking about the rational person, I could have spoken about the rational man. I could not do that today: even the plea that the language determines that "man" in such a context stands for "human being" is suspect. The reason for this is not merely that feminism is fashionable. It is that we have begun to recognize that, when we asked questions about the nature of man, most of us really were concerned with *man*. We took behaviors associated with *men* to be behaviors characteristic of *humans;* and we concluded that those who did not share these behaviors (that is, women) were not as fully or as equally human. It is not so much that we ignored women, or uniformly rejected their demands. We simply did not think very much about them and their particular concerns when we created moral and political arguments. We discussed moral values in a male context.

For example, in constructing their arrangements, Rawls's contractors make no special provisions for the birth and nurturing of children. Nevertheless, Rawls thinks of the contractors as heads of families and gives them the concerns—largely economic—that he thinks heads of families would have. But why have they no concern with birth and nurture, which surely must concern heads of families as much as, say, the need to save? Why are they not conscious of the special problems attendant upon them? In the absence of special social provisions covering birth and nurture, it is hard to see heads of families as being anything but men; for if nurturing as well as birth is left to women—as it must be in the absence of special social provisions—women must come to occupy a dependent and therefore socially inferior place in society. The need to come to terms with such a situation creates a serious problem for Rawls, for it implies that the negative conception of freedom he shares has unintended patriarchal consequences. To give women equal freedom with men it is necessary to do more than equally lift restraints on conduct or guarantee that all claims of freedom be reciprocal. It is necessary to provide for women in ways that men need not be provided for—to make special communal provision that alone enables them to act on equal terms with men. It means that we must tie freedom to communal supports for action and acknowledge an obligation to enable people to be free. (I shall discuss these points at length in Chapter 6, when I pursue the implications of defining freedom in terms of action.)

Now Rawls does not endorse patriarchy. He does not call his contractors "men," but mostly uses the neutral term "parties." And these parties do not know whether they will be men or women in the society they create; they are supposed to choose principles that will apply equally to both. But Rawls does not realize that they have not done this. For the rational contractors, not knowing whether they will be female or male, would have to opt for a more communal conception of freedom than Rawls suggests, as soon as they confront the implications of birth and nurture. It is likely that they would choose to count the "inability to take advantage of one's rights and opportunities as a result of . . . a lack of means generally" as a direct deprivation of liberty rather than, following Rawls, as a thing "affecting the worth of liberty."[6] They might even, being cautious, insist on tying freedom more closely to a concept of a common good or common ends, reasoning that only thus could they protect their indispensable need for special provision. They would certainly not trust to the difference principle to correct the problem, since the priority given to liberty would prevent it, except where the disabilities were immense.

I have argued that moral ideals are ineluctably ambiguous and that this ambiguity is introduced into ideals by their connection to action. The coherence of this argument depends on the further argument that the use of ideals in practice shapes them and that their meanings cannot adequately be specified except through the analysis of practice. The discussions of Rawls were intended to exemplify and clarify this argument. Of course, much more remains to be said. But I shall not say it. I believe the point has been established and full discussion would deflect attention from the main line of argument.

Let me return to this main line and ask how ambiguities are introduced into ideals. Clearly, our inability to characterize action in an exclusively valid way need not do it. It may prevent me from saying that a particular ideal (stated in the form of a rule) necessarily governs the situation. My refusal to tell the police that my friend Jones was at the proscribed meeting may be a lie, an affirmation of mutuality of concern, an act of courage, and so forth. In each case, a different ideal may be thought applicable. But this says nothing about the coherence of any of the ideals.

However, to the extent that our inability to characterize actions in exclusively valid ways prevents us from rigorously identifying the central terms of an ideal, it can introduce ambiguity into the ideal itself. That is, the subjective origin and nature of the description of complex actions or practices is a critical source of such ambiguity. Coherent and reliable understandings of such actions and practices cannot originate in a set of impersonal perceptions. "Beware of the man whose god is in the skies," warned Bernard Shaw, and he might have included the social theorist whose vision falls from Olympus. Understanding experiences and practices begins in personal and subjective interpretation because there is no other place to start. It is of course true that these interpretations can be refined and developed; and where they are refined and developed in a context of rigorous intersubjective inquiry, along the lines of science, the personal element may be reduced and a more disinterested conclusion emerge. This conclusion may be thought of as objective in the limited sense that it represents a broad agreement in which the original interpretations have been replaced by a common one. In this sense, an objective understanding is an understanding that is produced by a process of intersubjective communication leading to agreement, and that can be identified with the public or institution where that process took place, rather than with the view of any one member of that public. To say that an understanding is objective is, therefore, only to say that it is to be found not in private intuition or esoteric evaluation but in a particular sort of public consensus. It is not to say that it is true or worthy of acceptance. It is, however, likely to be more considered, more nuanced, more reflective, more responsive to ambiguity, than non-objective ones.

But an objective conclusion does not lose its subjective character. The description of complex actions and practices retains its evaluative character, however rigorously vetted it is, and, in the absence of a mode of creating true evaluations, remains at least partly problematical. And if justifications must be fashioned so as to incorporate the central terms of the description, they must be fashioned so as to incorporate the problematical elements as well as the more certain ones, and therefore become ambiguous.

AMBIGUITY, CONFLICT, AND VIRTUE UNALLOYED

It is probably in law that the presence of ambiguity is most obvious. Legal argument is known for its formalistic, arcane, even arch qualities. The image of lawyers haggling endlessly over petty technical points is probably the most popular image of law, an easy and tempting object of satire. Even where the issues are not minor technicalities but matters of urgency or vast public import, legal argument seems to be mired in pettiness and to turn on the narrowest of points. There are probably several reasons for the overlay of artificiality that characterizes legal argument, but one reason surely is the difficulty it encounters in dealing with ambiguity. This will undoubtedly come as a shock to many lawyers who believe that both legal education and practice are dedicated to dealing with ambiguity. To some extent, their objection is well taken: the legal process is designed to weigh ambiguous evidence and decide cases on the basis of probabilities. But this characteristic is mostly confined to factual decisionmaking. When questions of legal doctrine are at issue, the judge's need to render a clear-cut decision means that he cannot recognize ambiguity, but must pretend that there is, or that he can create, a certain outcome. This imposes requirements on logic that logic cannot meet except by providing counsel with the means to caricature itself.

Nowhere is the ambiguity of ideals more visible than in American constitutional law. Consider a simple problem: the ambit of protection provided by the freedom of speech clause of the first amendment. Does freedom of speech, for example, include the sign language used by a dumb person to communicate? If it does, what other physical signs does it protect? The amendment, after all, does not undertake to protect all forms of communication, even forms known to its drafters, such as the placing of lights in the belfry of the Old North Church. Does it protect me from prosecution for burning the flag, as it would if I *said* the flag deserves to be burned? No one thought so until recently. If it does not, what are its limits? The speech referred to in the amendment includes writing. Why does it stop at this form of non-spoken communication? Does freedom of speech imply that I may tell state secrets to the enemy, or, for that matter, family secrets to the newspaper, without penalty? As instances multiply, we are made more and more aware of the complex and often contradictory implications of this simple ideal and of the need to develop a jurisprudence sufficiently subtle and capable of addressing them. Such a jurisprudence has, of course, been developed and widely used over the past half-century in response to the perceived ambiguity of constitutional ideals. Clearly, that jurisprudence, which reduces constitutional rights to the interests supposedly composing them, may be thought critically inadequate. Indeed, I think it is, because it shifts all consideration of rights into a utilitarian context; and this is wholly arbitrary, if not directly contrary to the intimations of the fundamental constitutional scheme. But I am concerned less with the adequacy of any particular way of coping with the ambiguity of constitutional ideals than with the acknowledgment that some way of doing this must be devised.

Consider a different sort of problem: the relation of individual and community. The day is past when we could speak of either by itself: our individuality is that of communal beings and our commonality that of individuals. Yet does this not introduce a serious ambiguity into our pictures of social practice? Does it not complicate the question of when norms and practices should reflect the needs of single individuals or groups, of when the demands of the *I* should get more weight than the demand of the *we*? It is true, of course, that both individualist and communitarian theorists often reject these impurities and impose on their particular visions a clarity the rest of us fail to see. But we need not follow that lead. There is nothing wrong with confessing that we cannot resolve this dilemma. Neither logic nor fate nor nature dictates that all such opposition and conflict be resolvable. Perhaps as we work our way through the relation of individual and community we must come to recognize that it renders moral and political obligation more complex than we believed. The concept of liberty might include, as Toqueville believed, certain things we can call "collective rights," which obligate individuals in ways different from those usually thought of. It may be that we cannot understand freedom if we merely ask, "When am I free?" but must find a way to tie it to the question, "When are *we* free?" And such a question requires us to ask what individual or personal obligations, other than reciprocal recognitions of each other's rights, may be imposed in the name of freedom. Such a question seems at least paradoxical from an individualist point of view, which while granting that we may be justified in imposing obligations, requires us to see them as limits on freedom. But the paradox may be only apparent, and the capacity to see beyond it the condition precedent for reasoning about freedom. Conversely, however, we should ask, "What limits are imposed by individual desires and interests, needs and rights, on the common good?" To ask these questions separately is to repeat the course of traditional political argument. The point is, they must be asked *at the same time*. Individual and common claims, insofar as they are rooted in questions concerning the nature of our selves, each possess a crucial validity and exist in a symbiotic relationship with each other.

One of the crucial blunders of rationalism is its refusal to recognize that conflicting moral positions may each be valid. I do not mean simply that there may be elements of validity in each, or that each may be valid in different ways. I mean that it is possible for each to be valid in the same way—for both to occupy some of the same theoretical space. Neither reason nor coherence requires that valildity be exclusive. Romantic thinkers, particularly Hegel, had no difficulty with this idea at all, and it is a staple of much of literature.

There are elements of community and individuality in our selves and in our culture that respond to legitimate needs of both. If their demands are sometimes in opposition, that opposition may simply reflect the conflicting needs of our selves and our culture.

And it may be not simply arbitrary but harmful or wrong to choose one over the other. We may want to enlist the virtues of the conflicting forces and take the best from each, but if we do, we must remember that these virtues (or ideals) are themselves ambiguous. So this tactic may end, as it so often does, in rationalizing arbitrariness. We may have to accept the fact that, even in a society of one, the conflict is not resolvable, that we face a moral question without an answer that we can even give to ourselves, and that our best alternative is to try to contain the conflict by arranging a logically suspect, but rationally defensible, accommodation. How we do this is not now clear. In Chapter 4, I shall argue that we can at least create a concept of moral rules that comes to terms with this conflict. But this is clearly not enough. We need to be able to see what accommodation means in social practice, and this I discuss in the final chapter. At present, I merely want to set out the view that perpetual conflict over some issues in morality is not merely inevitable but rational, at least in the sense I use that term.

The story is told that a husband and wife go to the local rabbi to resolve a problem in their marriage. "Rabbi," says the wife, "he doesn't work, he drinks, he lies around the house all day. Our problems are his fault."

"You're right," says the rabbi.

"But you haven't heard my side," says the husband. "You should see the house. She doesn't clean, she doesn't cook, she's always out with her friends. Our problems are her fault."

"You're right," says the rabbi.

The rabbi's wife objects. "You say she's right and he's right—that's ridiculous. They can't both be right."

"You're right," says the rabbi.

Now this story, as I have heard it, is set in Chelm, a mythical village of fools. But is the rabbi indeed a fool? Quite the contrary: the point of the story, as I see it, is that the rabbi is also right. He is faced with a dispute that, on the evidence he cannot resolve, although we think he should be able to do so. What does he do? He sets the basis for possible reconciliation by hearing all sides sympathetically. This may not simply be sensible; it may be *right*. Where demands conflict and the evidence is ambiguous, accommodation is sometimes the *only* principled solution.

The history of morals suggests to many people that the enterprise of moral action, being riddled with ambiguity, is characterized by the presence of irresolvable conflicts and that the resolution of any such conflict is the exception rather than the rule. But how are we to react to this if we think of rationality as first of all making such resolutions possible? We are likely to regard the presence of irresolvable conflict as a sign that we have reached the borders of principled argument, that we can no longer confront the chief problems of morality directly but must take them on the quarter. If neither Kant nor Aristotle works, we must give up the idea of prescribing moral rules and turn instead to side issues, such as cultivating enlightened and tolerant dispositions.[7]

But this is not all that can be said. It may be that Aristotle and Kant no longer work because we see the lack of clarity in moral action as something endemic and inescapable, because we can no longer even imagine the idea of virtue unalloyed, and because we cannot imagine morality to be possible without the idea of virtue unalloyed.

The absence of this idea seems to us to signal the defeat of morality. We can live with the belief that self-interest impels us to identify the morally good with the personally profitable, that morality reflects nothing deeper than the norms our culture has gotten us used to, that there is no uniquely correct way to settle moral disputes because morality cannot be true or false, that the right or the good represents nothing deeper than an emotive reaction or an individual preference. All of these things can be handled because they tell us that we cannot justify moral principles. But they do not deny that we can identify or state them. When we say that there is no such thing as virtue unalloyed, we usually mean that motives are mixed and actions ambiguous, that mistake mixes with vanity and unintended consequences with unacknowledged self-interest. Or we mean that there is no final or true answer. What we do not mean is that we cannot define principles clearly.

But I want to argue that that is exactly what we cannot do. We cannot define a moral ideal with sufficient clarity, or isolate it so that it can be used in a rigorous argument. Yet this does not justify our leaping to the conclusion that we cannot prescribe moral principles. Within the sorts of limits I have indicated, we can do this. We simply have been going about it the wrong way.

Is there such a thing as virtue unalloyed? The central message of deductive rationalism is that there is—or at least that we can conceive of it even if we cannot practice it. For if we reject the possibility of virtue unalloyed, how is it possible to justify the demand for a rigorous, indeed, categorical, morality? What else could justify translating morality into precepts and rules that correspond to, and answer, moral challenges? Why should we seek to demonstrate, as rationalists do, the possibility of clarity in the articulation of moral principles?

If this message is not very convincing, it may be because rationalists fail to ask the sorts of questions we must ask if we are to understand the impact of ambiguity on ideals. To understand it, we need at least to take account of the confusions created by the conflict of ideals, especially the self-conflict; to see the many-sidedness of intentions, beliefs, feelings, and perceptions; to trace consequences that are not merely problematical, but hidden from anything more precise than intuition; to be constantly aware of the immense impact of context and circumstance; to grasp the developmental, narrative nature of action. Now contemporary philosophy is particularly weak when it tries to address these questions, especially together. It is concerned, even obsessed, with issues of meaning, logic, language, evidence—in short, with rules of discourse. And the rules it has developed provide weak avenues of approach to these critical questions. Indeed, to some philosophers they are not critical at all, but barren, even meaningless. To consider them, we might better turn to the poet, who, unconstrained by the philosopher's inhibitions, happily deals in obscurity and confusion and sometimes succeeds in giving the discourse of moral conflict a comprehensibility the philosopher cannot match. I do not mean that the poet makes morality easier to understand, or more real in a vulgar sense. I mean that, by making moral action concrete, by building up, however unsystematically, examples and narrative possibilities, by investing moral conflict with motives and feelings, the poet enhances our capacity to *see* moral conflict and to discover, through an act of recognition, the varied and complex nature of its claims.

There are some who might consider an appeal to the poet premature. They might want to argue that, while we probably could not conceive of broad or general ideals that are free from contradiction, perplexity, or uneasiness, we might be able to conceive of narrowly framed ideals that are. Or perhaps we could take a fairly narrow ideal and, by introducing a sufficient number of modifiers, avoid critical ambiguity. I might be able to argue that a rule such as "Never kill an innocent child" is sufficiently clear and pointed to be regarded as unambiguous.

There is a serious question whether such rules really do have those attributes or whether they are merely framed in such conventional and easily approved-of ways that they discourage serious analysis. Consider the rule I have just mentioned. Is the word "kill" as unambiguous as it seems to be? Certainly, it is more straightforward than a word like "murder," but it may contain problems nonetheless. Suppose killing an innocent child is the only way to prevent the outbreak of a plague? Does the rule imply an intention to deal with this killing on exactly the same terms as with an entirely arbitrary killing? Does "innocent" mean "innocent in intention" or "innocent in effect?" It is consistent with some usages of "innocent" to exclude from its scope a person who is a (perhaps unwilling) agent of potential harm to others. Does this exempt the child carrying the plague bacteria from the rule? Such questions may be elementary, but they are not insignificant.

Which meaning of "innocent" does this narrowly conceived rule contemplate? I suggest that the proper answer is, both and, therefore, that we cannot say. It may seem that this answer is excessive. Why can we not stipulate a meaning, or restate the rule to apply to cases where the child is innocent in intention, perhaps adding exceptions for certain instances of innocence in effect? We may surely do this. But we must recognize that we would not be resolving the ambiguity, but merely by-passing it. This is difficult to justify. To stipulate a meaning (either openly or, in the course of restating the rule, tacitly) is to base the rule on a wholly intuitive definition of one of its central terms. And if we did this, how could we answer the charge that we were proceeding arbitrarily?

Someone might object to the farfetched nature of my example, although it is not as farfetched in the Third World as in the First. But the central issue of the ambiguity of the concept of innocence comes up in any number of other examples. A soldier who loathes the idea of killing and seeks to avoid it may still threaten the life of an enemy, in spite of his intentions. A fetus incapable of intending it may threaten the life of the mother. An infant with a highly contagious disease may be a mortal danger in a camp of malnourished refugees. Now if "innocent' could only mean "innocent in intention," we should be hard put to justify causing the death of these persons (assuming we consider the fetus a person). But we can justify it, however reluctantly, because we separate the reality of the threat from the mental state that accompanies it.

A Kantian might want to argue that "innocent" can only mean "innocent in intention," since "innocent in effect" requires us to introduce contingent matters into moral judgment. But it is one thing to say that the inclusion of contingencies deprives a moral law of its categorical force; it is quite another to say that contingencies do not affect the meaning of the terms of that law. Categorical morality does not eliminate ambiguity so much as restrict the meanings we can employ. And it does so arbitrarily. If the meaning of an ideal is revealed only in practice, and if our language is so structured that an ideal's practical uses are critical aids in defining it, then saying that we cannot consider contingencies solves no issue of meaning. It merely says we must ignore one sort of usage. But as Kantians have not shown that linguistic usages are rightly subject to moral constraints, we may suspect that this way of limiting the definition of an ideal is illegitimate. In short, a Kantian may be able to argue that we should not take consequences into account in making a moral law, but he cannot argue that this eliminates the ambiguities consequences impart to the very meaning of the law. Ambiguity is in part the result of doubts and confusions that experience imposes on us and, however we may choose to ignore them, we cannot unlearn them.

THE CASE OF DON JUAN

What sort of light can poets cast on ideals? Clearly, they can deal quite effectively with issues such as hypocrisy, naiveté, stupidity, and the like, but this is not the point of my question. I am concerned with their capacity to frame the nature of ambiguity, to dramatize our difficulties in the face of it, and so forth. The writer's job, said Conrad, is to make us see. It is by showing us ideals in action, in the context of a narrative, that the writer can best enable us to see ambiguity. This is not to say that philosophers cannot think in terms of narrative. Alasdair MacIntyre does so superbly in *After Virtue*. But there is a kind of insight we can get from seeing in narrative, from following the course of a moral vision as it develops. I want to indicate what this involves, but to do no more than indicate, since a full discussion would take us too far afield.

Where should we begin? Why not with personal favorites? In *Don Giovanni*, Mozart dramatizes the ambiguity of rebellion, among other things. Mozart, of course, sees the Don as a rebel and his rebelliousness and rejection of hypocrisy are heroic as well as charming. But, after all, he is not a tribune of humanity or the uncompromising realist of Shaw's dream scene, but a seducer. He seeks liberation from the stifling bonds of social convention, but for largely selfish and hedonistic purposes, and he is not scrupulous about the consequences of his actions for others. If rebelliousness is, in the circumstances, a virtue, it is not a virtue unalloyed. This is not to say that Mozart values the virtues of his other characters more highly. When the Don, unrepentant to the last, is pulled down to Hell, his pursuers—Anna, Elvira, Ottavio, and the rest—remind the audience that it is always thus with dissolute scoundrels and rightly so. They are with God, but Mozart makes certain that *we* are with the Don. Even as he feels the icy hand of the Statue, even as he is warned that it is his last moment of life, he refuses to repent; and there is here a moment not merely of the serious, but of the tragic. That moment is not sullied by the final sextet, which, in its obligatory sententiousness, is as close to ordinary music as Mozart's genius permitted him to get.

But for all of his courage and heroism, Don Giovanni is not a Sarastro and Mozart takes no pains to hide this. The Don undoubtedly has his quota of dignity. At the end of the first act, for instance, he meets his pursuers' threats of punishment with nobility and courage: even if the world should fall on my head, he tells them in music that makes the point as strongly as the words, nothing could ever daunt me. Yet there are limits to this dignity and Mozart makes us aware of them. However much he sympathizes with the Don's rebelliousness, however brilliantly and powerfully he portrays his moments of courage, Mozart takes care not to write for him an aria like "In diesen heil'gen Hallen." The

Don's music is magnificent, but it is not music that, as Shaw said of Sarastro's, would not sound out of place in the mouth of God.

In *Man and Superman*, Shaw gives us a similar Don Juan—not surprisingly, since Mozart's was his model. John Tanner is honest (even, to some extent, about himself), decent, open, fairminded, contemptuous of respectability. He recognizes the extent to which we avoid facing up to the horrors of social reality by clothing that reality in the language of ideals, by making of ideals not high principles to aim at but masks to hide behind. He is a flawed man, as we all are, but superior to all around him. But the fact is, he is rich, and that means that he lives, as he says, by robbing the poor. And his willingness to admit his, while disarmingly honest, adds nothing to the well-being of the poor. Nor does he abandon his gentleman's status in order to work: he pretends to philosophy, but is merely, as John Stuart Mill said of Thomas Carlyle, an afforder of guidance. He is ready to threaten Ann's happiness to save his own. Richard Dudgeon nearly dies because he can not take his head out of a noose and put another's in. But Tanner can—which is why *The Devil's Disciple* is melodrama and *Man and Superman* comedy. What saves Ann is Tanner's inability to cope with his sexual drive, which the prudish Shaw could not divorce from the procreative. It is Tanner's will to satisfy *his* needs, not hers, that makes the resolution possible. For all of his revolutionary ardor, he is more like his antagonist Ramsden than he would like to admit.

What is the moral of the story? Nietzsche wrote that any custom is better than no custom. And in the face of stifling conventionalism, any rebellion may be better than none. More than this, however, the rebellious temperament is the support of decency and civility when the overwhelming mass of people is only too willing to obey, no matter what is demanded. The artificiality, pretension, and constraint that characterized the aristocratic Europe of Mozart and the England of Shaw fairly cried out for Giovannis and Tanners. This is why these works speak so powerfully to us today; for we, while disparaging the fear of conventionalism as old-fashioned, are thrusting ourselves headlong into an age of appalling conformity. We have convinced ourselves that this is not so, even that we live in an era where the avant-garde is the pampered child of the best society. But this is self-delusion. The avant-garde indulges in trivial self-promotion, fooling no one but itself, the press, and the academy. Its excesses are tolerable precisely to the extent that they are harmless or, worse, encourage the fantasy that there exist real points of resistance to the aggrandizing power of corporate liberalism and bourgeois civilization. In this context, the rebel, if not exactly the hero of the hour, is at least a carrier of virtue, and rebelliousness a quality much to be prized.

But as Mozart and Shaw remind us, rebelliousness by definition brings with it a powerful sense of individualism, a resistance to the view that, in better times, the claims of community deserve to be treated with respect. Now a powerful sense of individuality leads its possessors to assume risks as the price of self-assertion. And the assumption of risk enables us to justify imposing risks on others. Nobility, after all, seeks not merely to express itself in action but to *ennoble:* to be noble is to make demands on others as well as on oneself. But those others may not be ready, or willing, to act in this way, nobility being, to some extent, a matter of taste. And if they cannot resist the noble actor, they will likely find themselves put at risk by him. The courage and nobility that allow Don Giovanni and John Tanner to stand against the smothering stupidity of their times also enable them to injure others, not out of evil intent, but as a by-product of their overpowering need for self-expression. Like Jove, they cannot help hurting others with their thunderbolts. When the hero acts, the rest of us had better look to our defenses. But the danger of injury may be a poor reason to contain such spirits in dark times.

Virtue unalloyed? The need to rebel and the need to take others into account simply do not fit together. Yet no persuasive moral law can ignore either or harmonize both. The virtue of individuality is also its vice. That is why community is such a dubious alternative to individuality and individuality to community. Each is ambiguous. Each exists in tension with itself and with each other. This, I argued at the outset of this chapter, is inescapably the fate of ideals. *Don Giovanni* and *Man and Superman* exemplify this brilliantly, let us see it, which is why I have discussed them.

We live in a world without clarity and it is this that makes impossible virtue unalloyed. When God asked Job who made the earth, Job knew the answer and knew that it implied submission to

God's will. But when God gave us a code of laws, we had to argue over it, and not merely among ourselves, but with God himself.

The woman of Canaan begs Jesus to cure her daughter and he, after vainly trying to ignore her, tells her, curtly, that "it is not meet to take the children's bread and cast it to the dogs." But she will not be dismissed: "Truth, Lord, yet the dogs eat of the crumbs that fall from their master's table." Jesus, rebuked and touched by her faith, heals the daughter. (Matt. 15:22–28; Mark 7:24–30 makes her a Syrophoenician).

A generation later, there is a great rabbinical dispute over the interpretation of a section of the law. A voice from Heaven tells the rabbis that one of them, Eliezer, is right. But Rabbi Joshua protests that since we have been given the Torah we should pay no attention to heavenly voices, for "thou hast written into the Torah to decide according to the majority." This causes God to rejoice: "My children have won against me, my children have won."[8]

We argue with God because God's law is unclear. But what do we hope to gain by arguing with him? After all, even if we win, we can only win small points; the main structure will be left intact. We hope to gain clarity, to impose on ambiguous materials a degree of limit, a focus, a measure of intelligibility. We hope to reach an accommodation that allows us to resolve tensions within the moral law. We need to know what the boundaries of God's claim to universal authority are, or how seriously to take his promises. We cannot act as God's agents without such knowledge and we cannot get it without human intervention in the divine law. And the resolutions of these tensions, the stories tell us, are the results of our reconstruction of God's law. For in one regard, God's moral law seems remarkably like our own: its ambiguities and tensions must be revealed through human action. And it is thus only through human intervention and human participation that they can be resolved.

IDEALS

Perhaps "resolved" is too strong a word. I use it merely to indicate that we are not rendered helpless by the ambiguity of action and ideals. Suppose we can argue that a particular moral ideal is consistent with *any* reasonable characterization of action, or with a characterization that may be employed in any moral theory. We could not pretend that such a characterization would resolve the ambiguities of action or synthesize contradictions. Indeed, if what I have argued is valid, it could exist only on a level where ambiguities and conflicts have not yet made their appearance. In other words, such a characterization would have to be very broad and general—too broad and general to serve as a model for rational deduction. But if we could bring such a characterization together with an otherwise satisfactory argument justifying an ideal, we should have been able to remove some of the ambiguity present in that ideal. (I shall show how this can be done in Chapter 5, where I discuss moral principles.)

But we can do this only at a price. We must state such an ideal in terms consistent with the breadth and looseness of the sort of characterization I have referred to. If ideals are articulated and shaped in action, and if our characterizations are broad and general, then we can only state ideals that have been shaped by general characterizations. And this is to say that we can state ideals that have only been imperfectly developed or incompletely articulated and shaped. It is important to distinguish ideals that are imperfectly or incompletely developed from those that are merely general or vague. A general or vague ideal is one whose ambit of application is unclear, and that can, therefore, be affirmed by people who at the same time have serious reservations about it or about some of its applications. An ideal is vague when its meaning is left open, when it is little more than a symbol that points nowhere and leaves open the possibility of being seen in entirely inconsistent ways. An imperfectly developed ideal, on the other hand, can point in a particular direction and, therefore, can narrow the field of justifiable action. But within this narrowed field there remain implications in tension with each other and ambiguities that cannot be resolved by referring to the ideal itself. To say that an ideal has been incompletely developed is to say that it has a character different from the character we usually associate with moral precepts, however general these latter may be. It is to say that it cannot be seen as much more than a rough outline of an ideal. Now such an outline can do only limited service in moral argument. It can provide us with a broadly described vision—an attitude, a mood, a temper. Such a temper can indicate the sense of a justifiable moral ideal, create a viewpoint that can guide moral decision, permit us to reach—within limits now broad, now narrow—justifiable conclusions. It can guide the course of moral argument and constrain moral choice. But it cannot entail particular conclusions or determine moral decisions. We can see moral ideals so defined as neither rigorous precepts nor vague generalities but as commanding intuitions.

By "commanding intuition," I mean simply a basic moral force, a center of gravity. A commanding intuition is a vision that pushes or drives our arguments in a definable, if general, direction. It also can be thought of as a disposition to *see* things in a definable, if general, way. Thus, it helps to account for the much-noted phenomenon that people holding different moral views tend not only to evaluate and judge actions differently but to see them differently. A moral temper is also a perceptual disposition.

If it is possible, at least in principle, to justify and deploy in practice imperfectly developed ideals that have the character of commanding intuitions or moral tempers, we still need to know how we may develop them. How can we frame an ideal in such a way that it is consistent with any characterization of action or with a characterization that may be used in any moral theory? We cannot do this by using traditional modes of rational theorizing. Traditional modes of theorizing hinge on our being able to take particular characterizations of action and particular statements of ideals as definitive, and to use them as a basis for reasoning. But we cannot do this. We cannot reason forward, as it were. We must settle, at best, for characterizations that have a strong (though not exclusive) claim to validity. We must assign meanings to ideals knowing that they are not definitive or conclusive meanings, and seek to impose coherence and unity on them. But this is, in effect, arguing backwards. *We engage in a process of constructing ideals and characterizations and then retroactively refining and reshaping them so that they fit together.* We should not pretend that we have developed an argument that, when completed, fits together in such a compelling and logical way that it appears to reflect an inherent or unassailable truth. Nor, since we cannot characterize action in uniquely valid ways, should we think that the coherence of the argument, the unification of its disparate elements into a consistent and compelling conception, can be the product of rational deductions. Coherence and unity can only be imposed on ambiguous material by an *act of creation*, in which we continually adjust the meaning of the ideal and match it with the way (or ways) we choose to frame our characterizations. Like Rawls's notion of reflective equilibrium, we engage in a process of continual adjustment until we reach a statement of the ideal that seems coherent and persuasive—perhaps better, more coherent, more persuasive than other, or all other, statements. But our judgment that the statement is coherent and so on is not a judgment we make by evaluating each step in the argument according to the canons of rational deduction. We cannot do this because we cannot test the separate steps or moves we make in moral argument by those canons. The test of rationality may be applied when the argument is complete, when it is framed up. At that point, we can look back into the argument and judge whether its elements fit together sufficiently, cohere adequately into a unified statement. At some moments, of course, a particular move needs to be, or pretends to be, logically justifiable, and here we may certainly criticize it for falling short. But the elements of a moral argument may be and, whatever the claims made for them, ordinarily are introduced because the arguer judges them to be important or relevant or compelling. Whether they fit the argument rationally is to be decided only when we have some sense of what the argument is.

In the fourth chapter of *Utilitarianism*, Mill makes his well-known argument that, just as "the only proof . . . that an object is visible, is that people actually see it," so "the sole evidence . . . that anything is desirable, is that people do actually desire it."[9] Generations of first year philosophy students have never tired of discovering this supposed fallacy. And their teachers as patiently explain that it is not a fallacy at all, but a significant statement of the utilitarian position that the evidence for moral propositions can be found, not in logical argument, but only in the facts of human nature and experience. What is this explanation but a retrospective construction of the sense and flow of Mill's argument? And it is in this construction that we can grasp the significance and meaning of this argument and understand its coherence.

This is the sense of my argument that rationality is a *recon-

structive mode of thinking. Rationalism in morality involves, not the deduction of moral principles, but the imposition on the materials of moral action of a structure that *makes them into* a coherent unity. The rational thinker reconstructs moral ideals and in doing so creates, as an artist does, a world in which they fit. The rational thinker shapes his world, gives it life. He alters or bends or molds ideas so that they will finally reveal a dominant and powerful unity, a unity that is not, as Justice Holmes might say, a brooding omnipresence in the skies but the result of a skillful and purposeful construction. At the same time, however, he is limited in what he can construct. The materials of moral argument are too refractory to allow him to fill in the details of his world. All that he can do is indicate its content.

PART TWO

THE CONSTRUCTION OF MORALITY

3

THE USE AND ABUSE OF COMMUNITY

THE COMMON GOOD

The examination of moral action is complicated by the fact that, as moral actions are done and moral claims made by persons who are deeply shaped by social relations, and who cannot be defined apart from their relation to others, moral action cannot be understood without reference to the communities of human beings that give them life. Now, although this is hardly a new or striking perception, it presents a number of difficult problems. The first of these, in my view, is that community has many sorts of meanings. It may say something about the nature of morality itself (as in common good theories), or it may say something about the setting of moral action (as in arguments for intimate communities), or it may say something about both (as in arguments for tradition). I want to argue that the first sort of meaning is the proper one, but I also want to reject identifying it with the common good. Part of my objection to the common good, as well as to the other sorts of meanings, rests on their incompatibility, in greater or lesser degree, with freedom. Now, as I have not set forth an argument justifying freedom, the use of the term here may be regarded as improper. But I do not think that it is.

In the next chapter, I argue that the construction of morality necessarily begins with the recognition of certain limited common elements in moral action and that it leads us to see freedom as a constitutive principle of morality. No part of this justification of freedom rests on the criticisms I make of other uses of community. The justification rests, rather, on implications drawn from a minimal reading of the concept of community that is independent of those criticisms and that I set out at the end of this chapter. It would be perfectly possible to set out this argument, move directly to the argument of the next chapter, and leave the critical analysis of community for later. But these criticisms might help the reader to place my argument in perspective, to see it in relation to the appropriate traditions of communitarian discourse, or to understand just how it differs from more commonly used approaches. Being aware of such things in advance might help readers to see the argument more clearly. That, at any rate, is why I adopt the strategy of dealing with the concept of community now.

Where does the concept of community lead? We can dismiss at the outset any claim that it leads logically to a reduction in the strength of the rights we may assert against society. That claim is ordinarily based on the argument that to rebel against society is to rebel against ourselves and, in some cases, against our freely willed choices. But this is superficial. It is more convincing to argue that it strengthens, even authenticates, that rebellion. I know both sides, said Nietzsche, because I am both sides. To rebel against oneself is the profoundest of all rebellions because it forces one to become aware of the presence of others within one's persona and, therefore, to confront the ambiguity of one's demands and the limits of moral righteousness.

Some people would want to make such a perception the basis of an argument that moral and political principles must be communal principles whose validity is a reflection of the common good. I want to argue that this carries us *too* far. But in arguing this, I want to forgo any advantage that may accrue to me from relying on older organic conceptions of the common good (such as Léon Duguit's construction—out of Durkheim's materials—of social solidarity, or D.G. Ritchie's theory of social utility), or on more recent conceptions that, in their attempt to integrate individuals in groups, manage only to submerge them.[1] The authors of these theories may not have intended the authoritarian consequences seemingly implicit in them any more than Sidney Webb did when he identified the development of the individual with "the filling, in the best possible way, of his humble function in the great social machine."[2] Nevertheless, the consequences are only too plainly there. They are there as well in the arguments of those who say "common good" when they mean only to refer to the interests of a particular group or class, or who impute universality to a bundle of favorite policies, or who take the common good to be the principal implications of a social compact or agreement they happen to have constructed. I refrain from discussing these because they are easy targets. And, being easy, they mislead. It is painfully obvious, after all, that not all common good theories rely on organic metaphors or contemplete illiberal politics. These are the theories that challenge us.

One conception of the common good that plainly sought to avoid authoritarian consequences was advanced early in this century by Leonard T. Hobhouse. Hobhouse argued that liberalism involved more than the mere sanctification of the pursuit of their interests by individuals. Following Mill, he took the universalization of self-development to be the chief value of a liberal social order and he drew the moral that such an aim can be attained only where we can harmonize the individual's good with the common good. "The fulfillment of each personality," he wrote, "is a constituent element of the common good, and the individual may justly claim the conditions necessary to it, the forbearance of others, and their aid in so far as the general conditions of the community allow."[3] The most obvious objection to this formulation is, of course, that the conditions necessary to some people's personal fulfillment may impinge on other people's goods—that is, upon their well-being or their rights. Now, by "good," Hobhouse meant a harmony of feeling and experience. Practical reason, he wrote, "is the impulse to develop harmony, on the one hand, by extending the control of the mind over the conditions of its life, on the other by establishing unity of aim with the world of consciousness itself." In other words, practical reason must develop harmony within the world of feeling and, by acting on the social environment, bring experience into harmony with feeling.[4] And Hobhouse never doubts that this harmony of feeling and experience can be sufficiently universal to make possible a shared system of life. It is true, of course, that this harmony is not a possibility to be assumed, as in early liberal thought. It is an end to be brought about by purposive and democratic social policy that seeks to synthesize conflicting claims. But the possibility of such a synthesis is not subject to doubt. Consequently, Hobhouse can conclude with assurance that "the individual has no moral rights which conflict with the common good, as therein every rational aim is included and harmonized. . . . In general terms, a true right is an element in or condition of the real welfare of its possessor, which on the principle of harmony is an integral part of the common welfare."[5] Harmony, then, provides us with a practical answer to the objection that, in the resolution of conflicting claims, the goods of some individuals will be sacrificed. It makes possible not merely the accommodation of conflicting claims but their synthesis.

The strategy of making the welfare of individual persons a key element in the common good allows us to escape the dangers of making the well-being of the social order itself the highest law. But it does not tell us *how* to integrate, or synthesize, conflicting individual goods. The problem here is critical. If we want to synthesize conflicting claims, we need to do a special kind of operation. We need to translate the claims into common and measurable terms. That is, we need to translate the individual claims into terms that allow us to compare them and measure them by the same standard. A claim for improved educational practices that can be satisfied only by imposing new taxes needs to be stated in a way that enables us to judge how much of the former justifies how much of the latter. Now if we are resigned to resolving this conflict by means of ordinary political accommodation, we need not do this. Since ordinary accommodation merely tempers, but does not eliminate, conflict, and since it pretends to be no more than a rough judgment of what constitutes a minimally acceptable compromise, specificity in the statement of claims is not required. But a synthesis is not merely an accommodation and it is certainly not a compromise; in any particular case, a synthesis of conflicting claims may involve giving one claim far greater weight than the others. Consequently, an attempt to synthesize claims according to a standard of right cannot work with the same crude methods as accommodation. It requires that claims be measured fairly according to a standard and, therefore, that they initially be reduced to common terms of measurement. And this creates a critical problem. We need to be able to quantify these claims in a rational way—that is, to introduce a measure that is coherent and compelling, rather than merely convenient and available. Individual claims do not arise accompanied by built-in and self-evident numerical weights or indications of what they are to be weighed against. The weight we give a claim and the claims we measure it against are ordinarily products of conventional assumptions and common sense. We weigh claims for better education against claims for reduced taxes because that is the way the conflict is usually perceived. But this perception is not necessarily the perception of the claimants. It may—indeed often does—represent the perception of those who seek to accommodate rather than synthesize the conflict. The claimants may see it as a matter of the obligations of the fortunate to the deprived or of the invasion of one's property rights. Now how *should* these claims be stated? It is abundantly clear that they cannot be stated without first being interpreted. That is, they need to be translated into common terms of measurement. Who is to do this? Who determines the measure by which they shall be weighed? If the individual claimant herself does, then how may society decide between conflicting interpretations or terms of measurement? Clearly it cannot, since the standard of judgment is the judgment of each individual. In this eventuality, we should not be able to delegate to an institution the right to speak for society on the issue: there would be no legitimacy in a democratic determination, except where the outcome is unanimous. If, on the other hand, a social institution (playing a role similar to the impartial observer) is to interpret or decide on the terms of measurement, are we not merely substituting an institution's evaluation for the individual's? And in that case, how can we say that we have *synthesized* conflicting individual claims? What indeed remains of this synthesis? Have we not rather resolved the conflict by using institutionally defined terms of measurement? And harmonizing or synthesizing conflicting individual claims means more than superseding them with an institutionally defined standard. It may be that such supersession is unavoidable, or even desirable. But we cannot employ it without tacitly abandoning the project Hobhouse requires us to engage in. Nothing remains of the integration or synthesis of individual goods into a common good: we have lost the element of harmony and, while the common good remains a viable concept, it is an altogether different sort of concept than Hobhouse wants.

There is another reason why the attempt to integrate the individual into the common good does not work. A person who is normally self-interested will never approve of a course of conduct or make a choice merely because she values the fairness or worth of the particular process of choosing. That is, she will normally not adhere to a process for the sake of the process, however admirable it is. Of course, we are occasionally placed in circumstances that induce us to choose a process for its own sake: in an environment of anarchic barbarism, people are likely to favor any government that promises to impose civil order. But situations like this are unusual. In the ordinary case, we approve of a process because of the outcomes we expect of it—the benefits and improvements in our well-being we believe it will bring. Rawls argues this. We choose the two principles because we think they will enable us to realize our primary goods.

Now even where people cannot be *certain* that reliance on a common good standard will benefit them, they may accept it where they can reasonably *expect* that it will. We can expect people to adhere to such a standard, therefore, where it promises improvements in well-being for a substantial portion of the population. The common good need not be perceived as Pareto optimal, but it must be seen as widely beneficial. Now this condition cannot be met where a substantial number of people face serious poverty, alienating social environments, radically constricted opportunities, and so forth. Those living in these conditions will want (and, indeed, need) substantial aid in the form of transfer payments. These payments involve, generally, the transfer of wealth from those at least more than marginally better off than the poor. The category "better off," then, tends to comprehend a rather large number of people. Even though some of the better off will transfer very little wealth, they do not ordinarily see this as being in their interests. They may be willing to do it occasionally, or temporarily, or minimally. But they seem to want to reserve their right to suspend it when they think it desirable. They want to regard transfer payments as voluntary rather than obligatory, and the claims of the poor as based on charity rather than—as Hobhouse himself insisted—on justice.

It may be that abstract rational persons would favor a common good standard because it benefits the most needy, or because it is fair, or because it is in the long-term interests of society. But these reasons rarely move real persons beyond charity. They will fail as arguments for rights where the individual goods to be synthesized are not the constructive goods of hypothetical persons but the perceived goods of real ones. In conditions of serious poverty, these perceived goods conflict radically. There is strong opposition between the claims of the poor and the claims of the better off; otherwise, serious poverty would not exist. Nothing in our experience allows us to say that we can synthesize these conflicting claims. In conditions of substantial inequality, better off persons simply cannot be said to identify the common good with expected benefits. Undoubtedly, some people will regard the consequences of the common good as beneficial because they value the claim that altruism makes on civilized people, or because they get psychic satisfaction from altruistic behavior. But many will not. They will identify the common good with the attempt to deprive them of their justly acquired goods and will therefore see no compelling reason to adhere to it, however abstractly justifiable it may be. Hobhouse, like most liberal advocates of the common good, does not understand how dependent the liberal version is on an *antecedent* condition of reasonable equality. Rousseau understood this perfectly. *Equality is a prerequisite, not a consequence, of the common good.* The common good will reinforce equality; but no common good that is supposed to incorporate rather than supersede the good of individuals can come into being, or gain widespread approval, where people's goods are as discordant as they are in conditions of serious inequality. The possibility of the common good, then, depends on a transformation of society that it is supposed to anticipate, and on the legitimation of a belief (that the individual's well-being is powerfully implicated in the general well-being) that it is supposed to promote. The synthesis of individual goods and the common good is most likely to occur precisely where the claims of individuality are weakest—which is to say, where the synthesis is least needed.

THE OTHER

Objections are not the same as solutions. The concept of a common good may be weak or dangerous or incoherent, but the problem of community remains. For the problem of community is the problem of the "other"—of the existence of an other's needs, wants, perceptions, and so forth.

The problem of the other in modern social theory is formidable, in the light of our concentration on the self. MacIntyre and earlier communal theorists such as Dewey are right to see that this problem may only be approached by emphasizing the social locus and context of moral action. In arguing thus, they mean to strip traditional liberal individualism of its persuasive power and to reveal the hollowness at the core of liberal pluralism. But, as I have already suggested, the strong communal alternative to liberal individualism, where it is anything more than a fiction enabling us to design and develop a morality, is potentially quite as dangerous as the position it seeks to replace. It threatens to create a sense of the unity of human life. But this sense is not a widely shared conception, as Dewey and MacIntyre insist, but a narrowly shared one. Moreover, it is not a conception that can be justified by appealing to a natural end of human beings, since both Dewey and MacIntyre reject this notion of a *telos*. And, as William Connolly, following Michel Foucault, perceptively noted, the attempt to retain this sense of unity in these circumstances is likely to result in the punishment and confinement of those others who do not share this conception.[6]

Dewey and MacIntyre seek to avoid this possibility by restricting the scope and meaning of the pursuit of both the common and the common good. The unity Dewey seeks is the pursuit of moral agreement through democracy and progressive enlightenment. For MacIntyre, the unity consists largely in pursuing the idea of a common life. Now, neither assumes a shared conception of the good or of the virtues. But they suggest that, in the absence of such shared conceptions, we can still share a *process of creating* them. And this process differs from the liberal individualist process because it seeks to realize, not individual goals compatible with minimal social relations, but common goals compatible with sufficient room for individuals to pursue separate lives. The emphasis, in other words, is radically different and this difference has great consequences.

So much, it seems to me, is admirable. But when we ask how we are to pursue such a process, and what contexts will support the communitarian project, we are left with dramatically limited alternatives. Dewey, like Benjamin Barber today, puts great stock in communication.[7] But this appears naive, for the conditions necessary to allow widespread democratic communication among citizens imply a reorientation of economic and political power radical enough to constitute an entirely different social order. That is, such communication presumes the existence of the sort of social practice that it is supposed to help to create in the first place.

MacIntyre, to his credit, does not pretend otherwise: he sees modernity as a new Dark Age and closes his book with the recommendation that we follow the example of those "men and women of good will" who turned from supporting the Roman *imperium* and sought to construct "new forms of community within which the moral life could be sustained so that both morality and civility might survive the coming ages of barbarism and darkness." Yet this new monasticism, this attempt to resolve ourselves into "local forms of community,"[8] is unlikely to lead us out of darkness. Intimate communities, as I shall argue in a few moments, sustain conformity and narrowness of vision more often than moral enlightenment. Monasticism led to dark ages and to the constriction of civilization. Why would MacIntyre's communities be different? More than that, MacIntyre's solution is an abdication of responsibility by the sons and daughters of privilege—as they must inevitably be—to those who, being less favored, will be unable to follow them into communities of light. For who will gain entrance? The illiterate farmer of India, the starving peasant of Ethiopia, the wasted addict of the urban slum, will not apply. This is likely to be a moral revolution for the few, and moral revolutions for the few reinforce paternalistic and ultimately authoritarian forms of community. Neither of these alternatives is attractive.

I shall argue that the alternatives presented by Hobhouse, Dewey, and MacIntyre do not exhaust the implications of community. It is fortunate that they do not, because the individualist alternative is incoherent and badly at odds with historic reality. This is true even of the most sophisticated versions of individualism. F. A. Hayek, for example, argues that "the most important of the public goods for which government is required is . . . the securing of conditions in which the individuals and smaller groups will have favourable opportunities of mutually providing for their respective needs."[9] Now even if we do not read this to suggest a social order that is characterized by what Hayek calls "spontaneity" and that "enables the individuals to provide for their needs in manners not known to authority," to facilitate the "pursuit of unknown individual purposes,"[10] we still have to assume a rationalist conception of such an order. We must assume that we know the conditions that make this possible. But how can we know this? Can we refer to history? Historically, even democratic market societies facilitate the pursuit of the purposes of some individuals only and, far from being unknown, many of these individuals and purposes are very well known. Words and phrases like "owner," "colonist," or "upper class" correspond to such knowledge. Not *all* can be known and it is true that democratic and market societies provide greater openings than others. But these are not as significant as they may appear.

In the first place, liberal market orders are not spontaneous. They depend on the existence of authority and on the exercise of that authority being described, in appropriate cases (such as the devolution of public authority on the corporation), in individualist or non-authoritative terms. An entirely artificial and deceptive vocabulary develops, feeding a spurious reality into an otherwise sanitized model of social practice and, in turn, being justified by that model.

Second, purposes cannot be individual. We are socialized beings, and our purposes therefore reflect societal influences. These influences (traditions, conventions, and so on) are clearly affected, although not determined, by the society's structure of information and learning: educational, religious, and informational institutions disproportionately influence traditions and conventions and, with that, our conceptions of our purposes. If these institutions are in the hands of elites with generally common interests, values, perceptions, and so forth, these conceptions of purpose will be strongly infused with the elite's vision. Therefore, individual purposes will, to some extent, reflect and reinforce elite interests. Hence, we no longer have an individualistic or spontaneous order, but a structured order. This order may not be "planned" in a conscious sense, or structured as a society governed by a rigid dictatorial regime is structured, but it reveals a pattern that can be accurately described only in the vocabulary of control and order. It is an order that is hierarchical, inegalitarian, and constrained in the sense that, if all ideas and values can be presented for acceptance, only those conforming to certain interests are generally given institutional support. This is surely preferable to an order where unwelcome ideas are suppressed and their advocates imprisoned or killed. But it is not the sort of response we associate with unplanned or spontaneous social behavior. In a complex society, where the expression and communication of ideas and interests is vitally affected by the presence or absence of institutional support, those with the capacity to command, or disproportionately influence, the giving of such support exercise a crucial power. And where that power is persistently exercised in a way that denies support to interests in conflict with the interests of those who control those supports, one can hardly conclude that the outcomes result from serendipitous agreement.

The existence of common interests among elites, their perception of this commonality, and their action upon it—even where it is not coordinated or the result of common planning—results in a defined order in which certain individual purposes are given an official standing or preferred status. Now, as I have said, this is preferable to coercion by the secret police. But it does not correspond to a spontaneous definition of purposes by individuals. And it cannot be described as a system in which individuals make free choices: the conditions under which they choose and which crucially influence or affect their choosing are not chosen *by* them, but *for* them. And freedom, as I shall argue in Chapter 5, means that the conditions of choice must themselves be freely chosen. Freedom is not secured by having the ability to choose among alternatives structured by others, but by having the ability to affect the structure of choice itself.

Individualism, therefore, fails on its own terms. It speaks of individuals, but delivers power into the hands of elites, whose defined community of interest provides a focus for their exercise of power. Individualism is not opposed to community, as socialists have argued for over a century, but to a specific type of community—a community of all classes. Both the history of individualism and its rationale confirm the assumption that common experience is the basis of human life and that recourse to the supports offered by community is the prerequisite to the capacity of individuals to act and choose.

There are those who see this connection as so integral that they regard it as the very basis of human freedom. Like the seventeenth-century social contract theorists, they regard the freedom possible outside of communion with others as random and abstract—so speculative that it is scarcely worth talking about. And the alienating conditions of mass society, with its economies of scale, impersonal bureaucracies, and overwhelming social processes, magnify the need for recourse to communal supports. Two contemporary versions of this position are especially important: conservatism, with its newly developed concern for integrating freedom and tradition; and a revised radicalism that stresses the need to develop face-to-face communities or, where this is not possible, to encourage the growth of intimate groups in workplaces and localities. Each of these positions presents a significant vision of human community and its relation to freedom, and I want to consider them in turn.

THE CONSERVATIVE THEORY OF COMMUNITY

Liberal critics of conservatism typically attack it for holding freedom hostage to the authority of tradition and the integrity of institutions. Conservatism, they argue, limits freedom arbitrarily by giving traditions and the collective conscience greater consideration and weight than they deserve. Now if the liberal critics are right, not much remains of the question I want to investigate: the belief that human beings cannot be understood apart from their communal relations leads to a politics of restraint and conformism, if not obscurantism, and the only open questions concern the degree of restraint desirable and its most efficient institutional form. So we need to ask whether the general liberal criticism is valid.

Conservatives from Edmund Burke to Robert Nisbet have bitterly attacked it as superficial. They have argued that, if we are to specify the range of freedoms a person ought to have, we must place those freedoms in a context of authority. Authority here means not merely political authority but the authority of the various social institutions that mediate between the individual and society. That is, the integrated, non-alienated human personality needs to develop in a context of family, neighborhood, village, religious, and work institutions, each of which receives some loyalty and exercises different types and degrees of authority. These institutions constitute an environment that is variously described as private or personal or intimate but that might better be called "proximal." It is an environment, in other words, where the individual's involvement seems to him more direct, more comprehensible, more immediate than his involvement with institutions like government or a corporation or the army. These institutions we think of as impersonal. They exercise a grudgingly given authority, appear "distant." Proximal institutions create a complex set of rules that helps us orient our private conduct and seems to reflect values we have internalized. We cannot free ourselves from the authority of proximal institutions and still remain unalienated, although we can always reject particular rules and demands. To burst free of the authority of proximal institutions is to hurl ourselves into an anomic darkness, to disable ourselves psychologically, to shatter the internal controls that allow us to distinguish satisfying liberty from anxiety-breeding license. And since both the authority of proximal institutions and the norms they press us to internalize are the products of tradition and slow development, since neither authority nor norm is absolute master of us but can variously be rejected (although at some cost), the danger of tyrannical authority is muted.

Freedom in this view cannot be seen as an abstract concept but as concrete forms of action taken by concrete persons and rooted in concrete patterns of authority and tradition. The exercise of freedom implies a relationship between the desires and interests of the individual and the norms she has internalized: without these norms, her desires and interests would be rootless, arbitrary, self-contradictory. And the point is that she would *feel* this rootlessness, arbitrariness, self-contradictoriness. They would not merely be feelings attributed to her by another. She would *feel* anxious and confused. The individual's freedom, therefore, is bound up with the proximal institutions among which she lives. She is, in a very concrete sense, a member of a social community and her freedom is inescapably that of a member. As an individual, she is an alienated person inhabiting an anomic universe. As a member, she is an integrated person whose choices reflect the balance she has constructed between the authority of proximal institutions and her desires.

Enlarging on this, conservatives treat political freedom and rights as products of a complex process of organic development known as tradition, and substitute for the abstract statements of rights so dear to liberals tables of concrete freedoms and rights. These concrete freedoms are the products of a long process of accommodating the diverse needs for order, security, self-expression, experienced by the members of a society.

There is much that is attractive in this version of freedom, not the least of which is its concreteness and its willingness to see freedom as a concept that can only be defined in action. It is true that the price one pays for this concreteness is a loss of conceptual clarity and a certain fuzziness about just what sorts of actions we mean when we speak of freedom. But that might be a price worth paying. Conceptual clarity is by no means as unalloyed a virtue as some philosophers like to think. It can narrow our field of vision, encourage us to overlook crucial relations, transport discussion into a range of abstraction that is at a considerable remove from the actions and experiences to which freedom is supposed to relate. And the loss of clarity is not necessarily fatal to an understanding of freedom. The conservative vision can be constructed so as to convey a mood or temper that enables us to deal with the social world and that reflects the richness and diversity of human experience. Why, then, reject it?

The reasons are not far to seek. They lie in the incoherence of the conservative defense of tradition. Traditions gain their moral force from the belief that each reflects a kind of agreement made among past and present members of society. This creates a particular sort of social contract, a tissue of agreements composed, in effect, of the individual agreements represented by individual traditions. But we cannot take the idea of individual traditions too literally, because each individual tradition reflects the texture, the mood, of the entire tissue. The traditions of a society, if not organically related, nevertheless reveal a common moral vision or mood—a set of internalized norms that, being considered together, are generally given an identifiable and moderately consistent definition. And this moderately defined set of norms gradually defines the traditions and institutions of society, modifying and shaping them so that they reflect its consistency. When we seriously alter institutions or traditions, therefore, we create strains in the common moral vision that informs their texture.

The problem with this argument is that the traditions and conventions of society tend to reflect elite interests and values. While specific elite groups occasionally disappear or lose power, the identification of rightful claims to privilege, and to awe and deference, with the disproportionate possession of resources and authority remains. This, together with the wielding of the power that comes with resources or authority, makes it possible for elites to influence disproportionately a society's formalized beliefs. The persistence of the elite in status or power creates patterns of action that persist and eventually come to be accepted habitually. In addition, where a group held in awe and deference exercises disproportionate influence—indeed, sometimes control—over the means of communication and education, and over the institutions of religion (civic and otherwise), it is hardly surprising that the moral conceptions and characterizations of action widely held by its members become the conceptions and characterizations that dominate the process of the reflective elaboration of norms. This does not mean, of course, that the traditions of society are simply the interests of elites writ large. It does mean that the content of traditions is critically shaped by elite interests and values, and that in the process of developing traditions elites play a more decisive role than the rest of society.

But this deprives traditions of much of their moral force. Traditions have moral force precisely because they are supposed to be, in effect, broad social agreements and widely valued ways of tending to society's business. But if these agreements are manufactured by elites taking advantage of their superior power and strategic position to manipulate general opinion, not much strength remains in the conservative moral argument. The authenticity of tradition is compromised and with it the integrity of the conservative position. Compromised, of course, does not mean destroyed. It is exceptionally difficult to say just how far general opinion has been manipulated, and it is probably impossible to deny that a degree of integrity remains in traditional arrangements. But this degree of integrity is demonstrably less than the defenders of tradition need. The capacity of tradition to withstand the assaults of liberal or radical moral demands must be diminished by the realization that the claim that traditions represent *societal* agreements is, to a crucial extent, a pretense. Freedom, in the conservative view, reflects a relationship between individual desires and the authority of proximal institutions. If that relationship is largely the product, not of the mutual interaction of the members of a society, but of the authoritative action of social elites, we are back in Sarastro's temple, somewhat redecorated, but fundamentally intact.

It may be objected that elite manipulation, as opposed to dictation, does not prevent traditions from being sufficiently voluntary to be considered legitimate agreements. Similar attempts to dilute the requirements for determining when an act is voluntary are not unknown to moral philosophy. There are good reasons for rejecting them. As I have already said, I shall argue in Chapter 5 that agreements made in circumstances where one of the parties has no say, or has a critically inadequate say, in defining the conditions or the structure of agreement cannot be defended as freely made. Nor can the ascription of freedom of choice to such a party be made in good faith. This argument, suitably modified in obvious ways, applies in these circumstances as well.

Critics may also object that my argument here is entirely contingent and that I have proved nothing in principle against traditionalism. That is hardly a serious objection, since traditionalism is largely based on the need to make political argument an entirely contingent enterprise. However, in Chapters 4 and 5, I present more rigorous arguments justifying the need to constrain agreements. If these are valid, and if we regard traditions as forms of agreement, we must regard traditions as subject to the same need. But as I do not want to anticipate this argument, I shall have to postpone considering this objection.

There is a second problem with the conservative attempt to integrate freedom and community. The conservative account of freedom assumes that the free individual is indeed a member of society—that is, a person integrated into the community. But much of the history of traditional society is a history of imperfect integration or resistance to integration. Strangers, outcasts, members of despised racial groups, followers of different religions, may be, and frequently are, denied membership status and, consequently, the freedom enjoyed by members. Even if strangers are admitted to membership, they present a serious problem. For if strangers have been socialized differently, have internalized somewhat different norms, it is hard to see how, once they have entered a community, their situation can be different from that of the alienated individual. Indeed, the conservative model, if it is to be coherent, practically demands this conclusion. Thus, the conservative concept of communal integration breaks down as soon as mobility becomes a real social possibility—as soon, that is, as society advances from a primitive state of static agricultural communities to a state where some form of market relationship makes its appearance.

Consider next the status of women. Even if members of the community from birth, women ordinarily find themselves subject to entirely different statuses of membership. Conservatives may account for this by developing a theory of parallel integration and membership. Such a theory may clearly be coherent. But it does raise a question about the conservative account of freedom. Where the norms internalized by half the population render them inferior to, and subject to the domination of, the other half, one may begin to wonder just what sort of freedom there is in the arrangement.

The conservative model also stresses the commonality of norms. This does not imply the equality of all members. It means only that all members internalize pretty much the same norms and strike the balance between the authority of proximal institutions and their personal desires in significantly similar ways. But internalizing a norm is not a simple matter, like digesting a meal, in which internal bodily functions combine with food to produce a result. It is more like a process where the body produces chemicals that, at the same time, aid and retard the digestive process. The human mind is a place where conflict reigns, where opposing drives clash and are incompletely reconciled. Internalization, therefore, produces anxiety as the person strives to reconcile norms in a psyche characterized by conflicting drives. But if these drives are fundamentally similar in all persons, the only way we can assume that social norms will be internalized in the same way—the only way we can assume that the authority/desire balance will be struck in the same way—is to assume that the norms apply to all in the same way. Thus, we cannot speak of commonly held norms, but of norms that speak differently to different groups and create different, and often conflicting, responses to authority. But if we cannot assume that all people internalize social norms in the same way, we cannot assume that all are capable of striking authority/desire balances that satisfy them. We must realize, then, that the internalization of norms may really be an adoption of habits of submission—often, as we have finally come to realize, a resentful adoption. Far from seeing rooted, integrated personalities creating a context in which a more authentic freedom can exist, we must recognize the existence of disabling alienation among some—perhaps many—members of the community and a consciousness of one's loss of freedom.

The conservative model, in speaking of "the individual's relationship to the community," of "social" traditions, of "the individual's internalization of norms," speaks in universal terms. It speaks of *the* individual and *the* community and *the* traditions of a society. And that is its attraction, its nostalgic charm. But the reality is disappointingly different. The traditions of society turn out to be, not norms formed by the general practices and agreements of its members, but norms formed by the practices and agreements of its elites and imposed—or, if that is too strong a word, impressed—upon the rest. The individual's relationship to the community vanishes and in its place we see different and radically unequal relationships of different groups to each other and to authority. "The community" begins to look suspiciously like a structure of authority and power relationships based on dominance and inferiority. Indeed, it is only by poetic license that we can call it a community at all. In short, the language of conservatism is radically inappropriate to the social reality it purports to describe.

The reality of conservatism is an order of different types of membership, different degrees of integration, and, therefore, different accounts of the balances individuals strike between community norms and personal desires—which is to say, different degrees of freedom. To restore the conservative concept of community (with its implication of common integration), one would have to create rules fostering the integration of all—strangers, women, outcasts, and so on—into a society that shares common norms and traditions. But this is possible only in a society characterized by a good deal of social, economic, and political equality. And to create such a society, we would have to abandon tradition in favor of a very radical form of social planning.

I raise a final problem. To strike a balance between personal desires and the authority of proximal institutions one must have some capacity to influence those institutions. Without such a capacity, one would be able to do no more than alter one's desires to conform to the demands of authority. Now, training myself to desire only what I am allowed to desire, and to will what I am required to will, may ultimately allow me to do voluntarily what is demanded of me. And in some sense, I might be called free. But unless the process of training itself meets the test of freedom, it is hard to see how my ultimate condition *can* be called freedom. If a ruler required lobotomies of all of his subjects, we would hardly call the resulting voluntary obedience to his rule freedom. We can call a person's actions free only where the process of creating voluntary behavior, as well as the behavior itself, satisfies the requirements of freedom.

Now let us suppose that the proximal social environment is controlled by outside forces, such as absentee landlords or "impersonal" corporate or government bureaucracies. Does the loss of a person's influence over this environment, or the serious attenuation of a group's capacity to influence it, not radically restrict his or its ability to strike a balance between the demands of authority and personal desires? There is substantial evidence that this loss creates feelings of inadequacy, inefficacy, and alienation.[11] Could we, in these circumstances, say that the process of internalizing norms corresponds to the process imagined by conservative writers? Or that the powerlessness of those who have lost influence over their environment is irrelevant to the question of whether the process of internalizing norms meets the requirements of freedom? If freedom is to be thought of as emerging in the concrete actions of people who have internalized a balance struck between the demands of authority and their personal desires, it requires a social order where the manipulation of the process of internalization by dominant classes or groups is absent. In short, it requires a social environment in which the actors—whether individuals or groups—have substantially equal power to create norms and to resist the imposition of norms. But no societies exhibit such equality; and to create it where it is absent, or to begin the process of creation, means undoing traditional arrangements and, therefore, abandoning conservatism by way of rescuing it. Of course, we can try to distinguish "apparent" traditions, which do not meet these requirements, from "true" traditions, which do. But such a distinction, even if not arbitrary, would move us away from the results of concrete behavior and toward a rationalist and abstract construction of behavior and, consequently, would contradict the nub of the conservative philosophy.

Thus, the conservative attempt to combine community with freedom fails. It either offers an idealized account of community that is contradicted by the reality of social action, or rescues that account by undertaking to introduce reform measures that contradict its most basic recommendations.

THE POLITICS OF INTIMACY

In recent years, advocates of community have sought to encourage the growth of face-to-face politics in neighborhood and workplace groups, and in local government where possible.[12] They have done this because they have seen how the conditions of modern mass society frustrate democratic participation, attenuate communal relationships, and introduce deep strains of alienation. The results of decentralization cannot be stated with confidence, but it is clearly reasonable to expect it to generate a wider sense of personal efficacy than currently exists. In addition to encouraging greater participation in voting, it might reveal to the participants the extent of their common interests at a time when the credibility of common interests is at its nadir. Although this would reflect interests related to the concerns of the small society, it might awaken a sense of the existence of common interests even in the national society, and encourage the development of a more benevolent attitude toward cooperative political behavior than presently exists.[13]

Yet decentralization may not address the issue. In the view of some radical theorists, the issue is the state itself and its tendency to suppress any form of popular expression that threatens its authority. What is required is a new view of politics altogether, which stresses the substitution of small cooperative communities for state organization.

There are good reasons for adopting this argument, romantic as it may seem. We may accept the fact—as a fact—that the state is not about to be replaced by a congeries of small communities. But we may argue, with Robert Paul Wolff and Peter T. Manicas, that the intimate community best exemplifies the moral requisites of politics and is, therefore, the appropriate model for the future we should want to build.[14]

I find this argument in some ways compelling. It is certainly not an argument that yields a program of practical political action, but that is hardly a serious claim against it. Its purpose is not to set out the conditions for political reform but to sensitize us to the values we have lost in the maelstrom of modern state politics. It stands as an island of moral opposition to the state-worshippers who dominate our political and intellectual life; to the descendents of Burke who mistake techniques of control for traditions of liberty; to the heirs of Mr. Worldly Wiseman who see freedom of enterprise in an economy dominated by great firms; to the bureaucratic socialists who propose to bring all social power but the state's under control; to the galaxy of social scientists for whom empiricism is the handmaiden of convention. Yet it is ultimately an argument we must reject. We must do so not out of an access of realism, nor even out of admiration for the state. We must reject it because a politics of intimacy is inconsistent with the freedom it purports to advance.

In one sense, the "politics of intimacy" is a misnomer. People do not seem disposed to forego some of the things that the modern economy has given them, nor is it unreasonable of them to refuse to. Consequently, when we think of small communities, we must think, not of social units of a few hundred people, but of units capable of supporting economic activity sufficient to satisfy existing demands. Such activity supposes indigenous economic institutions of adequate size or institutions run cooperatively by several communities. So the communities we speak of must already be of considerable size—say, the size of small cities. Such communities retain a great deal of participatory potential, but not necessarily of the face-to-face variety.

But my purpose here is not to measure communities of various size against each other. It is to consider what the relation is between intimate communities generally and freedom. And here, I think, we encounter conflicts closer to conflicts of principle. In examining these conflicts, I shall address myself to those encountered both by face-to-face communities and by communities the size of small cities, which I shall call small communities. For the purpose of examining these conflicts, I shall take both to be examples of the politics of intimacy.

The first conflict probably concerns face-to-face communities more than small ones, but can appear in both. It revolves around the role of formal procedures. The closer a society comes to the condition of intimacy, the more social action is based on custom and cooperation, rather than on formalized procedures. Procedures, to be sure, need not be absent. But because the conditions of intimacy are subverted by formality, their importance must be comparatively small. Voluntarism, custom, actions based on shared understandings, characterize the intimate community. Now if this order of custom breaks down—as it often does—and if there is no set of procedures sufficient to bind the members of the community, how is the order of the community to be preserved? The obvious answer would seem to be by force, exerted by the most powerful coalition. But then what is to restrain that coalition, to guarantee that it will respect the freedom of the dissenters or, indeed, the conditions of community? There must be some formalized and enforceable constraints. It may be excessive to identify formal procedures with the maintenance of freedom itself, as some do, but it is not excessive to say that, in times of social unrest, they are a necessary, if not sufficient, condition of it. So the intimate community's need to rely on custom rather than form means that it can preserve freedom only where the order of custom is not seriously threatened—that is, where social unrest is largely absent. But periods of unrest are precisely the times when freedom is most threatened and protection of freedom most required. The association between political intimacy and the order of custom, therefore, turns out to threaten the maintenance of freedom precisely at the point where it needs the greatest protection and where it is so often lost or compromised.

Second, intimate communities create bonds between intimates, limiting their circle of sympathy and concern. As Rousseau said, I grieve more on hearing of the death of a neighbor's child than on hearing of the death of a hundred children in Cathay. Such feelings may in some sense be natural. But an intimate community does not simply rely on them—it reinforces them by making care for, and obligation to, one's intimates the highest law. This is magnified in face-to-face communities, although it is present in small ones as well. And this is a dangerous step. It may easily lead—as it has led in innumerable instances in the past—to the creation of rules governing relations between ourselves and strangers that are different from the rules governing relations between ourselves and intimates. It can lead to a rejection of newcomers who threaten, by their numbers or natural or ethnic characteristics, the existing conditions of intimacy. It can lead to a denial of the political and social status and, therefore, the rights of strangers.

I do not mean to suggest that these things are universal and inevitable experiences—merely that they are disturbingly frequent. The exclusionist and nativist tendencies of political intimacy are evident in much of the history of communities and populist movements in nineteenth- and twentieth-century America. Localism does not extend merely to distrust of newcomers; it frequently invites denials of rights or of elementary toleration. In America, it was the overriding of localism by state and ultimately national institutions—to the accompaniment of chapters of abuse hurled at tyrannical "outsiders" who ignore the will of the people—that reversed this trend. It is at best poignant and at worst sobering to recall that respect for local traditions, freedom of association, and the integrity of communities were the last refuges of segregationist ideology.

Even where it does not extend so far, constricting the circle of sympathy and concern leads to a radical reduction in the possibility of altruism. "Who is my stranger?" asks Richard Titmuss in his extraordinary book on social policy. It is a crucial question precisely because social policy is "concerned with 'stranger' relationships, with processes, institutions and structures which encourage or discourage the intensity and extensiveness of anonymous helpfulness in society."[15] An egalitarian society is a society whose social processes make possible, even encourage, acts of altruism. Of course, one ordinarily mentions altruism at one's peril, since it is the signal for those with no other arguments to assume the mantle of realist and sage and warn against the dangers of social fantasy. So I shall state at the outset that I do not assume that altruism will become a major factor in human affairs. I assume only that, conceived in terms of "anonymous helpfulness," altruism is hardly an unknown factor in social life. Indeed, with apologies to professional realists, it remains a persistent characteristic of it. The willingness to act on the basis of concerns that affect strangers rather than friends is a central condition of community and a characteristic—if not the dominant one—of all of the great movements of human liberation of the past three centuries. For these movements have been characterized by the intense commitment and participation of many—sometimes, as in the case of the American civil rights movement, of millions—who in no way stood to benefit from their success. The fact that their motives might have included egoistic self-satisfaction is simply irrelevant. What matters is that their actions evinced concern for strangers and that the social environment encouraged this. One need not depend on a sudden access of universal good will to insist on the relevance of such concern to equality. One merely need agree that acts of anonymous helpfulness are both possible and desirable and that the institutions of society ought to be adapted to *promoting* rather than *restricting* them. We should extend the circle of concern to include strangers; and we can do this only by identifying that concern not with personal feelings of sympathy but with *impersonal processes*. And this is beyond the capacity of a politics of intimacy.

Third, a politics of intimacy centers people's interests on the concerns of the community. But communities, no more than people, are islands entire of themselves. It is not unfair to say that intimate communities have tended to prefer homogeneity to diversity, conformity to independence, moral rigidity to toleration. But how, in conditions of intimacy, can it be otherwise?

The interests of people need to be turned outward, away from themselves, to be opened to outside ideas and movements. The justification for this openness is not simply that it, rather than insularity, is a condition for the development of a significant or vital culture, although that is not a minor advantage. It is that such a culture is, in its turn, a spur to reflection and creativity, to the replacement of parochial visions with cosmopolitan ones, to the easing of the lineaments of conventionalist restraint, to the recognition of the humanity of strangers and to the widening of the circle of concern. But this describes a culture that values the maximization of moral enlightenment and that underwrites—if it does not guarantee—the practice of toleration. This openness is, therefore, a necessary if not sufficient condition not merely of freedom but of what I shall shortly describe as civility.

But if openness helps to produce toleration, it is produced by it as well. An open society can develop where conditions make it possible for people to tolerate dissent from convention. Dissent is easier to tolerate where it is not bound up with the social tie itself and where, therefore, it does not seem to threaten that tie. The tendency to identify dissent with the dissolution of the social tie itself is stronger in small communities, precisely because dissent *is* more destabilizing there. This magnifies the ordinary psychological and social causes of resentment of dissent and helps to explain why openness has not been a notable characteristic of intimate communities. It is true that openness is not necessarily characteristic of large societies either. It is simply that the possibilities of developing an open culture improve as we leave the conditions of intimacy behind.

The characteristics of political intimacy—the emphasis on custom rather than form, the narrowing of the circle of concern, the tendency to a parochial culture—may encourage participation, but they tend to hinder the attainment of freedom, and especially of equal freedom. For all of its surface attractiveness, the politics of intimacy fails as a way of integrating individual and community.

COMMUNITY

It seems, then, that none of the leading communitarian theories is adequate. Does this mean that there is no satisfactory indication of what the communal nature of human morality means or where it leads? That hardly seems credible, since the elementary communitarian perception itself appears to be well founded and coherent.

When our attempts to amplify such a proposition seem to fail, the sensible thing to do is not to abandon the attempt or to pursue a failed strategy with greater intensity but to try a different approach. Like a traveler who suspects that he has taken a wrong road, we should pause to consult our maps and consider whether there may be a right one.

One of the first things we should consider is whether the right road is a more limited one than we are used to traveling. After all, the common nature of our existence does not, by itself, suggest any particular style of existence, or any particular set of moral assumptions. Nor does it guarantee that any conclusions we can draw from it will be strong or comprehensive. The drawing of such implications was probably a reaction to the radical individualism of the early liberals and the tendency of later liberals to ignore the social dimension of human morality. But however this may account for the intensity of the communitarian reaction, it hardly justifies its particular moral arguments. Perhaps our problem lies in the fact that we succumbed to the temptation to build a grand theory out of insufficient materials, to place on communal theory a greater weight than it can bear.

The recognition of limits is the beginning of wisdom. It is a difficult beginning because it goes against the modern faith that enlightenment involves the transcendence of limit. Nevertheless, philosophy is in large measure a demonstration that there are mountains that faith cannot move. We cannot march as easily as we thought from premises concerning the social character of morality to the conclusion that moral ideals must be common ideals, or that justifiable benefits are common or shared benefits. We cannot justify embracing a radical communitarianism merely because we reject a radical individualism. Something else needs to be said. But this something else is not a set of additional premises from which we may draw conclusions. It is instead a construction of a moral theory into which we fit, retrospectively, our sense of the communal character of morality. We need to weld a theory out of the ambiguous materials at our disposal before we try our hand at drawing implications. We need, in other words, to argue rationally.

Now this does not mean that we are to forget whatever little we know about the communal character of morality. It means we are to use it, but refrain from deducing anything from it until we have constructed the theory into which it fits. Until then, we are to accept it for the limited perception it is and use it according to its limits. To speak of these limits, however, is not to admit to intellectual paralysis.

To say that there is a social or communal basis to moral life is to say that some concept of community must be part of any model used to construct a moral theory or set of ideals. Moral life is, in a sense yet to be specified, a *common life*. If this common life can be given a particular moral dimension, it can be taken to imply that we have some obligations to our fellows with whom we share that life. What these obligations are and to whom we owe them cannot now be specified. Some believe that they come to nothing greater than the obligation to create a minimal framework for the exercise of voluntary choice and otherwise leave others alone. I shall argue that this view—which is substantially Robert Nozick's—is not coherent and that the terms of the practices it describes cannot be incorporated in its justification. I shall argue that freedom must involve more than being left alone to act and, ultimately, that the communal element in the moral life is best seen not in terms of cooperation or participation but in terms of equality.

But all of this awaits construction and development. At this stage of the argument, the concept of community functions simply as a model, or part of a model, of the practices necessary to justify a moral theory. It works, therefore, in the same way that a model of the state of nature or original position would. It is a postulate that forms the context of moral reasoning. But unlike a state of nature, it is an open postulate, telling us very little about that context. We can make no assumptions about the nature of the situation created by this model besides the assumption that there is a communal element in moral life that no moral theory can ignore. We know nothing, and can assume nothing, about the character of the actors in that situation, the way they think or reason, the things they value, and so forth. All of this awaits reconstruction.

4

MORAL RULES

RULES AS BOUNDARIES

To speak of moral theory is ordinarily to speak of rules. It is true, of course, that we can frame a moral theory without rules. We may, for example, follow Nietzsche in seeing morality as a struggle for self-mastery that would be subverted and trivialized by being reduced to rules. And it is surely correct for MacIntyre to distinguish rules from virtues. Nevertheless, we cannot frame a theory designed to govern or guide transactions without at least contemplating its reduction to rules. Sooner or later, a social theory, or a moral theory intended to guide social action, must leave room for this possibility.

It is also true that moral philosophers who easily tolerate conflict and ambiguity in their general discussions of morality do not ordinarily carry this tolerance over into the discussion of rules. They rather think of rules as inescapably preceptual in nature, as having to be stated as summaries of exclusively correct ideal standards of behavior. Isaiah Berlin, not surprisingly, puts this position most clearly:

> In so far as rules are general instructions to act or refrain from acting in certain ways, in specified circumstances, enjoined upon persons of a specified kind, they enjoin uniform behavior in identical cases. To fall under a rule is *pro tanto* to be assimilated to a single pattern.[1]

Once we translate an ideal into a rule we seem to leave conflict and ambiguity behind and reject the possibility that the rule may be stated any way other than preceptually. Perhaps we believe that to state it any other way is to risk incoherence or inconclusiveness. Is this so? Can doubt, ambiguity, conflict, be reflected in rules? Will rules so conceived not lose their character as rules?

The belief that they will reflects a particular understanding of how moral rules function. In general, rules of any type—such as rules that state instructions, or precepts, or rules that constitute practices—seem to create standards. In this view, a moral rule is a statement of an ideal pattern of behavior, coupled with an injunction or recommendation that it be followed. Now it is clear that such rules leave very little room for ambiguity and doubt. They necessarily exclude all contrary moral standards; otherwise, they risk their coherence. At best, their scope can be limited by stipulating a *ceteris paribus* clause, or a reservation that the rule applies in "most cases," or some other similar qualification. But the inability to clarify such qualifications by specifying what needs to be equalized, or by defining "most" with particularity, simply renders the rule ambiguous or subject to *ad hoc* compromises over its scope. The clarification of the qualifications, on the other hand, threatens to render the rule incoherent.

The need for ideal-behavior rules to exclude other standards creates a serious problem. As I have argued, much of moral life is characterized by dilemmas precisely because we cannot, with confidence, exclude all other standards. The price of realism in moral philosophy is the admission that moral choices often do not resolve doubt and conflict, but are taken in spite of them, and thus give rise to feelings of ambivalence, guilt, anxiety, and so forth, that will likely affect—perhaps alter—future choices. Nor can we argue that, if moral choices cannot resolve human doubt, they can at least resolve logical doubt. If ideals themselves are ambiguous, even this line of retreat is cut off. Of course, we cannot press rationality into service to justify ideal-behavior rules. So we must conceive of moral rules that take doubt and ambiguity into account.

We can do this if we conceive of the moral rule as structural in nature, creating boundaries that confine the universe of possible good or right actions. It operates, therefore, by excluding certain possible actions but, within the boundaries so set up, leaves room for choice and variation. It creates a sort of conceptual space within which the rule holds. This conceptual space does not contain an ideal answer, but rather contains a number of acceptable answers, among which we are free to choose, provided we can come up with adequate justification. Thus, this concept of a moral rule accepts the view that there are often no right answers to moral dilemmas, but there are wrong ones; and it works to limit the boundaries (or scope) of indeterminacy. Its view is that morality is *indicative*—pointing to the range of acceptable answers, perhaps even to the range of relevant attitudes or motives.

In limiting indeterminacy, we do not create ideal answers, but accept the existence of doubt and ambiguity as legitimate. But it is possible to confine the boundaries of acceptable answers, to narrow the rule-boundaries, to engage in a process I shall call *closure*. I shall argue in this chapter that the creating and closing of rules must be done by a process of agreement, constrained by certain principles of a peculiar type. I discuss these principles at length in the next chapter. At this point, however, I want to emphasize the need to distinguish them from moral rules. This distinction is a hard one to make just now, since it is difficult to take account of certain features of a concept one has not yet encountered. Yet it must be done, for an awareness of the distinction between moral rules and the principles that constrain them is crucial to my argument.

Since a claim to rationality creates boundaries, we shall have to speak of both rules and principles in boundary terms. But I mean "moral rules" to describe the boundaries of moral judgment and action reached by agreement, and "principles" to describe the means of structuring both moral rules and the agreement process. So principles are the ground of moral rules: they limit the scope of rules and agreements. But they should not be thought of as categorical or architectonic. They constrain, but in less rigid or precise ways than we are used to. I have argued that moral ideals may be only roughly outlined and that the vision of an ideal is the vision not of a clearly defined standard but of a temper—a disposition that guides or directs moral argument and perception, but does not *entail* anything. The word "temper" does not mean that moral principles must necessarily be weak or vague. They may be strong, creating powerful presumptions in favor of certain moral positions.

Indeed, they may even be decisive, in the limited sense that we cannot now develop answers or deploy counter-principles of equal power (although we may in the future). But the point is that these principles do not entail answers to moral dilemmas; they guide the course of moral argument and constrain, but do not determine, moral choice.

So on whatever level we think about morality, we do not think about a deductive process. Morality is a continuous process of creating, closing, or opening rule-boundaries in response to our changing understanding of action and our sense of whether we should like to encourage or limit particular actions or sorts of actions. And while this sense may be initially formed out of our intuitions, desires, aspirations, perceived needs, experiences, and the like, the actual creation and closure of rules must be the product of agreement, constrained by the principles I have referred to. Within these constraints, rule-boundaries can be severely closed where there is extensive and widespread agreement over the characterization of particular actions, and agreement, consistent with the constraining principles, that choice ought to be restricted. They can—and ought to—be relatively open where such agreements are missing.

It is impossible to see morality as a cohesive and coherent set of rules whose basic postulates are sufficiently symmetrical to allow us to derive from them an adequate and consistent set of duties, evaluations, or preferences. The ambiguities and doubts that are inseparable from both moral action and our characterizations of moral action, together with the ambiguity of ideals, certify this impossibility. What we can hope to do is to limit indeterminacy. But this means, as I argued in Chapter 2, that we must give up the dream of a moral theory that prescribes answers to particular problems. There I suggested that the hope of creating rules that are narrow and well modified—such as those that prohibit particular sorts of arbitrary violence—is decisively frustrated by the ambiguity of ideals as well as by our inability to characterize actions rationally. Besides, in a world of ambiguity and doubt, a rule of such particularity sacrifices, along with its generality, its relationship to other rules.

Although the concept of a rule as a boundary-marker is relatively simple, perhaps the argument would profit from an example.

I shall choose a simple example, because my purpose is to show how a rule functions, rather than to examine the range of problems that boundary-marking presents.

Suppose we want to understand the rules concerning killing. We may want to say that the intentional killing of other human beings is wrong. Many of us believe, however, that there are exigent circumstances in which killing is not wrong; and this belief is neither arbitrary nor unreasonable. Some of these exigent circumstances will be pretty generally agreed on, such as a killing done in self-defense or to prevent the murder of an innocent person where there is no alternative to killing. But other circumstances will be the subjects of great dispute. Is euthanasia justified? Or capital punishment? Or killing to avoid a social calamity? Is the killing of a loved one, dying in pain, to be compared with the killing of a loan shark by a debtor? The very characterization of an act as killing may be open to question. How do we treat a surgeon whose patient dies during an unnecessary operation? Or a mine owner who refuses to correct certain hazards that cause the deaths of some miners?

It is not credible that a rule prescribing an ideal pattern of behavior—a rule on the order of "thou shalt not kill"—can deal coherently with the variety of actions and the range of (reasonable) disagreements involved. To state such a rule would force us to reduce a complex and ambiguous congeries of actions to a simple, abstract characterization (or a narrow set of characterizations). It would strongly limit the development of exceptions and foreclose the inclusion of new actions in the scope of the rule.

Suppose, instead, we recognize that we can do no more than create a presumption against killing. We may agree that arbitrary killing lies beyond the boundaries of justification, and we may define certain types of killing as arbitrary. For the rest, we recognize that it is possible to justify killings that lie within those boundaries. That is, we may agree that positions for and against euthanasia or capital punishment or killing to avoid a social calamity are legitimate, provided reasonable arguments can be advanced in their favor. We ourselves may be convinced that one or another of these arguments is determinative and, therefore, that a particular position is the right one. But unless these convictions have been very widely accepted after having been thoroughly vetted and rival views fairly considered, they cannot be translated into rules. Even then, there are constraints on this process that I have yet to consider. At this stage, we can merely say that both boundary-setting and closure—the narrowing of the boundaries and the restriction of the range of acceptable answers—should be slow and deliberate processes.

How do we decide what the scope of a moral rule should be? Should a moral rule concerning killing deal with killing in general and treat decisions on euthanasia or capital punishment as inferences from it, or should moral rules concern individual actions, such as capital punishment and euthanasia? I am afraid that I cannot say. We cannot identify the subject matter of rules, or create a conceptual mechanism that would do so. For that would entail making the sort of rational decision concerning the characterization of action that cannot be made. Any action, or type of action, whether broad or narrow, can be the subject matter of a rule. The agreements, the conventional understandings of a society, are, on this issue, determinative.

AGREEMENTS AND THE IMPOSITION OF RULE BOUNDARIES

If rules are to be thought of as boundary-markers, we must have some idea of how these boundaries are set. At the same time, we must remember that the boundaries to be set concern rules governing the behavior not of isolated individuals but of people who live in society with others and whose actions necessarily affect others. Thus, while we may envision moral values or ideals that concern individuals alone, or the discrete actions of individuals, we conceive of moral *rules* as something else—as norms that obligate, bind, and govern interpersonal actions. To justify a moral rule, then, is to justify something that sets boundaries for good or right action not merely for me but for others as well.

May we argue that the boundaries of moral rules should be set by specially designated individuals or groups? May we justify the imposition of boundaries by authority? Putting aside claims to divinity or divine guidance, this imposition may be justified in two ways. One of these ways is by arguing that the imperative of order is so great that it gives to authority a decisive entitlement to impose norms. This is a large claim. The entitlement to impose moral norms is an entitlement to appropriate exclusively the entire realm of morality, so that, except for what is said or implied by authority, there is no morality. Such a position is tenable only when we can believe that the meaning and implications of, and the need for, order, as well as the means of attaining it, are clear, that no confusions and ambiguities attend the attempt to characterize the actions involved in maintaining order, and that doubts about the relative importance of order can be decisively overcome. In my view, these are claims plainly falsified by human experience and contradicted by the arguments presented earlier in this chapter.

The second way authoritative imposition of rules may be justified is by assuming an entitlement based, not on order, but on some particular moral virtue or advantage—say, the possession of valued attributes, such as superior wisdom or goodness, by an authoritative elite. But this argument also fails. I have argued that referents influence the way we understand moral terms and actions and that, while we can somewhat transcend their influence, we can never be certain that our understanding is uniquely or universally valid. I have also argued that an exclusively valid characterization of action depends on our ability to frame an exclusively valid theory of rationality, which we cannot do. Now, to justify the authoritative imposition of rules on this second ground, one would have to assume such a uniquely or universally valid understanding of moral terms and actions. As we cannot do this, we have no warrant for assuming that the virtue or advantage on which the entitlement in question rests has any relevance. For example, if my superior wisdom or goodness does not allow me to understand moral terms or to characterize action in a uniquely or universally valid way, I have not put forward a reason why my wisdom or goodness justifies replacing your judgment with my own. At the most, I may have put forward an argument that it would be prudent for you to pay close attention to my judgments (supposing, of course, that you accept the superiority of my wisdom or goodness). But this is a far cry from authoritative imposition.

Alternatively, we might assume that the doubts, ambiguities, and disagreements that characterize moral life can, in some way, be synthesized and encapsulated in the understanding of the authoritative elite. But this is equivalent to taking that group to be some kind of ideal or hypothetical rational person, for this process of synthesis and encapsulation still depends on unique or universal understanding (although of a different type from the one discussed in the last paragraph), or on the existence of an exclusively valid concept of rationality. Hence, it, too, must fail.

In the absence of justifications of moral rules as cognitively true or authoritatively imposable, a moral argument is merely a reason for my holding a particular moral opinion. That reason may be powerful. But the justification for *my* holding a moral opinion is not the same as the justification for *your having to hold it*. Some justification for your having to hold it must be offered. But if no such justification can be made, then my argument—whether based on natural law, tradition, categorical theory, contract, utility, or whatever—*can be nothing else than an appeal for acceptance, an argument seeking to persuade.* (Even theological justifications may be seen in this light, so long as the vehicle for their acceptance is faith rather than fear of earthly punishment.) Absent acceptance, I can offer only an account of my moral opinion. Since this is not adequate to establish a rule, we must conclude that rules can only be established by persuasion and acceptance.

Establishing rules by persuasion and acceptance suggests that the reason for your holding a moral opinion is your agreement (where agreement includes such practices as the accommodation of disagreements, voluntary and intentional adherence to conventions, and so forth). Now, if moral arguments are appeals for acceptance, and if rules are to be established by agreement, the moral terms and characterizations of action relevant to these rules must reflect the understandings of those appealed to. For we cannot expect people to agree to a rule if the terms of that rule and the characterization of the actions to which that rule is relevant appear to them to be incomprehensible or inappropriate. So moral concepts and characterizations must be stated in terms that reflect *common experiences* or that allow people to draw on common experiences. Where can we find such understandings? It is in the actions of people—that is, in the choices they actually make—that we discover their impressions of the ambiguities and doubts that constitute the tissue of moral dilemmas. And we can infer their conceptions of moral terms and characterizations of actions from these choices as well. We may, of course, make mistakes, but there is no better place to look.

If we are to establish moral rules, we cannot content ourselves with merely accumulating these conceptions and characterizations. We must sooner or later create generalizations sufficient to allow us to establish rules. This process is also subject to error, and for this reason we must tread lightly. In many cases, the generalizations must be very general and the rule-boundaries very wide. But some such process is inescapable. And if generalization is inescapable, when we talk about appealing to people's characterizations and conceptions we must mean appealing to a *common store* of human experiences—that is, to experiences shared by those appealed to. I am not concerned with how this is to be done; perhaps, as Abraham Edel has suggested, we can utilize social science in the effort.[2] My point is more obvious: in the construction of rules by agreement, we must make the common store of human experience the basis for our construction of moral concepts and our characterizations of actions.

No doubt the agreement process does not *entail* appealing to this common store of experience. Nor may the need to appeal to a common store of experience entail further conclusions. But, as I have argued, we should demand not that our conclusions be entailed one by the other but that they be consistent with each other and with a coherent and persuasive moral vision that they mutually reinforce. In that case, the need to appeal to a common store of experience, coupled with the establishment of rules by agreement, suggests a process in which common experience can be enlisted in the creation of rules. If such enlistment is to be more than a mask for authoritative imposition or a pretense swept aside by arguments establishing a theory as cognitively true, does it not suggest a conception of morality as (in some sense yet to be specified) a *common enterprise?* That is, does it not suggest that moral rules are to be established by a process in which all participate together? This, it seems to me, is precisely what makes the argument a coherent one.

Before I deal with the implications of considering moral rulemaking a common enterprise, I want to deal with certain problems presented by the concept of agreement. In the first place, one may wonder whether agreement does away fully with the imposition of rules. Does it not merely alter the character of the imposing authority, or convert imposition by a minority into imposition by a majority? Agreement can do away with the imposition of rules in two circumstances. The first is the circumstance of permanent unanimity of moral opinion. But this is clearly a utopian circumstance; we must assume continuation of disagreement. The second circumstance is this: we show that agreement implies toleration and extend the concept of toleration so far that all dissenters are relieved of obligations they have not agreed to. Or else, we frame a theory of moral obligation in such a way that no one is rightly bound by rules she has not agreed to.

But this second alternative runs up against a formidable objection. There is a purpose to the enterprise of morality. It is not a purpose immanent in the concept of morality considered abstractly, or in nature, or in the metaphysics of human existence. It is, rather, a tacit purpose that informs the enterprise of morality precisely because of the altogether contingent but crucial fact that people invest it with that purpose. But we have no warrant to consider the enterprise of morality apart from the purpose with which people invest it, precisely because morality is a product of that purpose. Unlike the circulation of the blood, or the breeding of sparrows, or the decay of elementary particles, morality is an invention of human beings and its scope and meaning are inseparable from that elementary fact. Morality reflects the human need to provide an alternative to barbarism—to arbitrariness and anarchic violence in the conduct of human affairs. We may accept the logical possibility of an order of barbarism as we accept its historical manifestations. But it is a possibility without compelling force. The force—or, better, the urgency—of morality is found in the need to create a basis for the existence and maintenance of a culture opposed to barbarism—that is, in the need to create civility. By "civility," I mean nothing more than human life as a life of association and interaction that seeks to substitute norms for arbitrariness and violence. The creation of such a culture makes it possible to consider—in fact, to conceive of—human needs, aspirations, and ideals, to develop and transmit values—in short, to do the things that characterize human life.

At this point, I must pause to consider a possible objection. Does the concept of civility not require a characterization of action? And if it does, why is it not subject to the critique I offered earlier?

The short answer is that it is subject to that critique. But this only means that my argument does not pretend to the specificity, clarity, and universality that claims to rationality do. Like Hume, who employed the concept of proof after he demonstrated its impossibility, I use characterizations in limited and tentative ways. I do so because, like Hume, I have found it impossible to discard the concept. I accept its ambiguities and offer my characterizations as rough summaries of experience or imperfect statements of concepts based on such summaries. I believe that the characterizations that go into developing the concept of civility are general enough, and rely sufficiently on common experience, to be comprehensible to most people. This belief may be false. And the meaning I give to violence or arbitrariness, the weight I place on civility, will not be shared by everyone. But that is what makes my argument an argument, rather than a demonstration. And in this, my theory does not differ from any moral theory, Kant's included. A moral argument, delivered with whatever conviction or passion, is simply part of the drama of moral philosophy and it is a mistake to reject it if it does not take the form of a revelation of the Absolute. It is an act of creation, structured in a form that makes it possible to show its coherence. So I shall acknowledge that acts of judgment appear at crucial points in my argument. It would be strange, indeed, if a theory that argues the need for agreement, that sees arguments as attempts at persuasion, would do otherwise. Civility, therefore, may retain its place.

The threats to civility are not simple and known. The possibility of the disintegration of a culture into a condition of arbitrariness and violence is ever-present. And the means by which this disintegration may occur vary greatly. Disintegration may arise, unpredictably, from forces at work in society that are unrecognized, or only dimly understood, as easily as it may arise from forces—such as war—classically associated with barbarism. In addition, we understand that the disintegration of civility is not merely a matter of the fall of cultures or social orders. It is also a matter of the introduction of strands of barbarism into the workings of a social order—the subjection of people to arbitrary treatment, the encouragement of violence, the growth of alienated and anomic masses.

Indeed, this selective disintegration remains the greater, because more real, threat. It may be true, of course, that threats of violence lie behind all order-creating social systems and that strands of barbarism exist in every culture. If that is so, the crucial question comes to be the extent of their appearance, the point at which they start to have serious consequences for the culture. These are questions of the greatest importance, although beyond the scope of this book. We may take it as true that civility cannot be fully attained, and that the real question is how closely it may be approached and with what means. But these reservations do not compromise the desirability of adopting such means if we know them; they merely caution us not to make civility a perfectionist demand.

It may be thought that I have given civility too specific a content. Calling the subjection of people to arbitrary treatment a strand of barbarism sounds like a condemnation of illiberal practices translated into the language of civility. But the strength of a moral argument is not reduced merely because it has become central to a particular political theory. And there are good reasons to support opposition to arbitrariness. Besides undercutting the very idea of norms, arbitrary behavior usually contemplates the employment of more than ordinary violence in its defense. For if we assume that people do not care to be treated arbitrarily, the resort to arbitrariness carries with it an implicit affirmation of the willingness to act in the face of their objections.

It may also be thought that, as any use of violence introduces a strand of barbarism into a social order, and as coerced obedience to social rules clearly rests on violence, coercion is inimical to civility. If this means that civility entails a preference that norms be voluntarily accepted and freely obeyed, I would not object. But if it means that norms not voluntarily accepted are somehow invalid, or that society has no right to enforce them, I do. Such a view seems to me superficial for very traditional reasons. In the first place, the individual's freely chosen norms may run counter to the interests, preferences, or needs of others, and there is no *a priori* reason why his freely chosen norms should outweigh or negate theirs. If having to obey a norm not freely chosen is being coerced, then one or the other side here must be coerced. So the issue is, necessarily, the justification of coercion, not its abandonment.

Second, the individual's freely chosen norms may contingently require the subjection of some people. So only where those norms are consistent with the freedom of all can they be defended. But this trivializes the argument or else ignores some difficult questions. Is this consistency anything but a formal possibility? Does it entail a utopian harmony of interests? How are we to determine that the individual's freely chosen norms are consistent with the free choices of all? Who makes this determination? If the individual does, will he not be biased in his own cause? If public authority does, its right to make this determination can be no more extensive than its right to make laws in general. Thus, it either will be unable to make some determinations or will have to exercise greater power than is consistent with the idea of freely chosen norms.

So, in the absence of a general harmony of interests, the issue of coercion and violence is very complex. It is this complexity that forces us to develop theories of freedom that will allow us to determine if and when coercion is right. Civility is not rich enough to do this. From civility we can only draw the conclusion that we ought to minimize arbitrariness and violence and, if we must employ coercion, to choose the alternative that promises the least violence and the introduction of the fewest strands of barbarism into the social order.

I introduced the concept of civility in the course of asking whether imposition could be avoided by the unlimited toleration of dissent. While I have not yet completed the full discussion of imposition, I am able to dispose of the intermediate issue: unlimited toleration of dissent is not justifiable. Nor is it justifiable to relieve people of obligations merely because they have not consented to them. Toleration must end at the borders of civility, at the point where particular courses of action clearly threaten to introduce strands of barbarism into a culture—to magnify, rather than contract, tendencies to barbarism already in place. But how do we recognize those borders, and who is to say when they are encountered? Does this not raise the specter of imposition once more? These are critical problems; but before I discuss them, I want to introduce another problem that also raises the specter of imposition. For to defend an agreement process, the issue of imposition must be more clearly defined and met.

In meeting it, I shall present an argument that may be misunderstood. I shall argue that agreements are forged in action and that this action may reflect conventions created by authoritative elites and passively accepted by the rest of society. While it is hard to deny that such actions and acceptances are in some sense voluntary, it is also hard to deny that they are in some sense imposed. Finally, I suggest that, as civility limits the agreement process, some sort of imposition appears to be inevitable.

Now, without more, this appears to require me either to compromise the utility of agreement or to deny (quite arbitrarily) that conventionalist pressures are forms of authoritative imposition. But I wish to do neither. So I think it best to indicate in advance just what I do want to do and how I shall proceed. I shall argue that the agreement process, standing alone, is unworkable and self-contradictory—hence the dilemma just referred to. But I shall also argue that the agreement process cannot stand alone. It must be tied to, and be consistent with, the concept of the common enterprise. This requires me to develop principles from the concept of the common enterprise that constrain or structure the agreement process to create such consistency. The development of such principles is indispensable and I shall undertake it in the following chapter.

AGREEMENT AS ACTION

The concept of agreement is generally developed in a communicative or discursive context. Agreements, that is, tend to be seen as forms of discursively arrived-at exchanges. The rules governing agreements—the sorts of assents that constitute agreement and the constraints that must exist to make these assents possible—are then sought in rules governing the use of language or in rules applying to discussion. But agreements in society are not products simply of discussion. They are forged through, and revealed in, action. When we speak of a morality of agreement, we speak of a set of practices apparently done in recognition of certain values to which the practices are thought to conform. This forces us to meet a difficult question: how do we know when agreement exists?

To answer this question, we try to discover signs of agreement. Ironically, most signs of agreement turn out to be voluntary—or ostensibly voluntary—acts of obedience to authority, custom, or convention. But if agreement is supposed to be a *source* of moral rules, should we not be able to discover signs of agreement in the *making* as well as the *observing* of rules? Should we not be able to detect the role played by agreement in the process of creating responses to problems facing society? In the overwhelming majority of cases, we cannot do this.

Nor is such consistency as we can detect in the observance of rules free from ambiguity. Agreements, like accommodations, ordinarily reflect the influence of habit and convention. But the practices for which the words "habit" and "convention" stand are usually given a special force by society. Societies tend to see existing practices not merely as desirable but as compelling. They ascribe ideal purposes to practices—assume that they are directed toward, and can be defined in terms of, the highest ideals, rather than in terms of preferences and interests. Thus, there arises a subtle identification of conventional practices with the noblest moral ideals, making it possible for societies to denounce serious criticisms of conventional practices as attacks on the ideals themselves. So a market system is supposed, ideally, to combine maximization of wealth with maximum protection of personal freedom, despite the fact that its actual practices deprive many people of both. But it is to the ideal—or, in contemporary terms, the rational model—rather than to the practice that its supporters turn to prove that radical restrictions on market practices will reduce freedom. On a simpler level, opponents of women's rights take the demand for those rights to be an attack on the ideal of the family. In these circumstances, we cannot be certain that the minimal conditions for agreement exist; and this is certainly one reason for the ancient suspicion that social conventions resemble moral compulsions more than mutual agreements.

Again, people ordinarily hold only vague feelings or intuitions about values. These are hazy notions, characterized by ambiguity and contradiction, rather than coherent beliefs refined and systematized by reflection. "Perceived needs" are not always needs perceived in the same way by all. Contradictory evaluations of human experiences are not uncommon. Aspirations often cohere only at the outer edges of generality. Referents rear their confusing heads. As Rawls suggests, our intuitive moral ideas must be refined by extensive reflective analysis before they can be employed in the social world. But if such reflective activities are undertaken, they are usually undertaken by members of elites and, as I argued in Chapter 3, tend to reflect their values and internalized referents. Now, as most of us rely on conventions to refine our feelings and intuitions, conventions also determine much of the content of our agreements. And our agreements thereby reflect a disproportionate elite influence.

But the argument that values must be validated by agreement ordinarily supposes a more universal contribution to the process. For that is why the notion of agreement is attractive. When philosophers say that the validity of moral values is established when "we" agree, they do not usually mean that "we" is an elite minority, that agreement is nothing more than a passive or deferential acquiescence in elite decisions, or that its validity is unaffected where it is born out of deceit or manipulation. For how compelling would agreement be then, how superior—or, for that matter, different from—the imposition of rules by authority? It is of course true that some philosophers tend to read too many requirements into agreements, to argue that only agreements made under conditions of full freedom and equality can count as agreements. And I believe it is true—as I shall shortly argue—that such requirements are largely illicit, that agreements require only a limited amount of freedom and equality. Still, they require some, even if not enough to satisfy liberals and egalitarians. So we may rightly demand that "our" agreements be agreements *we* have made, rather than pretexts for an elite minority to justify imposing a moral code on us that *it* has made. At the very least, we should *distinguish* this latter sort of agreement from the sort that emerges from the actions and decisions of the general membership of society. And we should understand that these two sorts of agreements cannot be justified in the same way. The latter sort must be justified by the claims of order or superior wisdom; or else the agreements it refers to must be *constructive* agreements, reflecting the decisions of a hypothetical rational observer who speaks for all of us. The former sort of agreement, on the other hand, suggests that a morality of agreement is justified by the argument that the creation of moral values ought to be a common enterprise, and that the imposition of certain values on dissenters is justified, in part, on the ground that they have had a substantial, rather than merely formal, opportunity to contribute to that enterprise.

Is it possible to argue that the concept of agreement should be narrowed to refer only to those agreements that in fact emerge from the actions and decisions of a community, that reflect a common moral enterprise? Apart from further justifying the commonality requirement (which I shall address shortly), we should still have to decide *how* we can recognize such agreements. If the concept of agreement refers to action, if agreements are forged and revealed in action, what can we look to to determine whether agreement exists?

Perhaps we can look to consistencies in action. But the concept of agreement can be employed only where the people acting in a consistent way are aware of their acting consistently and intend that consistency to constitute agreement. To discover these intentions, we may resort to asking them to vote on certain moral propositions, or examine the creeds they nominally assent to, or do intensive opinion polling. The problem with these methods—apart from their sheer physical difficulty—is obvious. Even if we could get a set of consistent, symmetrical responses, and even if those responses dealt with complex moral issues as well as with simple ones (such as murder), we would only be consulting statements of beliefs. Now moral philosophers must be aware of the extent to which our stated beliefs often conflict with our actions. We may, after all, mistake our motives or actions, or lie, or deceive ourselves, or simply be confused. Besides, the purpose of beliefs is to guide action. That is why, in discussing a person's moral beliefs, we prefer to seek what Shaw called "the assumptions upon which he habitually acts." A person's moral beliefs are revealed in his actions. It is by drawing reasonable inferences from his actions that we can define his beliefs.

But if we look at the actions of the members of a community, we may be able to see nothing but certain consistencies. What inferences are we warranted in drawing from this? We need to go beyond the mere perception of consistency and say something about the reasons for, or causes of, that consistency. Following a well-trodden path, we might want to say that the only practicable way to conclude that agreement exists is to identify very basic underlying structures that shape actions and that bind various activities together. These structures might allow us to interpret actions and draw inferences from consistencies. Assuming that we can employ this method, it is open to the objection that these structures help to shape and influence agreements, and, therefore, that what we are identifying are patterns of convention-inspired obedience rather than considered and freely formed agreements. That is, these structures serve to limit the scope of individual challenge to, and reflection on, conventions, and thus, to some extent, to impose values. Even if we accept the argument that agreement is consistent with a less-than-optimal freedom of choice, we may see that freedom limited by the impact of underlying structures. So the very factors that help us to recognize agreement compromise its value in a familiar way. Agreement now comes to be seen—in some, perhaps, large measure—as a function of the directive impact of convention; and this may be insufficiently indistinguishable from various forms of authoritative imposition.

We seem, then, to have come to an impasse. We want to justify the agreement process, but discover that civility—the central purpose of morality—imposes limits on that process and that, under all but utopian conditions, imposition of some sort seems inescapable. So it appears that we cannot employ agreement after all.

But that conclusion is excessive. I have rejected the authoritative imposition of rules. But it is worth recalling that, by "authoritative imposition," I mean the imposition of rules by a group *in virtue of its being specially designated or entitled* to impose rules. I have rejected such imposition on the ground that it entails a claim to an understanding of moral concepts and actions or a theory of rationality that cannot be sustained. I have not rejected it on grounds of freedom or on any grounds that could be called absolute. Indeed, I cannot consistently do so.

Now, when we conceive of a practice, we conceive of a set of related activities. The justification of that practice implies that the activities denoted by the justificatory theory reasonably correspond to the activities identified with the practice. The justification of a practice, therefore, is at the same time a statement of the constraints imposed upon it. I have not justified the agreement process by citing the demands of freedom. I have justified agreement by claiming that moral argument is an attempt to persuade, that in persuading we must appeal to a common store of human experiences, and that this implies that morality is a common enterprise. I have also argued that the requirement of civility is a constraint on the entire enterprise of morality. Taking the argument that morality is a common enterprise to include the need of persuasion, we can conclude that the agreement process may be constrained to prevent that process, or the rules produced by it, from undercutting the requirements of civility and the commonality of the moral enterprise. Rule-making by agreement remains the presumptively appropriate course. But imposition is legitimate where the agreement process fails to meet those requirements and where imposition functions to constrain the agreement process to meet them. Imposition, therefore, remains a viable but limited alternative, and resort to it is not presumptively valid.

Now this is admittedly a dangerous game, but it is a game we cannot avoid playing. We cannot avoid it even if we adopt the limiting view that moral obligations must always be self-imposed and that no obligations may be imposed upon dissenters. For are we to imagine that, in a society of wholly autonomous people, no person or group ever has any claim upon another person or group? Are we to assume that every moral controversy concerns wholly permissive behavior, or that a person's voluntary acts never affect the lives or actions of others? Moral controversies do involve claims on others. Voluntary actions do, sometimes, affect others. If we assume that not every controversy is amicably compromised, the resolution of such a controversy must involve the imposition of one will upon the other, even if that imposition is the result of a rejection of obligation. Suppose I am injured by your careless act. To say that I am obliged to suffer my loss and may not force you to answer for it is to say that your view of the obligations involved in the controversy is to prevail over mine. To say that we play a dangerous game is, therefore, to state a sad but inescapable truism. The question is whether we can control the way the game is played—whether, that is, we can contrive to contain the inevitable need for imposition so that it stops short of tyranny and works within a general practice based on agreement. Can such an accommodation be conceived? I turn directly to that issue, reserving discussion of the institutional arrangements for doing this for Part Three.

5

STRUCTURING PRINCIPLES

THE JUSTIFICATION OF STRUCTURING PRINCIPLES

I have argued that agreements are forged in action and that we can know what agreements exist when, armed with knowledge of underlying structures that allows us to interpret action, we perceive certain consistencies in action. But these consistencies may be due to the directive impact of those structures (conventions, for example) and may, therefore, reflect authoritative imposition. This difficulty vanishes if the underlying structures themselves support those things necessary for agreement—that is, if they meet a moral test. The moral test is obvious. We are entitled to call a relevant consistency an agreement—and not obedience to authoritative imposition—only where it proceeds from a common enterprise. Now it may be difficult to say whether any particular relevant consistency proceeded from a common enterprise; and, indeed, it would be surprising if all did. But the argument I have made is not that every rule must be certifiably common in origin. The argument I have made is that the *enterprise of morality* must reflect this common participation. What we need to know is something about the structures underlying rule-creation in a society. We need to know whether the *process* by which rules and closures are created supports the commonality of the moral enterprise.

Agreements and moral rules must, of course, be consistent with the requirements of civility. Thus, to repeat the argument, we have two requirements—civility and the commonality of the moral enterprise—that act as constraints on the agreement process. Now to say that there are constraints that may validly be imposed on the agreement process is to say that there are moral principles outside of agreements that structure—or, rather, ought to structure—that process. That is, the process by which rules and closures are determined should in fact reflect these principles. (I shall shortly argue that the constraints on the agreement process cannot be said to follow intuitively from the concept of agreement.) Furthermore, these moral principles do not simply constitute standards that structure agreements. The principles that structure agreements will clearly impose restraints on the rules we may agree to: we should not be able to agree to rules that threaten civility or that contravene any of the constraints we ultimately decide on, since such contravention will affect the agreement process or undercut the purpose of the moral enterprise. The influence of the structuring principles (as I shall now call them, abbreviated as "SP's") will be felt throughout the moral system. Constraints on agreements will be constraints on boundary decisions and closures as well.

If SP's are not arrived at by agreement, how are they arrived at? And does the idea of SP's not seem to violate the assumptions that lie behind an indicative morality?

If I were to argue that the SP's are analytically valid or entailed in some antecedent principles, the answer would be obvious. But I do not want to argue this. I want to employ the looser version of rationality I spoke of earlier and present a conception of the SP's whose claim to rationality is based on coherence and persuasiveness.

Rather than being analytically valid or rationally entailed, the SP's are merely the basic inferences drawn from the presumptions of civility and morality as a common enterprise. These presumptions are not analytically valid, either. My use of civility is justified by a simple argument. However we characterize any human action, the need to subject human actions to limits is the most persistently advanced and intersubjectively approved conception in moral theory. Agreement, however characterized, is the only way to create such limits, consistent with the ambiguities of human action. The controversial move is the conclusion that morality must be conceived as a common enterprise. But this, I argue, is the most coherent way of establishing and institutionalizing an agreement process. The argument, although not forced, presents what I conceive to be the most convincing and coherent response to the problems of moral theory.

Now if we consider these presumptions, we may encounter certain principles that appear to be indispensable in reducing the presumptions to practice. That is, the creation of most, if not all, other moral rules hinges on their existence, so that if we did not presuppose them we could not create moral rules at all. These principles structure the other rule-boundaries.

To say this is not to suggest that the SP's are merely categorical principles in a different guise. They lack the logical compulsion and universality of categorical principles and share an ambiguity suggested by their origins. Furthermore, while the SP's cannot be identified without characterization of action, they require a very limited characterization—indeed, only such characterization as may be employed in any moral theory. It may be thought that the same argument can be made for Kantian rationality—and perhaps it could, except for the fact that the need to create an exclusively valid theory of rationality forbids it. Furthermore, the Kantian conception of rationality cannot be employed in moral reasoning without characterizing action. This creates ambiguity, which vitiates the concept of *a priori* categorical rules. The SP's can tolerate ambiguity, however, precisely because they are not architectonic and do not provide the foundation for the *deduction* of moral rules. The SP's are designed merely to indicate a general direction, to justify relying on a mood or temper or attitude in the making of moral decisions. They must be conceived in such a way that they do not implicitly determine those decisions, resolve the doubt and ambiguity that define moral life, or contemplate any particular characterization of action.

The SP's are universal in form, although clearly we cannot know the extent to which our understanding of them is restricted by referents. It is obvious that I have already called upon experience to lay the foundation for their derivation. On the other hand, if these arguments reflect persistent perceptions and intersubjectively conceived values, I can make some claim to have transcended the restrictions of referents and the ambiguities attendant upon characterization of actions, and to have presented defensible summaries of relevant experience. These summaries are inescapably part of the argument that the fabric of moral life depends on civility, just as they help us to understand the role that doubt and ambiguity play in moral life. Both civility and the vision of morality as a common enterprise can follow only from arguments that tacitly include summaries of experience. And these and similar summaries can be used to draw further inferences.

FIRST PRINCIPLE: CIVILITY—MAXIMIZING THE POSSIBILITIES OF MORAL LIFE

The most obvious inference we can draw comes from the requirement of civility. Moral rules are crucial weapons in the struggle against barbarism, inseparable from that limiting of violence and arbitrariness that is the condition for the survival of a culture of civility. And this, I think, constitutes the fundamental project of morality: the subjecting of human action to limits, the regularizing of what otherwise would become barbaric. Hence, the most obvious SP: maximization of the possibilities of moral life, of life lived according to norms and relieved of the threat of violence and arbitrariness. This is, in its general form, little more than a restatement of the concept of civility.

I use the concept of maximization for obvious reasons. As I have suggested, barbarism stands for more than the bald replacement of norms with an order of terror. It also stands for the strands of arbitrariness and violence existing in, or introduced into, a culture. The occasions for this introduction are many and frequently unpredictable, the causes not wholly known. Consequently, we must see the possibility of barbarism in every failure of civility and in every default in the struggle against violent or arbitrary methods of resolving conflict. This is not a once-for-all sort of struggle. The elimination of barbarism involves a continuous effort to assure the dominance of those things that preserve and advance the possibility of civility. But this is nothing less than a requirement to maximize the possibility of that dominance, to choose to support that effort at every opportunity.

It is possible to flesh this maximization principle out. Doubt and ambiguity create moral dilemmas, and the lack of a cognitively true morality suggests that resolving dilemmas and forging agreements are, like the articulation of moral theories themselves, acts of creativity. By "creativity" I mean more than the imaginativeness needed to evaluate and adapt traditions and conventions to unique situations. I mean things like the capacity to discover what is unique in a situation and respond appropriately to it, the capacity to examine moral language critically, to perceive the limiting impact of referents, to conceive of possible solutions to threats not clearly understood around which opinions may coalesce. But creativity must play its role in a morality of agreement. This raises the question of a dialectical relationship between the two. They support, but also threaten, each other—agreement by raising the possibility of the triumph of conventionalism over individuality, and creativity by inflating the significance of individual moral intuitions. Any possible reconciliation is, and always has been, difficult. It must begin with the understanding that creativity in morals, as in art or philosophy, is not merely a matter of individual intuition. It is also a matter of gaining enlightenment or insight from others, of building on mutual contributions. Who these others are is not always clear. We may wish to stand on the shoulders of giants; but giants are not so easily found and, besides, the thin air of great heights can make us giddy and foolish. So we must prepare for these heights by first learning to stand on the more modest shoulders of people. Enlightenment begins on the ground. Before Newton wrote the *Principia*, he had to learn to do sums. The viability of joining agreement and creativity depends on a willingness to entertain the possibility of mutual contributions—of *intersubjective* forms of enlightenment—and on the existence of social processes promoting such enlightenment.

It used to be thought that enlightenment was the great weapon for combatting barbarism. That faith has fallen apart in the modern culture of despair. We have good cause to doubt the promise of reason and the impact of enlightenment. But we are thrown back on them because we have, so far as we know, no better weapons. If it is naive to think that reason and enlightenment are vehicles for moral regeneration, or that release from our mind-forg'd manacles promises redemption from an uncivil state, it is not naive to see them as our only means of perceiving and understanding the possibilities of barbarism present and latent in our social practices. This is something that faith, passion, intuition, cannot do and Providence will not do. Enlightenment and reason remain, as Dewey and Freud urged, practical necessities in the moral enterprise.

So civility must be seen as a complex principle. It requires, certainly, that we maximize the possibility of agreement, which is the chief means by which rules are created. But because the overcoming of barbarism requires enlightenment, and because we need to harmonize agreement with creativity, this principle must also include maximization of the possibility of intersubjective methods of moral enlightenment. This, of course, strengthens the concept of morality as a common enterprise.

SECOND PRINCIPLE: EQUALITY

The first SP, which I shall call the "maximization principle," is drawn from the concept of civility. We also need to draw inferences from the concept of morality as a common enterprise. Certainly, the idea of creating rules in common has certain implications. But we must be careful to understand the nature of those implications.

Consider, first, the concept of agreement. Agreement is frequently taken to require a high degree of equality and freedom among the participants. Is this requirement justifiable? It is not clear that it is: agreement may require an altogether more limited amount of equality and freedom. Suppose some people are disadvantaged, not in the sense of being wholly powerless, but in the sense of having less power than others to frame rules or to influence the content of alternatives. Does such disadvantage render agreements between them void? Why? So long as the disadvantaged people have a legitimate voice in rule-making, so long as they can ensure that the alternatives among which they choose are at least minimally acceptable to them (even if not the ones they prefer), they can be said to have agreed. For the alternative they choose is within a range of alternatives they willingly entertain, not merely as alternatives to death or force, but as acceptable in themselves. And surely we cannot argue that no agreement is valid unless all parties are in a position to realize their primary preferences, for we should hardly be able to consummate an agreement if we did.

Now suppose that, in the course of creating an agreement, A withholds from B information that would lead B to make a particular choice. In the absence of that information, B chooses differently. B's decision is surely a voluntary one, and to the extent that an agreement is the result of a voluntary choice, B can be said to have agreed. It is also clear that A has manipulated B's choice. She did not *force* B to choose as she did, but she altered the conditions of agreement. Had B been able to define the conditions of agreement equally with A, she would have chosen differently. By "conditions of agreement," I refer, first, to the norms that control the practice of negotiation and agreement and, second, to the circumstances of power and control over relevant resources attributable to the participants. To define the conditions of agreement is to determine both those norms and the extent to which power and resources can be used or may be neutralized. (The problem of the conditions of agreement is, of course, familiar to everyone who has thought about social contract theory, although it appears there in somewhat different form.)

The fact that B's inability to define the conditions of agreement may not invalidate the agreement can be given greater weight than it merits. It is surely a trivial conclusion. The important question is whether she should be *able* to define, or help define, the conditions of agreement. It is fairly clear that, if given the chance, B would want to exercise that ability. At least it is fair to say that most B's would want to do so. There seems to be no reason to assume that they would choose to be systematically inferior to others, or that they would be content to allow others to invest the alternatives among which they choose with value. Of course, people might be willing to entertain some systemic inequality or some restraints on freedom, but it is not reasonable to suppose that they would agree to their own permanent inferiority.

Must people have an opportunity to define the conditions of agreement on equal terms with others? If the concept of agreement does not require this, perhaps the concept of morality as a common enterprise does. There is certainly a great temptation to use it so. For example, we can, without much effort, show how a moral enterprise with great differentials in capacities to define the conditions of agreement loses its common character. But this sort of argument proves nothing but one's ability to manipulate definitions. When I first offered the concept of morality as a common enterprise, I said that its sense was yet to be determined. The resolution of the issue of the conditions of agreement will certainly help to define the scope and meaning of that concept. It will give content to this somewhat open-ended concept, whose implications are vague and uncertain. But we empty both resolution and concept of significance if we merely absorb the former into the latter.

If morality is a common enterprise, it is a common enterprise among moral actors. And this is a matter of great importance. For if we can say something about moral actors and moral action, we necessarily say something about the common enterprise and help to define its scope and meaning. And if what we say about moral actors and moral action justifies a great degree of equality and freedom, then we can read this back into the concept of the common enterprise and enrich it to that degree—perhaps to the degree that requires that all people equally participate in defining the conditions of agreement.

Let us first consider moral actors. The most common way of justifying the contention that all people ought to participate is to argue that all people equally possess an attribute (usually a natural property) relevant to defining the conditions of agreement. That is, if the attribute or property relevant to defining these conditions is possessed equally by all, no coherent argument can be made to deny some the opportunity to participate in the process. But which property do we choose? Do we choose rationality, creativity, the capacity to suffer, maleness, featherlessness? Obviously, any argument must show that the property (or properties) chosen is (are) relevant to moral action. If we do this, we may conclude that people should be treated equally with respect to that property. On the other hand, the fact that a particular property is relevant to defining these conditions does not mean that others are not also relevant. So the argument requires a showing that no other property that is unequally possessed is relevant. Either we must show that all unequally possessed properties may be excluded as irrelevant, or we must show that the equally possessed property is so crucial that it outweighs all unequally possessed properties.

To make such a showing, we should have to define the selected property with reasonable particularity. This presents a problem. Consider, for example, how we would define the property of rationality. Let us (for the sake of this example only) take rationality to mean the ability to conceive of a purpose and take appropriate means to achieve that purpose. How do we know that this is a property of people except as it is revealed in action? Unlike featherlessness, it is not a property we can determine by observation in the absence of any action on a subject's part. People can be said to possess rationality because we can infer possession of a certain capability from their actions. We have no warrant for assuming that there is a single discoverable natural *thing* or bodily function that corresponds to the property called "rationality," any more than we may attribute its presence to a particular gene whose composition determines how much of this property anyone has. Rationality is a name we give to a capacity that is produced by a combination of natural capabilities revealed in action. That is, rationality is a relationship between ends and means that must be conceived of and stated in terms of human action, which is to say that we must reduce the universe of ends-means relationships to action. We can do this by creating summaries or examples of actions that describe or encapsulate those relationships. Since it is preposterous to demand that we create these summaries by matching up all possible ends and means with all possible actions, we may choose a more reasonable alternative. We may conceive of *representative rational actions*—types of actions that correspond to the range of ends we consider within the compass of reality (broadly understood) and the range of means we conceive of as appropriate. It is beyond expectation that we can create absolutely true, universal summaries. Consequently, our conceptions of representative rational actions wil be tentative, and will ordinarily be greatly informed by common sense.

No doubt this process has gone on—however unconsciously—long enough to enable us to speak generally of rationality with some confidence. But that is not enough to enable us to show its *exclusive* relevance to moral action. To do this, we have to be able to specify the range of rational actions with great particularity. Otherwise, we could be faced with the objection that much of what we take to be rationality could better be attributed to some other natural property, such as aversion to pain, imaginativeness, or creativity. And we should then be hard-pressed to show that rationality is relevant to moral action and these other properties are not.

Our ability to specify with great particularity the representative actions we associate with a property hinges on our ability to characterize actions. We must be able to show that the terms of the property—our conception of the typology of representative actions—are universally valid. But here we are frustrated by our inability to characterize actions universally. The ambiguity of action interposes itself. Take a simple illustration. In characterizing the hypothetical rational person in the original position, Rawls argues that he would be governed by a desire to avert risk that is manifested in his adoption of maximin strategy. But it is not clear that the hypothetical rational person—assuming we could coherently conceive of one—would have to be governed by this desire to the exclusion of all contrary desires, as critics such as Brian Barry have maintained.[1] It is consistent with Rawls's concept of rationality that the contractors be willing to accept a statistically low risk of economic deprivation in exchange for a statistically high possibility of increased benefit. So the contractors may be willing to accept the existence of inequality on terms other than the difference principle.

Again, in order to identify a property as exclusively relevant, we must be able to specify the representative actions associated not only with it, but with all other possible properties. For we must be able to show that what we take to be an excluded property is really not part of, or implied in, the relevant property. So even where we argue that the general, common sense conception of a property is sufficient to justify the judgment of relevance, we discover that we cannot show its exclusive relevance unless we are prepared to assume that general, common sense conceptions of properties are sufficiently differentiated from each other to permit the appropriate judgments. This, I think, we cannot do. Nor is it sufficient that we *agree* that a generally conceived property is exclusively relevant. For we would have to admit that rationality could be generally conceived also, and we could make the agreement argument only if no rational disagreement were possible.

Suppose we select something such as Gregory Vlastos' concept of "individual human worth." The advantage of such a concept is clear. Because "persons have [it] simply because they are persons,"[2] it seems not to be rooted in a property or properties, or to have to be an exclusively relevant attribute. It suggests merely that people need to be treated equally, not in all respects, but only in respect of their human worth. But in order to use it to justify giving all the opportunity to contribute to the definition of the conditions of agreement, it must be shown to be exclusively related to that purpose. And its intuitive nature and vagueness assure a most unsatisfactory looseness in the structure of such an argument. Finally, unless we can identify a property that individual human worth is rooted in (which Vlastos says we cannot do), we are faced, simply, with an article of faith that determines, by definition, both that the attribute of human worth is relevant and that all people possess it equally.

Thus, we cannot argue that all people should have the opportunity to contribute to the definition of the conditions of agreement because they equally possess a relevant property, since we cannot identify such a property in the way we would have to. Even if we could, we would find that we could not decide whether people possess it equally. For if the judgment that people do (or do not) possess it equally is a judgment of fact, we would have to create universally valid characterizations of the actions of all people. Of course, we may want to argue that the property need not be possessed equally. We may want to see it as what Rawls calls a "range property"—a property that need only be minimally possessed by all. But there must be a justification for regarding any property as a range property and this justification can only be given by a prior moral argument. In that case, the equal opportunity requirement would be a function of the prior moral argument rather than of any argument concerning the possession of a property.[3]

Thus, we cannot show that any property is exclusively relevant to the issue. And even if we could, we could not determine whether all people possessed it equally. Therefore, we seem unable to answer the question of whether all people, or only some, should be able to define the conditions of agreement. But this is unsatisfactory. Is there a way out?

There is if we can justify saying something about the person in her role as moral actor. In developing a moral theory, we must presume the presence of moral actors. The moral actor is a person considered solely in her formal relationship to moral action itself. Suppose we take the formal concept of the moral actor, purged of any particular references to personal properties or attributes, and framed so generally as to require only such characterization as may be used in any moral theory. If we did this, we should be going very far toward conceiving of the moral actor as an abstract construct, of which the person is a concrete representation. But what the person would be representing in her moral role would be the abstract construct called the "moral actor," and not an actor identified by particular natural properties or personal attributes.

Because we cannot know anything about the natural properties or personal attributes of the abstract construct known as the moral actor, we can identify that construct only in relation to moral action. Thus, the moral actor can be identified only as the subject and/or object of conduct informed by intention—that is, as the subject and/or object of moral action. And although the moral actor is a person, it is as a moral actor that she is perceived: it is in that abstract, constructive role that she can know or be known to other moral actors when they engage in moral action. No other means of identification is available, for any other means runs into the sort of objections raised above. Thus, whatever moral decisions, rules, rights and duties, or claims are made or legitimated, they must concern people identifiable only as abstract constructs called moral actors. No other sort of identification is possible, because no property we would specify can be shown to be exclusively relevant to the issue of moral action. The natural properties and personal attributes of people (including their beliefs, desires, feelings, merits, and so on) add nothing to their character as moral actors. *For the purposes of evaluating moral action, therefore, each moral actor, being only an abstract construct, is necessarily the equal of every other moral actor. And every person, being in respect of moral action only a concrete representation of a moral actor, is in this respect the equal of every other person.* So even where we can say nothing else about the claims a person may make, the rights she may exercise, the rules she may create, and the duties she may embrace or that may be imposed upon her, we can say that she does these things only as the equal of all other persons. Thus, the fact that we cannot identify moral actors by citing natural properties or personal attributes allows us to say a great deal. It allows us to say that *moral action is an activity of equals*. And if morality is a common enterprise, it is an enterprise characterized by equality among the participants.

Here, a possible objection may be raised. I have defined moral action as behavior informed by intention. To be capable of being the subject of moral action is, therefore, to be capable of having intentions. And the capacity to have intentions is surely in some sense a natural property. But, unlike other natural properties, the capacity to have intentions is used here as a deduction from the definition of moral action and is relevant by definition. If it is to be included in the definition of the moral actor, it is as a logical consequence of the meaning attributed to moral action, and not because it is a natural property. Its status as a natural property is coincidental and irrelevant and, therefore, the problems attendant upon identifying natural properties irrelevant as well.

It may also seem that the conception of the moral actor as an abstract construct contradicts the argument with which I began this book. There, I sought to show the actor as a person whose actions were mired in guilt, anxiety, ambivalence, confusion, and so forth. Now I reduce the actor to an abstract construct. And abstract constructs cannot be defined in terms of guilt and so on. But the two conceptions are quite compatible; indeed, the latter comes out of the former. For it is the very fact that we cannot identify guilt and so on with any set of properties or actions, that we cannot characterize actions without ambiguity or identify representative ambivalent actions any more than representative rational actions, that makes the retreat to abstraction necessary. We cannot therefore particularize guilt and so on, but must see it as a characteristic—in forms and degrees as yet unknown—of moral actors generally. So to call a moral actor an abstract construct is not to say that she does not suffer from guilt and so on. It is to say that we cannot identify intentions or mental states with particular actors and, therefore, must consider each actor as equally capable of having or experiencing them.

Having disposed of these objections, I want to develop the concept of the equality of moral actors. Equal moral actors are actors who can engage in moral action on equal terms. Now, this capacity to engage in moral action cannot be merely a *formal opportunity* to do so, but must be accompanied by the *power* to engage as well. That is, the equality principle (as I shall now call it) assumes that the capacity to engage in moral action refers to a capacity actually present, rather than to a formal or legalistic entitlement.

We may speak of the equality principle in terms of opportunities only where all persons are able to convert opportunity into performance on equal terms. Now, people may be on morally equal terms when their engagements in moral action are governed by their preferences or their natural abilities, even where they differ. But they are clearly not on equal terms where the opportunities of one are limited by factors over which another has some influence. Suppose that A can be said to have an opportunity to engage in a particular action or related series of actions, such as getting an education, but that that opportunity is affected by conditions of poverty. Suppose also that B—for whatever motive—strives to create, or intentionally contributes to the perpetuation of, a distribution of wealth that makes it harder for A to get an education than for B. Or perhaps B, aware that this distribution of wealth tends to block paths to education, intentionally supports it. And let us suppose further that it *is* possible for A to get an education, although he must work harder than B to do so. We might appear justified in concluding that, as A's formal opportunity can turn into actual performance if he does work harder, the equality principle is satisfied. But this would be a mistake. The circumstances suppose that, even though B cannot foreclose A's capacity to engage in moral action, he can affect it. A may have to postpone his education, or go to a school with poorer educational resources, or forego pursuing the course of study he wants. The equality principle implies that, if A is to have only a formal opportunity to engage in moral action, then B must have an equally formal opportunity. But if B is able to affect A's formal opportunity, it is clear that B has more than a formal opportunity. He has a relevant *power* that A lacks: the power to affect A's opportunity. And B has that power whether he can affect A's opportunity directly (by creating conditions that affect A's opportunity) or indirectly (by supporting or contributing to the perpetuation of conditions that affect A's opportunity). Where one actor has an opportunity and another has not only the same opportunity but a power—however indirect—to affect the first actor's opportunity, they cannot be said to be equal moral actors. This must be so even where the more powerful actor does not seek to exercise power over the other, but merely acts to further his own interests. The point is that his intentional behavior affects the other adversely and contributes to his own advantages, however unconscious he is of this. In order for inequality to exist, it is not necessary for the advantaged actor to seek to create or perpetuate it. Moral blame may be irrelevant.

People can be equal moral actors only where both opportunities and powers to affect opportunities are reciprocal—that is, where no actor can affect the opportunities of any other actor without being subject to the reciprocal power of the other. In such a case, the distinction between formal opportunity and power would vanish. The concept of the opportunity to engage in moral action would include the power to do so.

By "power," I refer to a capacity that is systemically related to the conditions of moral action. The fact is that a person may exercise power over another in a number of ways that do not affect the latter's capacity for moral action. C may, for instance, choose to marry B rather than A, or to buy B's painting rather than A's. These may be exercises of power, but they do not affect A's capacity to engage in moral action on equal terms with his fellow actors. Similarly, suppose A makes a chair and seeks to sell it to me. I choose to buy a chair from B. Neither B nor I has exercised a power that affects A's opportunity and power to sell chairs. It remains what it was before. This is why the simple market situation does not violate the conditions of equality and, indeed, may be a model for certain conceptions of equality, as Ronald Dworkin has argued.[4] But suppose A's opportunity to enter the chair market is restricted by a need for capital that only B has, or by a need to develop certain skills in carpentry that are denied to him. If A's inequality is created or supported by B's acts, B would be affecting A's capacity for moral action in a systemic way. The conviction that—whatever the virtues of the simple market model—this is how a complex market system operates makes the market model unattractive to egalitarians.

I began the discussion of equality by asking whether all people must be given the opportunity to contribute to the definition of the conditions of the agreement. I conclude that they must, and that this opportunity must be equal in the sense I have noted. The requirement of equality is not entailed in the concept of agreement, but is retroactively imposed on it. It needs to be justified by a specific argument on moral action, and if this argument is rejected, only a minimal conception of equality can be required. The minimal conception holds that only that degree of equality is required that would enable the participants to choose freely among the alternatives offered them. It does not require that they be able to shape the conditions of agreement. This latter requirement is imposed by the argument that, as the agreements we speak of are agreements made by moral actors, they must reflect the equal status of these actors.

Thus, while the occasion of the inquiry into equality was the question of defining the conditions of agreement, the conclusion of the inquiry carries us much beyond that issue. The equality principle clearly affects an enormous range of human moral action. I have merely hinted at that range in this discussion, because its purpose was only to provide a brief description of equality as an SP. In Chapter 7, I deal with the implications that this principle has for social theory and practice. At this point, we have little more than a bare statement: all persons must be considered equal moral actors, able to engage in moral action on equal terms with each other; and this ability must be understood to include the power, and not merely the formal opportunity, to act.

THIRD PRINCIPLE: FREEDOM

The concept of the power to act, however shaped and modified by the equality principle, raises critical questions and speaks to aspects of human action that the equality principle does not. We need to know, for instance, what actions may, by agreement, be restricted and promoted, and under what conditions, or when we may be said to be obligated and what the limits of obligation are. These issues raise questions concerning freedom, which I would like to define for the moment as the power to act. And if the power to act is basic to morality, we need to see freedom as a third SP.

I have suggested that the concept of agreement provides an inadequate justification for the existence of freedom because the concept of freedom so derived is ambiguous. Agreement does not seem to entail a conception of freedom that is particularly strong or rigorous, and it cannot be used to define the texture and extent of freedom. But we are no more tied to a logic of agreement here than we were with equality. To say that moral decisions involve resolutions of dilemmas, that moral rules are created by agreement among equal participants in a common enterprise, and that rules themselves are boundary-markers is to say that every stage in the moral process is informed by acts of choice. The very creation of moral rules depends upon—is made possible only by—the existence of choice on the part of the participants and, therefore, upon their freedom. Freedom is inseparable from the existence of moral life itself, and only the decision to do away with morality altogether and embrace barbarism can account for its rejection. And this, of course, would violate the maximization principle.

This, it seems to me, offers a much better account of the justifiability of freedom than traditional rationalist theories do. In the absence of an exclusively valid conception of rationality, there is no way to show that morality must *be* rational or that one should prefer a rational morality. And even if one could show this by appealing to a vague pluralistic conception of rationality, one could not show that there is a form of morality exclusively mandated by rationality that includes a requirement of freedom. The most one can do is to argue that any rational actor—however defined—would opt for freedom. But this means that freedom is justified by *will*, which is not quite the strong justification rationalists have in mind. For when asked why he *must* will to be free, the rationalist has no answer; and if he did, it would compromise the justification of will. It is just as plausible for the willing actor to follow Elijah and St. Paul and choose obedience to divine command and subjection to earthly authority as to choose freedom. Indicative morality, on the other hand, by identifying freedom with the creativity inseparable from moral action itself, by-passes this difficulty.

In the past, freedom was thought to be justifiable only by appeal to a natural or universal law, or to an argument that allowed us to draw compelling (if not entailed) deductions from generally accepted moral or natural premises. It is only in our own time that, spurred on by thinkers as diverse as Sartre and Berlin, we have begun to see that freedom is found, not in the certainties, but in the ambiguities of moral life. It is tied to the drama of ordinariness, the failure of system and certainty and the consequent need for creativity. The ambiguities and failures of morality make free choice a necessity if the enterprise of morality is to be pursued at all. We are all forced to be free by the decision to substitute norms for violence and arbitrariness. And we are forced to be free by our inability to create a basis for a determinate morality. Our freedom, therefore, is a product of the shortcomings and failures that characterize the human condition.

Hobbes might have appreciated the irony in this. He maintained that our misery was the product of the special properties that distinguished us from, and raised us above, the animals—our abilities to use language and to foresee the future by connecting causes and effects. And what we have now come to suspect is that, if our natural distinctions are the roots of our misery, hope for the relief of that misery may lie in recognizing our natural ordinariness and its implications.

The need for freedom among moral actors cannot be challenged without challenging the entire project of morality itself. But how far does this freedom extend? In one sense, it would seem that no limit on the freedom of moral actors is justifiable, except for the sake of freedom itself. After all, we cannot know *a priori* what amount of freedom is necessary in order to resolve dilemmas or create rules. We might try to select certain freedoms for special protection on the ground that they are particularly related to the rule-making process itself. But restricting *any* act may limit our capacity to engage in rule-making, however unrelated to that process it may appear to be. If the enterprise of morality is impossible without free choice, then any limit on free choice may create arbitrary or unanticipated limits on the rule-making process. And this would, it seems, violate the maximization principle.

But this view of freedom as a sovereign principle cannot stand. I may, after all, try to advance my interests in ways that undercut intersubjective enlightenment or the principle of equality. If these things are allowed, the concept of SP's constraining moral action falls. So some principle must prevent this. But the problem is that many of the strategies usually employed to limit freedom are not available to us. We cannot try to confine freedom to acts that meet some test of rationality, since we cannot frame an exclusively valid theory of rationality. We cannot rely on an intuitive case-by-case method to define constraints on freedom, since our intuitive judgments are confined by the SP's, of which freedom is one. And as we have rejected the possibility of cognitively true or categorical norms, we cannot rely on them to specify these constraints.

The justification of freedom is tied to the need for moral rules and to the commonality of the moral enterprise, so that the cruder conflicts with the maximization and equality principles need not trouble us. But the ambiguities of the SP's still leave room for significant conflicts, and it would be surprising if they did not develop. Some mode of resolving these conflicts must be developed if we are not to risk the coherence of the concept of the SP's itself.

PRIORITIES AMONG THE SP'S

The most obvious way to do this is to show that we can establish priorities among the SP's. This, unfortunately, we cannot do. For a priority rule can be established in one of two ways. We may show, first, that a moral theory contains an internal logical order—that the constituent elements of the theory arrange themselves (so to speak) in accordance with a principle central to the theory itself. Rawls does this when he relies on the concept of primary goods to justify the priority of liberty. For the built-in priority in primary goods—self-respect being "the main primary good"—leads quite logically to the priority of liberty.[5] But there is no principle of internal order in an indicative morality: any attempt to scale civility and the conception of morality as a common enterprise is clearly arbitrary.

The second way of establishing a priority rule is to refer to an external principle that structures morality itself. This principle may be intuitive or rational. An intuitive principle (in which I include principles of faith) cannot work for reasons cited earlier: our intuitive judgments are confined by the SP's and so cannot determine their relations to each other. And we discarded the possibility of a rational principle when we abandoned the idea of an exclusively valid theory of rationality. For the possibility of radically different theories of rationality points to radically different priority rules whose validity is no more exclusive than the theories of rationality from which they are derived. And the conception of a rigorous priority rule is critically inconsistent with the premise of ambiguity upon which indicative morality is based.

But that does not mean that conflicts between SP's cannot be resolved. There remains another way, consistent with the ambiguities of moral life: accommodation. Now, accommodation may signify nothing but an intuitive attempt to balance conflicting principles on the basis of *ad hoc* or common sense judgments. But this leaves us at the mercy of the balancer's subjective views of the situation. Where the conflict is revealed in action, the accommodation arrived at will depend critically on our characterization of the action. Where we perceive it through analysis of the principles themselves, the accommodation will reflect the emphases we give to the component elements of the principles. In neither case can we have much confidence that the accommodation will reflect either widespread agreement or coherent resolution. If, on the other hand, we try to create a rule governing the making of accommodations, we should be acting inconsistently with the entire thrust of an indicative morality. Such a rule is hardly possible without agreement on an exclusively valid theory of rationality. And if ambiguity characterizes moral life, how can we frame an unambiguous rule of accommodation? Such a rule would have to be a boundary-marker, in which case its utility would be radically compromised.

Accommodation is possible if there exists a fundamental harmony between the SP's. In that case, accommodating conflicts can be done by elucidating the basic implications of the SP's in advance of the actions in which they may be revealed. Remember that the SP's are not rational or architectonic categories, rigorously governing moral action or evaluation. They function to direct attention and evaluation, to impose a temper or mood on them. The harmony I speak of requires an elucidation of temper or mood, rather than an elucidation of the entailments of basic principles. Ambiguities and doubts will remain; more important, conflicts will remain. Accommodations, like moral rules in general, will serve only to confine and limit. This may seem a disappointing, even evasive, conclusion. But the ambiguities of moral life do not respond to the requirements of logic or fall away in response to our disappointments. They remain, like the speed of light, barriers to our best efforts.

125 Structuring Principles

The accommodations we may draw are not necessarily simple or self-evident. A good deal must be said before we can understand how to accommodate civility, freedom, and equality. I shall address this issue in the final part of this book. At this point, I shall answer my original question of how far freedom extends only in the most general and preliminary way. Freedom of action is limited by the requirements of equality and civility. We may thus far see that the equality principle requires at least a rule of reciprocity: each person's capacity to act must be consistent with every other person's capacity and each must have the same capacity to affect each other's actions. And the maximization principle requires that freedom of action be consistent with the requirements of civility.

INDIVIDUALS AND MEMBERS

A final point remains. It is a crucial point because, as we shall see, it is the focus of the accommodations made among the SP's. To say that morality is a common enterprise is to say, among other things, that we define our moral existence and the contours of our moral life by engaging with other moral actors. This engagement creates what we may call community: in this case, free moral actors engaged as equals in a common enterprise. And membership in the community of moral actors is inseparable from our own identity as moral actors. For when we engage in moral action we cannot be identified except as abstract constructs known as moral actors. This means, as we have seen, that every moral act is done, and every moral claim put forward, in the name of all moral actors. And, therefore, every moral act is an explicit engagement with the community of moral actors, a recognition that moral claims are asserted, not by the individual as individual, but by the individual as a member of a community of moral actors. The decision to engage in moral action implies an acceptance of the fact that we are, as moral actors, not merely persons, but members of a community of moral actors. Moral life is in this sense a common life.

So moral claims and choices must be understood as the claims and choices not of *individuals* but of moral actors who are *members* of, and engaged with, the community of moral actors. Moral claims and choices must be consistent with that engagement. So, of course, must rules and closures, which are, after all, the choices of the community of moral actors. That is, claims, choices, rules, and closures must be framed in such a way that they reflect the existence of a community of moral actors and reflect their engagement with each other.

In Chapter 3, I asked where the concept of community leads us. Rejecting the usual and best-constructed responses to this question, I concluded that all we could say was that community served as part of a model of the practices necessary to justify a moral theory. In Chapter 4, I argued that the necessity of agreement, the appeal to a common store of human experience, and the concept of morality as a common enterprise constitute a coherent and mutually reinforcing construct out of which we can draw certain fundamental, or structuring, principles. This is the communal element in the model of practices fleshed out. This richer communal element leads us further. We can see that it leads us, by a combination of deduction and reconstruction, into a more egalitarian conception of moral action, modifying the things we can say about both civility and freedom.

It is now time to examine these principles in greater detail. We need to know how far the arguments I have advanced affect moral practices. It should by now be unnecessary to remind readers that I shall pursue this inquiry not solely by drawing logical interferences but by incorporating such inferences as I can draw into other elements of an argument in order to create coherent conclusions. These conclusions will not be—indeed, cannot be—systematic and complete theories. They will indicate the nature and applicability of the relevant practices because that is the limit of moral argument. But this indication may be enough to set the broad boundaries of these practices, giving us a sense of the appropriate limits of social action.

PART THREE

THE STRUCTURING PRINCIPLES IN PRACTICE

6

FREEDOM

FREEDOM AND MORAL ACTION

I want to devote the remainder of this book to a delineation of the structuring principles in practice. I do not mean that I am going to show which institutional arrangements or policy choices they imply. I refrain from doing this, not because I think it is unimportant, but because, for two reasons, I think it is inappropriate. First, although the SP's occupy a central position in my theory, they are no more than commanding intuitions, indicating principally the moods or tempers that should constrain agreements and rules. As such, they cannot be defined with precision or set out in such a way that readers will easily be able to see where they lead. The SP's must, instead, be refined, felt out, developed—and it is by no means obvious that everyone would develop them in the same way. Ambiguities and conflicts exist throughout the argument and their resolution cannot be independent of referents and evaluative dispositions that, while capable of being overcome on occasion, still dominate our choices and interpretations.

Second, moral principles generally apply to institutional choices as well as to choices concerning action. The SP's resemble other principles in this regard, clearly constraining institutional choices and telling us something about their shape and texture. But they do not tell us very much. In this they also resemble other principles. It is true, of course, that some theorists believe that moral principles can be made to yield a large number of institutional deductions, or at any rate a clear set of them. But I think they are mistaken, buoyed for the most part by unsustainable rationalist assumptions. On the contrary, it is crucial to recognize how *few* institutional choices can be implied by the basic principles of a moral theory and how little discussion they cue. Two obvious points sustain this view. First, the SP's can impose no more rigorous boundaries on institutional choices than on any others. Second, institutional choices are radically contingent, limited by historical circumstances and knowledge. Moral argument can indicate the general direction of institutional arrangements, but little more.

The beginning of wisdom is to recognize that, as the SP's are the products of a common set of assumptions, operate in similar ways, set out only moods rather than architectonic first principles, and contain no priority relations, they cannot be understood except in relation to each other. This means that they must be delineated with an eye to the impact each has on the others and all, taken together, have on each. The SP's together create a context that limits the meanings we can assign to any one of them; and each has meaning only within that context. We cannot understand them alone, unrelated to each other. To define freedom, for instance, in a way that is not related to this context and to the other SP's is to define it abstractly and, as I shall shortly argue, to risk its justifying power.

On reflection, most people would probably agree with at least part of this argument. Except for the fanatics among us, we assume a plurality of ideals in moral life; and, while we understand that particular ideals may make stronger claims on us at particular times, and that some may make stronger claims most of the time, we see them as *elements* of a moral life. We know that we can invent moral arguments that make one ideal or value entirely dominant, so that it is a test of every action and judgment. But such an argument would be artificial and abstract in the very worst senses of those words, and would suggest a moral practice that most people would find objectionable, if not repulsive. The problem is that, although we recognize both the plurality of ideals and the need to balance the claims they make on us, we tend not to see them as interrelated. Instead, we see them as individualized ideals—ideals that can be understood and developed largely independently of each other, even if they spring from common assumptions. Thus, we have only the crudest idea of how to accommodate each to the other where it becomes necessary, and how to arrive at the most justifiable, rather than merely permissible, balances. It is true, of course, that the SP's do not solve such problems as they might if they were products of a rationalist theory; but being conceived as parts of a collective context, driving in a comprehensible, if general, direction, they create a defined sense of the boundaries of justifiable accommodation. The point of this and the two following chapters is to indicate those boundaries.

The SP's differ from most other sets of ideals—though not Rawls's—in another respect, and this respect aids the development of justifiable accommodation. Because they structure the way we create other ideals or values, the SP's are in a real sense *public* ideals. They are ideals that come out of an understanding of moral life as a common enterprise that reflects a need to have rules and, therefore, a culture that makes civility possible. Their role is to provide the bases for intersubjective action and communication, so that the various subjective beliefs of individual actors can be objectified—as far as it is possible to do so—into a set of rules. The SP's thus have an essentially political character. It is this public or political character that accounts for the fact that they do not deal with subjects like honesty, respect, kindness, courage, love, or any number of other ideals or virtues. The SP's may not be more central to morality than these virtues, but they are more central to the *process of building a moral life*, to the objectification of ideals, to making intersubjective action and communication possible. And this public character narrows the range of possible accommodations in the event of conflict among the SP's. It indicates that, far from being *ad hoc* or justifiable on any of a large number of grounds, accommodations must at least be consistent with the development of a culture of civility through intersubjective action and communication. Joined to the contextual understanding of the SP's, then, publicity helps to refine the boundaries of justifiable accommodation.

In short, to conceive of the SP's as public ideals that cannot be understood apart from their relations to each other and to the context of moral action is to conceive of each SP in a way that allows it to be conformed to the demands of the others. This means that we shall have to think of freedom, not in traditional liberal individualist terms, but in communal terms—in terms, that is, that fit easily with equality and civility. We shall have to think of freedom as applying, not to acts done by individuals, but only to acts that can be done equally by all individuals. Put into the language of this book, the term "freedom" applies only to the acts of the moral actor, who, as an equal member of a community of moral actors, may claim a right to do only what any other member may do. Similarly, equality must be thought of as an equality of actors who seek to choose and create, who must create and apply rules, and who, therefore, must constantly recreate civility in their lives. It is an equality whose concern must be with the capacities of actors to act rather than with the distribution of resources. Equality, then, takes on an entirely different meaning—a meaning that is rooted in action, just as freedom is. Civility—maximizing the possibility of moral life—must be understood as maximizing rules that underwrite or extend free acts of equal moral actors.

The question is, Can these understandings be justified? There are those who say they cannot—that freedom entails reciprocity, but not equality; that equality is a distributional concept; that civility suggests a degree of hierarchy and traditionalism inconsistent with equality and with robust conceptions of freedom. If they are correct, I am not; the two sets of views are fundamentally incompatible. Furthermore, the argument that these understandings are implied by, or come out of, the arguments of the first two parts of this book is hardly convincing. In the first place, it would require me to modify my views on the ambiguity of moral principles for what would—rightly—be seen as a mere tactical advantage. In the second place, it is unlikely that those who reject a particular definition or usage can be persuaded to accept it by a showing that is implied by a more basic argument. They are more likely to see it as a reason to reject the basic argument as well, however unreasonable that may be. So I must defend my understandings of freedom, equality, and civility in more traditional ways, and rely on my basic argument only where I am required, by the design of the theory itself, to use it.

FREEDOM AND COMMUNITY

My concern in this chapter is with freedom. Along with many others, I see freedom as inseparable from community. But this inseparability needs to be explained. Community creates a model for moral thinking—imposes a cast of argument upon it. It means that moral thinking—the creation of rules—is a common enterprise. But, as this common enterprise affects not only the act of agreement but the rules we may agree to, community imposes a cast upon moral life as well. I have argued that that cast of argument does not lead us to speak of freedom as action consistent with a common good, nor to limit freedom to acts consistent with the traditions of a community, nor to see freedom as emerging only as we associate with others in an intimate community. These meanings are mistaken or misleading. Freedom is communal in the sense that it is a public thing. It is justified by the need to engage the world, to choose and create moral rules, and is thus inseparable from moral life itself. But moral life is a common enterprise and our engagement with the world a common engagement. In the end, community refers to the equality that characterizes membership in the body of moral actors. It refers to the *common life* that can be created by the realization of, and action upon, the commonness of the moral enterprise.

The passions of community are the passions of equality. Equality is, in common sense, a way of realizing community. But in another, and profounder, sense, it is *the basic form community takes in practice*. To put it differently, the practical implications of community can be said to come down to the general features of an egalitarian society, so that egalitarianism is an effective substitute for community. To the extent that we are equal—socially, economically, politically—we are able to act with *each* other on the same terms as with *any* other. Free, democratic, and civil relationships become possible precisely because our rights and obligations are the same whomever we come into contact with. The practice of community involves the interchangeability of human parts, the extension of the circle of sympathy and concern. But this is not simply a matter of encouraging the development of affective associations or making people aware of the importance of the common.

All too often, communal thinkers seem to offer little more. But such an approach is inadequate, akin, in its naiveté, to the Dickensian belief that a good society can be made only by good people. The creation of community is accomplished by the integration of people into the body of moral actors by legal, political, and economic means. If any society should incorporate this integration and extension of membership into its basic practices, then the members of that society would engage with each other in transactions indistinguishable from ordinary communal transactions except for the degree of affect created by conditions of intimacy. But if my argument in Chapter 3 is correct, then the process of integration and the creation of appropriate practices is unlikely in conditions of intimacy; so the level of community characteristic of a common life is not merely satisfactory, but is, however limited, the fullest and best representation of community we can create.

The delineation of the SP's in practice is the delineation of the common life. It is common, once again, not in the sense that the same form of moral life is shared by all, or in the sense that we hold common conceptions of the good, or in the sense that, overcome with altruistic fervor, we accept greater obligations toward each other. *It is common in the sense that it is a public life that extends membership on equal terms to all moral actors, and this extension is a condition of justifiable moral rules.* Of course, many people may not want to act in this way. They may want to maintain their exclusiveness, privileged statuses, power over others, and so on. Nothing in the idea of the common life says that they will not do so, perhaps frequently. We may hope that, in a democratic society whose lower classes can mobilize some power, they will not succeed or will succeed only imperfectly. Otherwise, all that will occur is that they will compromise their moral standing, a fate few find disturbing. That the common life is the product of public ideals does not guarantee that we shall not daily subordinate it to private wants.

If freedom and community are inseparable, freedom contemplates the extension of membership as well. But that means that freedom is also inseparable from equality, understood in terms of capacities to act, rather than in terms of the distribution of resources. It means that we cannot be said to be free to do an act that derogates from the capacities of others to act on equal terms with ourselves. This, of course, is where controversy begins.

The strategy I shall adopt is to take some very common problems of freedom and show how freedom is at its most coherent when tied to equality. By this I do not mean that individualist versions of freedom—conceptions not tied to community or equality—are incoherent. I mean that they are not as coherent; if each version has its strengths and weaknesses, the communal version is, overall, preferable.

Because we are used to the locutions and forms of the individualist version, the consequences of the communal version sometimes strike us as odd and the individualist view appears closer to the root common sense of the matter. This is true even of the deplorable libertarian tendency to place the discussion of freedom in an exchange context, as though it were a branch of contract theory rather than the other way around. It is largely because we have trapped ourselves in a vocabulary of individualism that this confused reconstruction seems, if not desirable, at least sensible: it relies on a usage of freedom with which we are familiar. But to those schooled somewhat differently, it lacks credibility. When, for example, Publilius Syrus suggested that one who accepts a favor sells his liberty, he proposed a different understanding. Being neither trapped by the vocabulary of individualism nor hobbled by the formalism of contract theory, he saw little sense in assuming that, if one voluntarily makes a contract or agreement, subsequent encumbrances, however justifiable or foreseeable, constitute a strengthening of freedom. Now this insight might raise significant questions whose answers are by no means obvious. If there is a conflict between the expected consequences of one's choice and the continuation of one's freedom to choose, which ought the advocate of freedom favor? Is the voluntariness or moral significance of a choice (for instance, to accept a favor) affected by the comparative power or dependence of the chooser? If so, must freedom be thought of as sharable? Fortunately, none of this appears to have troubled Publilius Syrus. He seems to represent the common sense of his own time. And to speak of common sense, after all, is usually to speak of conventional wisdom. It is conventionalism dressed up, but rarely thought out. Of course, this omission of thought is precisely the advantage of conventionalism. It allows us to take for granted what we never would accept on reflection. It is, therefore, a pillar of the libertarian view and a comfort to its supporters. For by relying on the conventional identification of freedom with voluntary choice, and by denying that freedom must be sharable, libertarians legitimize their claims of privilege by converting them into expressions of liberty. One should not overlook the contribution of thoughtlessness to the continued vitality of confused ideas.

THE INDIVIDUALIST CONCEPT OF FREEDOM

Why is freedom something that can only be shared? Why can freedom not describe acts done by individuals, regardless of who else can do them? The question is a complicated one.

Let me begin by posing an example. Suppose A is able to act in a way that P cannot: A, let us say, can vote. May we say that A is *free* to vote? On the individualist model, there is no doubt that we can, even if, at the same time, we deplore P's disenfranchisement. On what ground can we reach this curious result?

We may, first, want to argue that freedom is a descriptive concept—that it speaks to the acts we are in fact able to do. We may then want to say that it is good or right that people are free to do certain acts (such as speak or vote) and not others (such as own slaves). We may also want to say that, in certain circumstances, a particular freedom may be overridden by other values or considerations. So it is perfectly reasonable to say that A is free to own slaves, provided we realize that it is not a freedom that can be justified. A ought not to be free to own slaves.

Now there are two things wrong with this argument, however reasonable it appears. The first problem is that, in everyday discourse, we do not use "freedom" in an entirely descriptive way, and we cannot in good faith assume that we can. For reasons cultural and historical, we associate the word "freedom" with something of moral worth. There is a conflict between the descriptive and evaluative connotations of "freedom" that is inescapable. More than that, this conflict may be part of the ambiguity of the concept. As William Connolly suggest,[1] the word "connotation" may be inadequate, for it fails to convey the point that the evaluative sense is something intrinsic to the concept of freedom itself.

To make this point more forcefully, we can see how we substitute other words for "freedom" in appropriate contexts—words that are more consistent with a descriptive intent. We might want to describe the activity of owning slaves in terms of *power*. While the concept of freedom is often related to power (to say that I am free to do something is often to say that I have the power to do it), the one need not, in ordinary parlance, be the same as the other. And we may be willing to sacrifice clarity in the usage of terms so as not to endow certain acts with apparent worth.

The evaluative sense of the word "freedom" is surely tied to the worth we assign to the concept. It is present in most of the referents of the word and colors the way we learn about its use. Freedom is, after all, one of the paramount values of the modern world—or part of it—and even those who hold it lightly see the wisdom of pretending to do otherwise. To call something a "freedom" is to endow it with a presumption of validity, at least—to say something about the act the word refers to that suggests a reason to consider it worth protecting. Freedom enters political discourse characterized by a sense of *anticipated justifiability*. By "anticipated justifiability" I mean that, prior to any usage in a sentence, the word is endowed with a sense of worth that we expect will be attached to actions in order to justify them. We are occasionally brought up short by a usage (such as "unlimited freedom") that contravenes our expectations. Yet even here what we condemn is the carrying of something to excess—having too much of a good thing. And we feel impelled to explain our condemnation as a special case.

Philosophers are not any less immune to the (often tacit) evaluative senses of "freedom" than the rest of mankind, even where they stipulate their intent to use it descriptively. Nor is this particularly lamentable. It merely reflects our inability to separate the descriptive and evaluative functions of the concept and specify the conceptual space each covers. This ambiguity is entirely apt. What better word to use to remind us of the need to make moral choices in an atmosphere clouded with doubt? What we mean by "freedom," how we define it, must always reflect its ambiguity, its two-sidedness.

There is a second problem with separating the descriptive from the evaluative in dealing with freedom. While we can still say that people *ought* to be free to do certain acts and not others, we cannot say that freedom itself has any *intrinsic* value. Therefore, we cannot use it as a justificatory principle.

If we adopt the descriptive version of the concept, we can say that A (and P) ought to be free to do a particular act (vote) solely because of the worth of the particular act, rather than because of the worth of acting for its own sake. It is the thing we do (vote) that carries the moral burden. There are two problems with this formulation. It tells us, in the end, that we are free only to do what is good or right—a principle not only inconsistent with the basic tradition of individualism but repugnant to its very raison d'être and pregnant with threatening possibilities. For, in the likely event of disagreement, who is to determine the worth of the act? If it is the actor himself, the issue becomes trivial; if a majority or some form of public authority, individualism comes to be hostage to the very worst version of the common good. The second problem is that the descriptive formulation never allows us to say that A should be able to act for the sake of acting, merely because acting without restraint is a good. If the rightness or goodness of an act is a function of something apart from the worth of acting itself, we can never say that freedom is intrinsically a good thing, that the ability to act without restraints is *itself* right or good. Such a view is not incoherent but, because it does deprive freedom of justificatory power, it is inconsistent with, and repugnant to, the individualist theory of freedom. For the moral center of individualist theory is precisely the worth of freedom itself: why else would the individual assume primary importance?

So while we can coherently separate the descriptive and evaluative notions of freedom, we cannot do this while affirming a commitment to individualism. To defend the individualist model of freedom, we must grant freedom a substantial degree of moral significance. But if we do this, we quickly see that, here too, we cannot make a persuasive case for the individualist version. The principal reason for this is that we cannot use freedom to justify an act *unless all actors can act in the same way*. (I shall argue later in this chapter that this is a *minimal* requirement and that freedom, properly considered, requires that no act I do impair any person's *capacity to act*. But I shall not develop and justify this point now.) But the litmus test of the individualist version is the contrary: a version of freedom can be called individualist if it allows us to say that a person may exercise freedom even if others do not. Freedom in this view is *serial*. It sees the individual exercising freedom not as a concrete representative of the category of moral actor but as a concrete person considered separately from, and independently of, all other persons. Each person's freedoms can thus be assessed and accounted for without considering the freedoms of anyone else. It is this separation that is the theory's distinguishing characteristic; that is why I call it "serial."

Why can we not use freedom to justify an action where some actors cannot act in the same way? As I have constructed the argument in the first two parts of this book, the reason is not far to seek. The equality principle requires that actors have equal power to act. Reciprocity means not merely that A and P can do the same acts but that each *has the same power to affect the other's opportunities*. Now as freedom is an element of justifiable moral action, and as justifiable moral action also requires an equality of moral actors, it follows (skipping a few obvious steps) that freedom may justifiably exist only among equal moral actors—moral actors who, among other things, have the same powers to act and to affect each other's opportunities.

We can reach the same conclusions using more traditional moral theory. Consider situations where all actors cannot act in the same way. The most limiting of these situations would be a case where A exercises power over P and deprives P of some or much of her ability to act. Clearly, A cannot employ freedom to justify his action. For to do so, he would simultaneously have to affirm and deny the worth of freedom, and that would render his justification contradictory.

Suppose that P is deprived of much of her power to act, but that A does not consciously exercise power over her. A merely goes along with social convention, seeks the best for self and family, and wishes everyone well. But if A is aware of P's deprivation, is his conduct not an intentional, if passive, toleration of it? More than that, such toleration, by substituting passive acquiescence in the actions of those who directly deprive P of her powers to act for possible resistance to them, in fact reinforces their actions and secures their positions. Thus, A becomes a silent partner in P's deprivation. Having tolerated that deprivation, and perhaps benefited from it (as a result of the decrease in competitors for status or position), he is in the same position vis-à-vis justification as he would be if he actively aided it. To defend his action, which includes support of deprivation, in the name of freedom is simultaneously to affirm and deny its worth.

This contradiction is not the result of A's *intentions*, but of his *actions*. Neither A's desire to deprive P, nor his sympathy with her, is the salient factor. What matters is the impact on P of A's actions. But if this is so, it seems that the contradictory nature of this justification vanishes if A acts to remove P's deprivation or to resist those directly responsible for it. That is, although P remains deprived of her powers, A's acting to enable her to acquire them allows A to use freedom as a justification for his own actions. This is hardly an anomolous result, for, in the circumstances, A's actions do not support P's deprivation and, therefore, his invocation of freedom is not contradictory. We are concerned, remember, not with the question of whether we can say that A "is" free, but with whether he can invoke freedom in justification of his actions. His attempt to enable P to act is, indeed, an explicit engagement with the community of moral actors, a recognition of the common nature of freedom. It constitutes an explicit rejection of the individualist model of freedom.

So we can use the concept of freedom as a justification in two sets of circumstances. First, we can use it where it is conditioned on all persons' being able to act in the same way. Second, we can use it where, although some people are deprived of it, we act to enable them to acquire it. In either event, we must reject the individualist model.

RECIPROCITY AND THE OBLIGATION TO ENABLE

Most of us believe that freedom ought to be characterized by reciprocity. Some, who reject the individualist view, agree that reciprocity is a condition of its justifiability. Even so, there is much disagreement about what the concept of reciprocity requires. It is not clear, for instance, whether our claim to freedom of action requires us to guarantee P an actual power to act, or whether we need guarantee her only a legal or formal opportunity. In most liberal versions, the latter is enough; so we may say (to borrow an example from R. H. Tawney) that, if P can afford it, she is free to dine at the Ritz. But what if she cannot afford it? Some writers (such as Rawls) seem content to state that this eliminates the worth of that freedom for P. But I do not think that that goes far enough. I think it is important to be able to say, generally, that no one can be free to dine at the Ritz unless all are.

Freedom is not an abstraction. It refers to the acts that take place in the realm of moral action. Taken in the context of moral action, an act can be expressive of freedom only where it is done by a moral actor: freedom refers to the acts of the construct known as the moral actor. It thus describes actions within the range of natural possibility that can be done by every person. Moreover, as I argued in Chapter 5, we must understand action in terms of the actor's power to act, rather than her opportunity to act. Freedom speaks to the power I can exercise in society. In exercising that power, I affect the interests of others. If they are in no position to defend their interests, or to affect mine. or if they are in a critically inferior position, they are deprived of an important power. And as I cannot justify a claim to freedom that simultaneously supports the deprivation of others, I cannot justify as freedom my ability to affect their interests. Justifying that claim requires equalizing whatever is necessary to correct the situation. If the mere existence of opportunities to act were sufficient to enable them to protect their interests, nothing more than equalizing opportunities would be required. But it is no longer possible to keep to such a pretense in the face of overwhelming evidence that disparities of wealth, resources, or status are also, and perhaps more, responsible. So the justification of my claim to freedom requires a sufficient equalizing of these.

In short, reciprocity contemplates a mutual capacity to do the act in question: no one can be free to dine at the Ritz unless everyone is. And this has a simple consequence. Where some people cannot dine there, my freedom to do so is contingent on my supporting their claim to be enabled to do so as well. If I refuse, I lose my right to justify my claim on the grounds of freedom. I can assert my freedom only as I acknowledge an obligation to enable those who cannot act to do so, and to do so in fact.

There are those who think that, even if we have a moral obligation to enable people to act, that obligation cannot be drawn out of the concept of freedom.[2] This argument, I think, turns on defining freedom as the absence of deliberately imposed restraints on action. If we define it this way, then inaction that does not make it impossible for P to act, but merely fails to make it possible, cannot be said to make P unfree. I want to argue that such a definition is wrong and then use that argument to support the obligation to enable. Unfortunately, the argument needs to be set out at some length and I must ask the reader to bear with me. Its relevance will become apparent.

RESTRAINT AS A CAUSAL CONCEPT

If we are to think of freedom in terms of action, we should want to say that, in any specific case, freedom is the ability to bring about a particular proposition regarding action. This proposition may or may not be brought about, and it is reasonable to ask why. The question is reasonable because in morals and politics we are concerned with persistent patterns of action and the way these patterns interact with rules of various sorts. We want to know whether a person's capacity to act according to her intention has moral or political meaning. So we say, "P was able to bring about the proposition regarding actions she intended because. . . ." But the difficulty of this formulation is obvious. There are an enormous number of reasons why P could bring about this proposition, some (such as her ability to use language or to reason) attributable largely to her social inheritance, others to her own actions, still others to the opportunities to act provided by society, and so forth. The range of possible reasons (including accident) is immense, the relevance of particular reasons contestable, the contribution of each suggested reason impossible to specify with confidence, the existence of unperceived or unknown reasons likely. The best we can do is create a few rough generalizations that seem to account, in tentative ways, for a large number of cases.

Moreover, it is frequently difficult to perceive *whether* the proposition P intended *has* been brought about, since many of the actions P does, or tries to do, will be ongoing, complex, or ambiguous. But we seem to find it easier to account for P's *failure* or inability to do an act, provided we know she intended to do it. At least, we seem to believe that it is easier to perceive that an intended action has not taken place and to account for the causes of failure. Among the most obvious, most perceptible, of these causes are the various restraints imposed upon P. So important is this type of cause, so persistent an explanation for failure, that we may be excused for seeing it as the most crucial of all explanations and for allowing it to figure so prominently in discussions of freedom. Yet this does not justify taking the explanation for the act or event itself. The concept of restraint is simply an explanation for failure. It functions, not as a means for defining freedom, *but as a way of accounting for the causes of incapacities to act*. If P is unable to bring about a particular proposition concerning action, we can say that she is not free to do so. *Nothing further is entailed in that statement*. It is only when we seek to know *why* she was unable to act that we need to talk about restraints.

How can we account for P's failure to act? The cause of P's inability must be attributed to human action. We are dealing with freedom in the context of moral action and the use of the word "free" is appropriate where the action P proposes to take is possible within that context. We do not say, "P is not free to fly by flapping her arms," because such action is naturally impossible and we recognize that P's inability to fly is irrelevant to moral argument. For P's failure to act must be morally relevant; it must involve moral action; there must be a functional relationship between P's incapacity and the action of human beings. A functional relationship can be said to exist where an alteration in the human action will significantly affect P's capacity to act. Coercion—the deliberate imposition of a restraint—is certainly one example of this sort of relationship. But it is wrong to think of it as the only example. Consider the consequences of P's being poor. If any action P might want to take depends on the possession of resources, and if P does not have those resources, then she cannot take that action. Her incapacity to act means that her freedom is diminished and her lacking the requisite resources is a way of accounting for that diminution. P may be unable to escape from an environment of violence, or may be unable to provide for her child's education. These things concern more than the distribution of property or the attainment of economic security: they concern action. Poverty is a way of accounting for the circumscription of a person's range of action.

It may be that P's poverty is not the direct result of anyone's action, deliberate or inadvertent. But poverty may be the result of *institutional* actions—of the institutional structure of society or the economy. Or it may be the result of certain social practices or traditions. Now one feature of institutional arrangements is that their operations do not ordinarily stem from anyone's deliberate action. Institutional arrangements normally exist prior to any one person's connection with them; they exist, as it were, outside of any one person's action. (I leave to one side the possibility that identifiable people may, in unusual circumstances, revolutionize or reshape social practices or institutional arrangements deliberately.) We are born into sets of institutional arrangements that transcend any person's participation in them. The language we use to describe them reflects this relationship. We think of them as impersonal forces, feel that they control our actions rather than our controlling theirs, and so forth. But institutional arrangements are, of course, products of human action. They reflect processes of acquiescence and participation. (I refer, naturally, to the actions of people who have a choice of acquiescing or not, and whose refusal to acquiesce will be subject to marginal sanctions.) Now acquiescence cannot be anything less than intentional, even where it is given passively or to avoid the bother of refusal. To say it is intentional is not to say that it is based on adequate reflection, knowledge, considered moral judgment, and the like. Acquiescence may be tacit, in the sense that it is not the person's primary purpose to signify agreement with a social system or practice. A person who wants to be wealthy, or merely support herself, may acquiesce in social arrangements even if she believes them to be bad. She may feel powerless to change them; or her passion for comfort may be greater than her passion for justice. Such acquiescence may be insufficient to constitute consent, but it clearly is intentional. That is, the person knows that she is "going along" with existing institutional arrangements. My point here is not to cast blame, or to raise the issue of justification. I merely want to say that those who acquiesce and participate cannot be said to be acting unconsciously.

If we account for P's inability to act by citing her poverty, and if her poverty is the result of institutional arrangements, and if those arrangements are products of human action, then P's inability to act is functionally related to the action of others, even if this action does not amount to the deliberate imposition of restraints by particular or identifiable persons.

Poverty is an example of the general principle that any incapacity that is functionally related to institutional arrangements is an incapacity stemming from human action. And, as that incapacity constitutes a diminution of freedom, the diminution can be said to be due to human action. No specific intent to impose restraints, no deliberate coercion, is needed.

RECIPROCITY AND THE OBLIGATION TO ENABLE (CONTINUED)

If this is so, we may distinguish the *lack of freedom* (which describes P's inability to act on her intentions) from the *suppression of freedom* (which suggests an action that causes, or is functionally related to, that lack). If we separate the causal explanation from the definition, we may conclude that not enabling P to act may not *make* P unfree, but it can *leave* her unfree. We may then ask whether our toleration of P's inability to act, or deprivation, is consistent with a claim of freedom. I have suggested several times that it is not, that it involves simultaneously affirming and denying the worth of freedom. It is true that the obligation to enable P to act cannot, without more, be drawn out of a wholly descriptive theory of freedom. But even if it is not misleading to think of freedom in wholly descriptive terms, an obligation to enable arises as soon as we seek to justify a claim to freedom or ground the justification of an action on freedom.

In the end, no one has freedom in her character as an individual. She has it, and can only have it, *as a member of a community*. As a moral actor, she explicitly engages herself with the community of moral actors when she makes a moral claim. And as an identifiable person in a particular community she is dependent on that community's practices for her ability to exercise freedom. And this is so whether that community is a locality or a state or a revolutionary party. The exercise of individual freedom depends on there being liberating activities pursued in common and realized in common. The common supports created by a community for the exercise of freedom—the laws, customs, institutionalized opportunities, and so forth—make that exercise possible. And this elementary fact does not only mean that freedom would not exist if the community did not adopt practices that make it possible. It means also that the capacity to assert one's freedom depends on the extent to which social practices enable individuals to become robust, integrated persons, capable of making demands and asserting claims. For freedom is not usually handed to us. Authority is only too willing to overlook it in its pursuit of deference or power or efficiency or stability or whatever else it seeks. We need to *assert* our freedom, to *claim* our rights. But we can only do these things if we can rely on others for aid, if we can count on support from our fellows. Isolated, we are helpless not merely against authority and its capacity to bend the law in its favor but against social pressure and compulsion. We need to be able to join with others and call upon their assistance to create islands of protection against these things or to build the countervailing power that may be the condition of the maintenance of our interests or the assertion of our claims.

The support we can count on increases in number and depth as it is given by a robust and assertive population. It is a truism that, other things being equal, educated and capable people, secure in their self-esteem and sense of efficacy, will protect their freedoms better than the ignorant, insecure, and alienated. But education, developed capacity, self-esteem, and the like, while not wholly products of a social practice, are greatly dependent on it.

As a practical matter, then, the freedom of individuals depends on the existence of communal supports and on social practices that nurture rather than repress the robustness of spirit needed to assert claims and demand rights. Freedom is dependent on other things as well; but if community is not a sufficient condition of it, it is a necessary one. Can we, then, reject an obligation to enable people to act once we realize that those who can act have been enabled to do so by common practice and common action? We can reject it by hypocritically pretending that it is otherwise. Just as we want to attribute our successes to ourselves and our failures to others, we want to think of our freedom as something we have won, rather than as something that has (partly, anyway) been won for us. But that way lies self-delusion and the self-serving and self-interested morality inevitably built upon that delusion. *All of us have been enabled to be free.* There is no blinking that hard truth. The only question that remains is how far we want this enabling to reach. With whom do we share our good fortune?

NOZICK'S CRITIQUE

The most powerful recent attempt to separate freedom and equality is Robert Nozick's.[3] Nozick's defense of inequality is rooted in the argument that freedom, understood in terms of voluntary choice, overrides all competing values, that a defense of freedom entails preserving the integrity of choice and of its consequences, and that equality entails restricting choice in a way that compromises its integrity. His most forceful presentation of this argument comes, not surprisingly, in his defense of unequal property rights. Beginning with the individual, and assuming that no practices of society are implicated in his attainment of freedom (although they may prevent that attainment), Nozick ends with a theory in which justice mandates the virtual vesting of property rights. If I have acquired something by the sweat of my brow, and without invading the rights of others, that acquisition is mine and its invasion for the benefit of others a violation of my rights.

Nozick's argument that the acquisition and retention of property constitute freedoms that must be respected comes to grief because it justifies as freedom what is actually an exercise of power over others. In saying this, I do not mean to suggest that the issue is whether my holdings entitle me directly to deny you opportunities to acquire property or to exercise other rights. They do not and Nozick does not say that they do. But consider the implications of his principles of acquisition and transfer (p. 151). A traditional criticism of market systems is that they are so structured that the very retention of substantial and stringent property rights ineluctably results in the wrongful restriction of some people's capacities to acquire or hold property. Now Nozick denies this. The implicit assumption upon which his principles of acquisition and transfer rest is that market systems do not operate in this way—that they retain the possibility of being wholly just systems (p. 151). Nozick thus rejects the possibility that a market economy must be systemically coercive and, therefore, unjust. True, he recognizes that violations of the principles of acquisiton and transfer have occurred in the past; and he accepts the need for a "principle of rectification" (p. 230). But a principle of rectification assumes that the injustices resulting from a particular system of property ownership are, at any particular moment, *retrospective* rather than *prospective*. That is, it assumes that rectification can be accomplished by relatively extensive, but temporary, state action. Following this, a system of ownership based on his principles of acquisition and transfer can reassert itself (p. 231). However, an unjust structure of subordination and dependence resulting from a particular system of property ownership may be *prospective*. That is, on any set of market practices, it is likely to reappear even after a period of rectification. In that case, justifying property ownership on the basis of the principles of acquisiton and transfer is incoherent. Either these principles themselves play a role in the creation of the prospective injustices, or they are powerless to prevent them from occurring and, therefore, lose most of their significance. In the latter case, we should have to say a great deal about the principles of rectification, for these would be the persistent principles of social organization.

Nozick might want to answer that the structure of subordination and dependence that characterizes the market economy of the minimal state is simply the result of voluntary behavior. There is a sense in which some subordination and dependence is voluntary. But subordination and dependence may also be voluntary in a superficial or thin sense. This would occur where the subordination and dependence result from a situation where one party has a power, which the other lacks, to define the conditions of the bargain or transaction. Such power closes the weaker party's options without any choice on his part. Clearly, as I argued in Chapter 5, the removal of coercion to an earlier step in the transaction cannot justify eliminating it from consideration. Why should this disparity of power—ordinarily based on the resources each party possesses—determine so much of the outcome and yet play no part in the justification of the result? Again, while I may have voluntarily chosen subordination or dependence, my children may not have; yet they are bound by them in fact, often into adulthood. Finally, the evidence that suggests that subordination and dependence actually result from voluntary choices rather than from one form or other of coercion is, to put it charitably, sparse.

Nozick argues that, as long as no one has intentionally invaded P's rights, the closure of his options is not a deprivation of freedom. But this is disingenuous. It confuses, in obvious ways, the actual constriction of P's freedom with the subjective desire to do so. Now these are certainly not the same: the fact that I inadvertently constrain your action affects the state of my soul, not the motion of your body. Second, as I have argued, it confuses a proposition concerning the availability of an action with a proposition concerning causality. So this evasion is not open to Nozick and voluntarism remains an inadequate justification. Third, and most important, Nozick's use of a rigid concept of intention leaves open the question of whether knowledge that our actions will invade P's rights does not convert our intention not to do so into a simple act of hypocrisy or bad faith. Immorality, as Leo Baeck somewhere noted, consists not merely in doing evil but in tolerating it with equanimity. In the simple and abstract social order Nozick describes, the combination of unintentional injury and ignorance of the consequences of one's actions may be possible. Indeed, since there is no practice to refer to to evaluate Nozick's state of nature, any combination of circumstances, however outlandish, is possible provided it is not self-contradictory or absurd on its face. But the world of action, alas, is not so kind to philosophers. Here, where we cannot suppose that no one will have mentioned the consequences of certain forms of action—say, the use of one's property for entirely selfish purposes—we cannot suppose a good faith ignorance of those consequences. That is, we cannot propose that one may do certain acts without knowing their probable outcomes. Now we may wish to justify those outcomes by arguing, say, that the invasion of some people's rights is inevitable and, considering the immense advantages that minimally regulated capitalism has over alternative systems, morally justifiable. Indeed, many people do argue this with considerable force. But this is not an argument open to Nozick because he cannot justify the invasion of some people's rights for other people's benefit. After all, such a justification would instantly legitimate taxes and transfer payments as well. So Nozick must either develop a theory in which knowledge of the invasion of rights is undiscussed and therefore, by tacit agreement, non-existent or assume that a market economy can be constructed so as to be systemically entirely just. In fact, he makes both assumptions, although neither can have even a remote claim to credibility.

This means that, to a much greater extent than is generally appreciated, the fabric of Nozick's argument rests, in reality, on his evaluation of the market economy. If it can be structured so as not to generate any systemic injustice, then his individualistic theory of rights can be coherent. If, however, this cannot be done—if, however better than any alternative a market economy is, it is also a structure of power characterized by coercion as well as voluntarism—then his theory fails. For the presence of holdings based on coercion calls for rectification. And if coercion is indeed systemic, then the principles of rectification become the principles of normal operation and that theory of rights deployed that is appropriate to the new norm.

The crucial issue, then, comes to be the entirely contingent one of whether the market system is or is not systemically coercive and, if it is, to what degree. To give this question anything like the attention it deserves is impossible here. Yet, following Nozick's example of summarizing a general argument (p. 172), something can be said in summary. Coercion is an integral part of any market system, however sanitized and purged of dominating enterprises it is. That coercion is not merely a matter of dramatic exploitation, imperialism, or grossly distorted distributions of power. These may, in principle, be overcome. But it is fundamental to a market system that one may legitimately bring into any economic or social relationship the resources one has accumulated. So exchanges may be critically influenced by the resources brought into the exchange process, and value distributions may reflect disparities in initial resources rather than in performances. And it is hard to resist the conclusion that, if these occur in an economy where the maintenance of the individual's livelihood requires that he participate in exchanges and value distributions, that economy is systemically coercive. If this is true (as the evidence, I believe, overwhelmingly indicates), then Nozick's principles of acquisition and transfer exist only in a realm of utopian equality or banal abstraction. It is his principles of rectification—whatever they are—that must guide the world of action.

So Nozick's critique does not work. The principled argument he presents fails and, while some of his subsidiary arguments retain some point, they dangle uncertainly in philosophical space, devoid of foundation.

FREEDOM AS THE CAPACITY TO ACT

I have suggested that, in any specific case, freedom be understood in terms of the ability to bring about a particular proposition regarding action. This is a passingly useful basis for beginning the analysis of freedom, but hardly sufficient to carry us very far in discourse about politics. We need to understand freedom as it refers to *general* patterns of action, to continuities of practice, to social processes and, of course, to action itself. It is true that when I say, "I am free to leave this room," I may be referring to an identifiable and individual act. That act certainly has moral significance, and it may have political. On the other hand, if politics is our concern, we should want to know more about that act. Shall I be free to leave the room tomorrow? Perhaps the room is an army induction center and, by tomorrow, I shall have been inducted into the army. That fact does not bear on the truthfulness of the statement that I am free to leave today, but it does bear on its political implications. If I say, "I am free to speak," I do not (ordinarily) mean simply that I am free to speak this minute, but that I am free generally, so that I shall be free next minute and tomorrow and next year as well.

This may seem excruciatingly trivial (not to say obvious), but occasionally a trivial point opens up a fruitful discussion. If we do, indeed, want to use "freedom" to account for patterns of action or for a general condition of social life, can we employ the same understandings as we do when we analyze particular or singular cases? Can the word "freedom" refer to the same things in sentences as different as "I am free today to leave this room," "I am free to publish my opinions," and "I live in a free society?" It must be obvious that, where we want to use freedom to account for a general condition of social life, to be able to say that we are free generally, or to characterize insititutional arrangements, we use freedom more open-endedly. We do not tie it to any particular act or to a related group or acts or to a long list of acts: *we tie freedom to the concept of action itself.* To tie freedom to the concept of action itself is to make action itself the subject of freedom. And to argue that freedom so understood has great value—that freedom has, therefore, intrinsic worth—is to suggest a manner of life where we are widely able to create and invent actions and alternatives in response to situations as they arise. Such a concept of freedom is one that can be extended indefinitely throughout the realm of action, and is, therefore, open-ended. This does not mean that there are no boundaries to freedom. It means merely that the actions that are the subjects of free choice are indeterminate and capable of extension (or contraction).

This is the concept of freedom that conforms to the requirements of a structuring principle. For the justification of freedom in particular is made possible by the justification of freedom as a structuring principle. The reason I can say that "I am free to leave this room," or "I am free to publish my opinions," is that they can be shown to be justifiable particular applications of the general principle that moral actors, confronting moral challenges in a context of ambiguity and conflict, need to choose, invent, create responses. It is not merely because freedom is a public ideal, applying generally to an innumerable number of actions, that we must understand it in general terms; it is because the very possibility of civility, of living with rules that limit violence and barbarism, turns on our ability to choose, invent, and create and, therefore, on a sense of the intrinsic worth of free action. Freedom, being a structuring principle, has to do with action itself, with the power of the moral actor to choose, invent, and create. It is not limited to particular acts, but is an open-ended concept.

When we think of freedom as open-ended, what is it that we mean when we say we are free? What is it that we refer to? At the very beginning of this book, I suggested that we could conceive of complex actions, composed of a sequence of interrelated behaviors, thoughts, and choices. In any serious account of any particular freedom (say, my freedom to speak), I should have to include statements about the laws, the behavior of enforcement authorities, the controls that society has sought to have me internalize, the experiences that become empirical referents for relevant moral concepts, the nature of education generally in society and of my education in particular, and so forth. I should have, in other words, to say a great deal about a great many things.

(In arguing this, I do not mean to raise any question concerning the automony of one's actions or the relation of autonomy to freedom. The issue of autonomy is difficult and treacherous even where we treat it—as I should—as a causal explanation rather than as a definition. I believe, however, that we can by-pass some of the difficulty if we ask, not whether people hold particular norms autonomously, but whether the conditions in which they generally internalize norms inhibit reflective evaluation or are accompanied by more or less severe sanctions. This allows us to avoid arbitrary assumptions about other people's states of mind and focus instead on the sorts of observable behaviors that social scientists and historians traditionally deal with.)

I should have to say a great deal more if my subject is, not a particular freedom, but the general freedom to choose, invent, and create. In that case, I should be referring to an extensive repertory of abilities, powers, and intentions—a repertory that is necessarily as open-ended as the freedom to act itself. I should, in other words, be speaking about a person's capacities to act.

So to say that a person is free to act in a general, open-ended way is to say something about her *capacities*. If I say, "She is free (in a general, open-ended way)," I cannot invoke the actions she is free to do: in the first place, I could go on forever; in the second, I would lose sight of the very open-endedness I want to describe. I can, however, say something about her capacity to act, for the concept of capacity is also open-ended and would fit easily with the open-endedness of the freedom I want to describe. Put another way, an open-ended concept of freedom refers to an open-ended repertory of actions justified by a claim of freedom. To be free is to be able to do this repertory of actions. Such ability is what I mean to describe by the word "capacity."

Freedom is, therefore, open-ended as well as particular. Significantly, it is as an open-ended concept that it is at its most vital;

for it is as an open-ended concept that it works to structure the process of creating rules and building a moral life. It is as an open-ended concept that it makes the justification of particular claims of freedom possible in the first place. If this is so, then the capacities we associate with open-ended freedom are the most crucial capacities and the most important to safeguard. They are the capacities whose constraint threatens to compromise the integrity of freedom in general and, with it, the justifiability of the entire moral process and, therefore, of all particular freedoms. This has serious consequences for the idea of reciprocity. Reciprocity must now involve more than a mere guarantee that any freedom claimed by A must be consistent with the same freedom of P. Reciprocity must also concern action considered generally and the capacity to engage in action generally. It is not enough that an action of A not compromise a like action of P; *it may not compromise P's capacity to engage in action generally.* A, for example, may not defend his power to vote as a freedom if he votes to deny P access to an adequate education or to an adequate livelihood (supposing they compromise P's capacity). A's action may not compromise *any* action that A claims to be free to do, or that A ought to be free to do, however remote that action may be from the action A is in fact doing. Freedom, in its fundamental sense as a structuring principle of morality, means that no action that impairs another's capacity to act may be justified by reference to freedom. In the end, therefore, *freedom means simply that A and P have equal capacities to act.* Far from being inconsistent with freedom, equality is at its very center.

If freedom requires equal capacities to act, I cannot defend my capacity to act on the ground of freedom without acknowledging an obligation to enable you to act equally. But does this not suggest an obligation bordering on perfectionism? If I act so as to support myself and provide for my family, I may also be supporting inegalitarian practices. And I may not be able to avoid supporting those practices and still provide for my family. Indeed, this is normally the case in inegalitarian societies such as our own. In a world of starving people, I may not be able to fulfil my obligation to them without reducing myself and my family to subsistence or without devoting all of my energies to equalization. That is surely a noble thing to do. But can it be an obligation? Can I be said to be obligated to live a life of pure service to others, to be a Saint Francis or a Gandhi? Would it not be confusing moral goodness with moral fanaticism to suggest that I am obligated to do this?

Putting the question this way can be radically misleading if it suggests that the obligation to enable is one that must be fulfilled by individuals acting individually. Clearly, some people support inequality actively and many others support it indirectly, by pursuing ordinary private goals and interests. But individuals acting as individuals do not produce inequality; individuals acting together, in a structure of social roles, produce it. And the creation of equality requires alterations in this joint, or social, action. So it is foolish to speak about equality as though it required me to give the interests of others an absolute moral priority over my own. What matters are the obligations that attach not to my private role *but to my role as member of a community*. In this latter role, I *may* be morally required to give a public good priority over a private one, so long as a reasonable sphere of private activity remains. As a member of a community—as a participant in its public processes and as a claimant of rights—I may be asked to support egalitarian measures even at a cost to myself. I may be asked to contribute to the establishment of practices that endow those who lack it with the capacity to act on equal terms with me. To the extent I do not, I may be held responsible—*in common with other members*—for their lack of freedom. I would have participated in the denial of freedom to others and thus have compromised the justification of my own capacity to act. The obligation to enable, therefore, must be seen primarily in terms of a social obligation; and the individual's obligation must be limited to the need to support egalitarian practices in his role as member of a community.

7

EQUALITY

SOCIAL EQUALITY

We must now ask what the practice of social equality involves. Fortunately, the answer is clear enough (given the discussion that has preceeded it) to make an extended discussion unnecessary.

All people must have an equal capacity for moral action. Social conditions affect this capacity for moral action. Therefore, the social conditions in which every moral actor lives must be such as make possible the equal capacity for moral action. *Social equality is that degree of equality of condition necessary to make all people equal moral actors*. Now, as the equal capacity for moral action does not seem to entail a degree of equality amounting to identity of provision, it clearly allows differences in wealth, status, even power. Equality is, therefore, consistent with the view that one's choices may have consequences for one's life-chances, that it is appropriate for society to offer incentives and rewards for certain sorts of activities and performances, that all comparative judgments are not invidious. It merely requires that consequences, incentives, and so forth attach to the activities of all and that income and property differentials not be great enough, or so structured, that they give to some qualitative advantages in the entertainment and realization of intentions.

It is important to underline what I mean when I say that equality describes the terms on which moral actors engage in action. *I mean that the principal concern of equality is not, as is customarily thought, with the distribution of resources but with capacities for action. Equality, therefore, occupies conceptual space similar to freedom, which enables us to create accommodations between it and freedom.* If freedom describes the capacities of members of a community to act, equality describes their capacities to act on equal terms. Therefore, the question of distribution is always an instrumental one. The equal distribution of resources is not justifiable in itself, or because people disinterestedly choose it, but because it is a condition of actors having equal capacities for action.

Social equality, then, is that arrangement of conditions and practices where every person has the power to engage in moral action on equal terms with every other person. It does not, therefore, envision equality of result, except as the result is the capacity for moral action. (And in this it hardly differs from the equality of result envisioned by advocates of equal opportunity: they assume that people will have equal capacities to exercise certain legal rights.) It does, however, envision an equality of condition—a situation in which the external conditions of life that bear, as far as we know, on our capacities for moral action will be sufficiently similar so as not to give rise to systematic advantages or disadvantages.

There are undoubtedly those who believe that this is a distinction without a difference, and one that contradicts my argument besides. If moral actors are equal when they can engage equally in moral action, can anything suffice but equality of result? If A has one hundred dollars and B ninety, they are unequal in the sense that A can act on an intention to spend one hundred and B cannot; if spending money is legitimately an intention, A and B can only be equal where each has the same amount of money. Spending money is legitimately an intention; but this is a bad objection. There is an endless set of differences that can be cited to the same purpose. If A takes the last seat in a theater, B cannot act on his intention to see the play. If A and B seek to chair a university department and A is chosen, B's capacity to act on his intention is frustrated. Do we then require all people to share their seats with each other, thereby creating a theater of chaos? Do we require A and B to share the chair? Or, for that matter, do we require A and B to share equally in a marriage to C, if C will agree to it? (And, if C does not agree, is this an example of the conflict between liberty and equality?)

Even if these objections were valid, they would not be particularly troublesome. Equality does not stand alone as a moral principle, but must be accommodated to the other SP's. And the requirements of the maximization and freedom principles obviously suffice to eliminate the claims of equality of result. But these objections are not valid. Their strength depends on our taking equality to be an unambiguous endorsement of complete parity of action. I have already argued that this is not the case. Equality concerns our capacities for action and requires that these *capacities* be equal, not that they yield exactly the results the actor desires.

How can we tell that A and B have equal capacities? We cannot discover this by comparing the entire range of their intentions, which, because intentions develop continuously, is beyond specification. And while we surely will differentiate important intentions from trivial ones in practice, and use this differentiation to draw the boundary lines of the equality principle, we cannot describe it precisely enough in advance, or in a way that would be agreeable to all. But it is possible to argue that A and B possess equal capacities for moral action where any differentials that exist are not so great as to overturn their reciprocal capacities to affect each other's actions. The existence of this reciprocity speaks to the power each has to act on his intentions in relation to the power others have. It thus acts as a litmus test of people's practical capacities. And such capacities speak to the issue of general condition, rather than to specific results.

What this comes down to is the demand that egalitarians have made for generations: insofar as people's capacities to act are dependent on external conditions, those conditions must be equalized. This requires two things. First, it requires a serious narrowing of the range of incomes and wealth so that, while greater incomes and wealth—reflecting a need for incentives, rewards, and other market features—will be available, they will not be able to buy disproportionate advantages or create disproportionate disadvantages. Second, the conditions in which people live, work, learn, and participate must be sufficiently equal so that they do not generate significant advantages or disadvantages in respect of action or affect in any systematic way people's capacities for action. For example, we should have to create housing that is equally healthful and decent, if not equally luxurious; structure health care so that, when they are ill, people enjoy the same hospital arrangements, see the same doctors, have access to the same treatments; eliminate privileged schooling, so that children attend the same types of schools; and provide adequate social services, including means of remediation for those disadvantaged by circumstance.

This does not mean that we undertake to *guarantee* that all people develop equal capacities. The equalization of health conditions does not give everyone a right to good health any more than the equalization of educational conditions gives everyone a right to a degree from Harvard. Equality gives them a right to equal external conditions of life, provided that these are reasonably within the competence of society to affect. Once this requirement has been met, society need grant them only equal opportunities to act. It is worth noting in passing that this assumes that there are weak and strong versions of equality of opportunity, with the strong version holding that equality of opportunity cannot stand by itself, but may only be invoked after a good deal of equalization of condition has already taken place.

A serious problem now arises. Equality of condition requires the implementation of social practices that would involve serious investment in public enterprises and services, as well as reductions in income for the well-to-do. Does this not seem to require a willingness on the part of people generally to endow public undertakings with serious value (an attitude less foreign to certain Western European societies than to American); to understand that professions of fairness and civility invite actions in accordance with them; to agree that, ultimately, a life based on mutual support is both freer and more satisfying than a life spent in racing frantically against each other? But such willingness, however morally compelling it may be, is not exactly rampant in the conditions of modern civilization; and attempts to inculcate it, where they have not withered, have too often come to rely on methods we associate with tyranny, if not totalitarianism.

Is equality, then, doomed by human nature as the market ideologues say? It was not long ago that conservatives taught that democracy was doomed by human nature, because it demanded a mixture of virtue and wisdom that no citizenry could possess. In the event, the conservatives were wrong. It turned out that people could develop a degree of commonality of action, limited though it was, that allowed democracy to work with passable success. This commonality developed gradually, as democracy developed gradually—its contours determined less by the passions of democratic revolutionaries than by the limited democratic practices they were able to introduce. These limited—perhaps primitive—practices, and the behaviors and actions that developed out of them, were gradually absorbed by people through experience. And, especially as they seemed desirable or advantageous, experience of them shaped new attitudes and demands. Democratic practices, to no one's surprise, both affected social action and developed in response to it.

Like democratic habits, the habits of mind needed to create equality must develop as responses to the perceived advantages of egalitarian solutions. With the institutions of education and communication disproportionately influenced by elites, with people's beliefs often affected by the need to appropriate elite values and manners, this process will be agonizingly slow. The habits of mind people develop will undoubtedly be imperfect, inadequately egalitarian, and infuriating to passionate believers. So, after all, it was—or indeed is—with democracy. But egalitarians believe that people do not easily give up the benefits they have won and the interests they have been able to protect; and as they come to see these benefits and interests as products of common action and communal provision, they are likely to want to retain these as mechanisms of their improvement. So egalitarians see a gradual acceptance of the values of community growing out of people's experiences of the limited egalitarian practices currently being taken or capable of being taken. Like democracy, the contours of equality of condition will affect and be affected by social action; and, like democracy, equality of condition may be approached—now badly, now passably—but not fully attained.

The extended provision of social services identified with equality of condition will undoubtedly create conflict among the types of services that can be provided. This is not a new problem, nor is it a daunting one. However, the rapid development of technology may make it appear so. Medical technology, for example, has made it possible for people to survive diseases that killed, not simply their parents, but their elder sisters and brothers. This care is expensive. If it is provided to everyone, the expense will likely cause other needs to go unmet. But if it is not provided to everyone, who will get it and how will the lucky few be chosen? If the care extends life, it will inevitably increase the expense of caring for the aged. How is this to be factored into the social equation?

The questions are new, but the problem is as old as politics itself. That does not mean that it cannot be addressed in a principled way. Of course, if by "principled" we must mean unswerving allegiance to a rigid plan or pattern, we cannot address it so and might do best by letting chance or the market rule. But no egalitarian is committed to such a conception of principle. Nor need we be, on pain of inconsistency. On the contrary, it is time to move the discussion of equality away from its dependence on descriptions of egalitarian futures and recommended systems and toward a process conception. Such a conception impels us to see a commitment to equality as a commitment, not to a model of a society, but to an attitude of egalitarianism—that is, to a commitment to articulate and press for those alternatives, arising out of particular social circumstances, which, in the circumstances, will push society in the most egalitarian direction possible. Equality is a process of constant equalizing.

We know that circumstances affect our capacities for action and often alter the relative importance of the conditions we seek to equalize. We must reject the idea that equality implies a particular social or economic structure or a definitive set of distributional relationships. We should not think of social equality as an abstract and mechanical formula imposing a self-defeating uniformity on social affairs. Instead, we should root our analysis of social equality in action.

Action, of course, does not take place in a vacuum, but in particular contexts and as a response to other actions. In turn, it affects both, thus creating a dynamic situation. So what is needed to create equal capacities for moral action depends on, and will vary with, the social practices and institutional arrangements of particular societies. Thus, while we can state the content of moral equality in fairly specific terms, we cannot state the content of social equality in specific terms. We cannot think of it as if it implied a unique set of relationships or a settled state of affairs. Instead, we must see it as a process. Social equality describes the on-going process of adjusting social conditions and responding to changing practices in order to produce equal capacities for moral action.

EQUALITY AS PROCESS

Even apart from its relation to moral action, social equality can only be defined as a process. Social equality describes a relation: A is, or ought to be, equal to B in respect of C, where C stands for a particular condition or practice. This relation can never be wholly specified so long as more C's than presently exist can be created—a possibility we must necessarily maintain. The most that we can do is to argue that A is, or ought to be, equal to B in respect of all known C's. To do this, we must specify each C in respect of which A and B are to be considered equal. But because social practices and conditions are interrelated, we discover that we cannot state any particular C (of all known C's) without entertaining the possibility that the equalization of A and B with respect to any particular C—say, C_1—will affect other C's: after equalization with respect to C_1, conditions C_2 and C_3 will be different from what they were before. But upon the supposition of the interrelationship of practices and conditions, the alteration of C_2 and C_3 is equally likely to affect C_1, and to require re-equalization of A and B in respect of C_1, and so on, *ad infinitum*. Therefore, any definition of equality in terms of a unique set of relationships or a settled state of affairs is incoherent, in the absence of a showing that all conditions can be stated and the manner in which each affects and is affected by the others can also be stated. If we cannot do this, we must see equality not as a set of institutional arrangements or defined practices but as a process—a constant adjustment of arrangements and practices in respect of C's.

This does not mean that it is illegitimate to say that A and B should be equal in respect of C_1. It merely means that we must understand this relationship and the conditions it refers to as subject to ambiguity and alteration. In every case, we must be prepared to make adjustments, to enlarge or contract the degree of equality, to redefine the relevance of particular C's to the problem of equality.

Let me illustrate this argument. The existence of political authority implies the existence of inequalities in power and in the rights that inhere in certain roles. For example, those with authority have a special entitlement to act in the name of a collective that the rest of the collective lacks. A literally equal distribution of authority denies this entitlement to anyone. But if no one has this entitlement, then the collective loses its ability to restrain individuals from aggregating economic resources sufficient to produce inequality of wealth, except in the unlikely conjunction of unanimous agreement and unanimous action by all non-wealthy persons at the same time. And as power is a component of authority, equality of power makes it difficult to understand how authority may consistently exercise its entitlement to act in the name of the collective. To equalize wealth, therefore, we must create inequalities of power and authority. But such inequalities may have serious consequences for the distribution of economic resources, whose re-equalization may affect the structure of power, and so forth.

If we do not want to speak of literal equality of authority, we may want to speak of approximate or substantial equality of authority. But how approximately, how substantially equal, can authority become before it begins to affect other sorts of equality? The answer cannot be given *a priori*. It can appear only as we engage in a process of progressive equalization of authority, examining the impact of each development and testing the adequacy of our decisions as they affect other sorts of equality. We may reach a state of equilibrium or, more likely, discover the existence of conflict or tension between different types of equality. But we cannot know this except as it emerges in the course of the process.

There is a tendency for the discovery of the conflicting nature of equality to lead to a resigned acceptance of inequality as a necessity. Perhaps this is a consequence of placing too much emphasis on equilibrium in our social and economic theories. But we need not be unduly affected by this discovery, if something so well worn can be called a discovery. Most of our concepts reveal, on examination, internal conflict; that is why too much liberty is as bad as not enough. Pure concepts, wholly consistent and clear, may exist in a

Hegelian heaven. Here on earth we make do with less. But this should only disturb millenarians. The rest of us may understand that the existence of conflicts among equalities is not fatal. It is not even discouraging. It does not prevent us from reducing some conflicts and accommodating others, so that real steps toward moral equality may be taken. It is not naive to believe so. And it is not irrelevant to the morale of egalitarians that, in pursuing these steps as strenuously as they know how, they satisfy the demands of the SP's.

OBJECTIONS TO SOCIAL EQUALITY

In practice, the western liberal tradition is only half-heartedly committed to equality, and then to a circumscribed version of it. And this hesitant commitment is easily overwhelmed by the massed protests of the adherents of the faith Tawney called "the religion of inequality." The precise tenets of this religion vary, but its basic form remains constant: equality is the great antagonist of some cherished value. The current favorites are efficiency, freedom, and individuality. But in the past, when these counted for less, or were even thought to entail some equality, equality was held to contravene the divinely inspired order of the universe, the just superiority of the "better sort" of people, the need for aristocratic political leadership, the perpetuation of a higher culture, and a host of other, now mercifully forgotten, dogmas.

There is, of course, no lack of rationalizations for the fear of equality. Writing of the seventeenth-century's hostility to it, J. R. Pole notes that "equality was an intuition rather than a doctrine, and had no comparable suggestions to offer on such questions as how civil society was to meet the needs of supply and demand, provide military defence, or organize systems of administration and justice." Egalitarians had to show that equality was "compatible with effective economic and political institutions."[1]

But, in the light of our knowledge of the seventeenth century, it is hardly plausible to believe that such a showing would have reduced the appeal of inequality. Nor is it likely that it would be decisive today. The all-too-obvious truth, I fear, is that the appeal of inequality is more likely to have a non-rational or irrational basis. Consider the impact of socialization. Conventionalism and patriotism create powerful pressures to approve of the existing system and the values identified with it. Those values constitute, among other things, a civic religion—a set of idealized values and practices that people identify with, and believe to be encased in, the social system. The civic religion critically affects the way people perceive their social worlds. I do not have time to discuss this in detail. Let me instead offer two examples.

The civic religion of market society tells us that each of us may suddenly find himself wealthy; and so long as existing inequalities are not literally catastrophic or destructive, many people seem willing to endure them for the sake of the dream of wealth. Egalitarians find this maddening. They know that it reinforces opposition to egalitarian policies, that the possibility of sudden wealth is ridiculously slim, that the great majority of people are much more likely to attain material comfort by supporting egalitarian measures, and that market mythology plays on people's dreams the way a casino operator plays on a gambler's. Nevertheless, few attitudes are more persistent.

More important, the civic religion of market society encourages us to attribute our failures and successes to ourselves. Frequently, therefore, feelings of unworthiness and self-condemnation accompany our failures and shortcomings. We imagine that they stem from our faults, flaws, mistakes. We are ashamed of them. The consequent feelings of guilt and inadequacy manifest themselves in a need to emulate the practices of those above us. For if we emulate their practices and values, we associate ourselves—however irrationally or vicariously—with the attributes needed for success and for lack of which we failed. We redeem our unworthiness by adopting the beliefs and attitudes of the worthy. And by placing their interests above our own, we punish ourselves appropriately for our failures.

The religion of inequality allows its adherents to accept without embarrassment arguments that they would reject as contemptible in other contexts. Fortunately, this relieves egalitarians of the burden of pitting reason against zealotry and allows us to direct our arguments at those whom passion has not disabled from hearing them. The audience I address in the remainder of this chapter is composed of this latter sort: people who, while willing to accept, or perhaps tolerate, a limited amount of equality, nevertheless suspect that the degree of equality required by the concept of community is more than a going social system can bear. They might fear, for example, that, however abstractly justifiable it may be, equality threatens to inhibit the cultivation of individual talents or ignore the need to reward effort. I should like to convince them that their fears are much overstated and that the common objections to the practice of equality have very little substance left in them. And I should like to start by reminding them of what equality means—or, rather, does not mean.

I do this for a very obvious reason. The best way to falsify a political argument is to take it literally. For this encourages us to ignore ambiguity and abandon awareness of the complexities of social practice for the homespun of verbal harmonics, thus marking ourselves as simple and our philosophy as naive. It results in arguments distinguished not by the conviction they carry but by the scorn they rightly engender.

It is not surprising, then, that no one takes equality as literally as its opponents, or is as anxious to define it as identity of provision, status, or power. For equality then becomes a principle that is not merely unworkable, but unthinkable—a perversion of morality. It threatens to abolish diversity and, therefore, liberty. It thrives only in a rigid, authoritarian social order, because only such an order can undertake the continuous manipulation of results, the constant supervision of people's lives, required to maintain identity. But such an order necessarily violates the ideal of political equality. So equality is not merely a bad idea; it is, in practice, a contradictory one as well.

It occurs to me to wonder what these critics would say to someone who, in evaluating the worth of liberty, insisted on taking it to mean license. They would object, I think, that this definition was a caricature that necessarily distorted analysis. And they would be correct. Yet Professor—now Judge—Ralph Winter suggests that "much of the distaste for inequality . . . seems based on assumptions about the validity of the claims made for absolute equality." Starting here, he concludes that the argument against "absolute equality of income" shows that "equality is by no means a value of established intrinsic worth in the resolution of economic issues."[2] That may be so. But arguments against "absolute freedom of action" cast the same doubts on the worth of liberty.

It is also true that the qualifications that may accompany philosophical discussion of equality (such as Winter's paradoxical admission that few people argue for absolute equality) are forgotten in the hurly-burly of popular controversy, where ideas tend to be reduced to relatively simple form. If philosophers and social theorists really want to influence the world, they need to recognize this. They need to ask not only what their arguments mean but what they may be taken to mean. If they want to confront equality, they should do so with the open acknowledgment that equality does not stand for identity of wealth or income any more than it stands for identity of hair color. They must give it a meaning that accords with responsible usage, which is to say, with the usage of egalitarians. I do not say this only because I think that my conception of equality as a process defeats the absolutist assumption. I say it because limited conceptions of equality are, historically, the norm. The tradition of treating equality as less than absolute identity is a long one, antedating Judge Winter, or Tawney (who called it an "arithmetical metaphor"), or even Matthew Arnold, from whom more than one writer on the subject has drawn sustenance.[3]

It may occur to the opponent of equality that, if the concept of the equal moral actor does not entail absolute equality in practice, it does entail a belief that all people are in fact equal. But, he will argue, it is simply false to assert this, for people do not share fundamental human attributes equally. And if they do not, we may expect the able and talented to rise above the norm, even where everyone starts out equally. To prevent this "natural" inequality from occurring, we should have to take steps to prevent the able from developing or using their abilities. But this is an intolerable infringement on their liberties.

I shall concede—rather with enthusiasm—that if we reduce the concept of the moral actor to practice, we produce a person equal to all other persons. And this equality is not merely a juridical or abstract equality but equality in some more fundamental, or natural, sense. Equalizing the power to act—as opposed to the opportunity—becomes trivial without the presumption of an equality fundamental enough to justify our expectations that it will have significant consequences for the actors themselves. But what do we mean by saying that people are equal in a fundamental sense?

We clearly do not mean that all people share all human attributes equally. Even under perfectly equal circumstances, we should not be surprised to find differences in beauty, strength, wit, energy, within a population any more than we are surprised to find them within the same social class—indeed, within the same family—today. Besides, it is not clear just which attributes are relevant to the claim that all are equal. We can always find particular attributes that we do or do not share equally, just as we can always find reasons to affirm or deny their significance. Perhaps it all depends on what we wish to prove about equality. If I offer as the relevant attribute one that is pretty equally shared, you can counter with another that is not. The lack of any agreed-on list of relevant attributes, and of standards for judging their significance, makes nearly every human attribute a candidate for inclusion.

But this is hardly surprising. To say that A is equal to B is not the same thing as saying it is not different from B. We accept quite easily the idea that differences can exist among equals, having observed from childhood that people we call equal do not look alike, or sound alike, or walk alike. But why are these differences normally irrelevant to judgments of inequality, whereas other differences seem to be critical? The answer cannot lie in the differences themselves, for if we consult only the differences, we should not be able to say which are relevant, critical, and so forth. We can make these judgments only by employing a richer theory that sets out the justification for evaluating differences and prescribes the terms for doing so. Such a theory contains a set of standards that determines how attributes are to be classified, evaluated, and ranked. In the absence of such a richer theory, differences are merely differences and no one can say which of our differing attributes is higher, better, and so forth. We can say this only where we can base our judgment on the richer theory. The judgment that people are unequal, therefore, is not a function of the existence of natural differences, but of a theory that impels us to evaluate those differences in a particular way. *The judgment that all are equal in a fundamental sense does not deny the existence of differences; it merely reflects a richer theory that denies their determinative significance.*

There are many ways to deny the determinative significance of differences. We might argue that our differences are not so considerable and are less salient than our similarities. Or we might argue that differences in personal attributes balance out, so that no one is superior to anyone else in everything. Or we might mean that we share crucial attributes merely by virtue of being human and that this sharing overrides all other differences.[4]

Without rejecting these arguments, I would like to propose another one. I believe that the denial of fundamental human equality requires the ranking of people according to the attributes they possess. And this should be rejected for three reasons. It is, first of all, pernicious. It encourages feelings of contempt for those in the lower ranks, and if experience is any guide, such feelings allow the upper ranks to restrict their liberties and opportunities in the name of common sense and economy. It may encourage outright rejection of their humanity, with the loathsome variety of consequences that ordinarily ensues.

Second, ranking is unnecessary. Both morality and social order require that we judge the worth of certain actions; but this does not require us to rank the beings who do them according to their attributes. The primary motive for ranking is to provide additional justification for differentials in reward or status. But if those differentials are justifiable, they must be justified by arguments regarding action. Ranking adds nothing to this argument but prejudice and superstition. If people are to be rewarded for their attributes, it must be because those attributes are crucially related to beneficial or desirable actions. Indeed, it is through action that we perceive attributes. And no one has yet made a serious case for rewarding undemonstrated attributes.

Third, ranking is incoherent. We are, as I argued in Chapter 1, unable to show that any property is exclusively relevant—or most relevant—to moral action. As the ranking of properties requires such a showing, and as an attribute is clearly a property, we cannot rank attributes. Nor can one object that the proper test is not the relevance of the attribute to moral action, but to specific actions that are higher or better than others. Even if that were so, ranking an action highly does not entail ranking attributes highly unless we can show that the action entails specific attributes that are exclusively relevant to it. And this requires the sort of showing that I rejected in Chapter 1.

This might not satisfy the critic of equality. He might respond that abilities and talents do differ and whether we call these differences inequalities is irrelevant. What matters is that people should be free to use their talents and abilities and that this freedom is unduly constricted by egalitarian policies.

But what we call these differences does matter, because it reflects deeply held beliefs about human abilities. A society that treated abilities as attributes of a common existence would value our similarities above our differences and would minimize, rather than maximize, the importance of differences in ability. No one, of course, expects such a society to appear in the near future, or at all. Nevertheless, we know that a society's customs and beliefs reflect, to some extent, its political and economic practices. And if this is so, we can expect the growth of egalitarian practices to modify current visions of human differences. These visions have already undergone serious modification; nineteenth-century assumptions about the "natures" of blacks, or women, or the poor, are at a considerable—though hardly sufficient—remove from our own. It is not utopian to assume that, as more equal conditions produce more nearly equal performances by individuals and groups, the perception of differences will diminish.

Nor need we take seriously the argument that equality threatens to decrease our freedom to develop and use our talents. On the contrary, it is the denial of equality that persistently does this. The demand that we be free to use our talents is justifiable where those talents have not been developed at the expense of others. It does not matter whether one's advantage over others is intentional or inadvertent. If A has a socially rooted advantage over B in developing his talent, and if that development helps A to realize some of his aims, recognizing A's demand to use his talent without helping B is permitting A to influence B's life without giving B a reciprocal capacity. Hence, A's use of his talent is an act of domination, or a support of domination, whatever his intention. Restricting A's use of his talent by as much as it takes to develop B's is depriving A not of freedom but of a capacity to take advantage of privilege.

Besides, when we talk of restricting A's freedom to use his

talents, we are not, strictly speaking, talking about his *use* of his talents. Equality is perfectly consistent with that use. What it is not consistent with is A's benefiting from that use in the measure he might like. So A's freedom to use his talents turns out to be A's freedom to profit from his talents, and that is a much different matter. It is not a deprivation of freedom to reduce A's profit by what is necessary to develop B's talent, given the circumstances referred to in the last paragraph. It is certainly a loss of privilege for A, a disappointment of his hopes. But these do not amount to a denial of freedom unless we are to take Ortega's spoilt child to be the very paradigm of the free human being.

Will equality restrict the expression of talent by removing incentives to its development? Does a market system, which is supposedly built on incentives, do better and, therefore, redeem the freedom to develop and use talents that egalitarian systems restrict? These questions are, I think, misconceived. They assume that talents develop primarily because of incentives society offers to their possessors. But talents develop first of all because society provides their possessors with the means to develop them. And where these means are radically skewed in favor of a class or group of classes, the existence of incentives becomes abstract for all but the most exceptionally talented of the disfavored.

Suppose a situation where the great majority of people remain in the social class into which they were born. In such a situation, there *is* a restricted possibility of social mobility but, as Morris Ginsberg put it many years ago, "the social ladder so far lifts only relatively small numbers."[5] And this would indicate that social arrangements impose serious limits on the opportunity to develop one's talents, or to benefit from that development. But, as Professor Ginsberg, among others, has shown, this was precisely the situation in pre-welfare state market societies and in market societies with extremely limited welfare programs. Mythology to the contrary notwithstanding, much of the improvement in the general opportunity to develop talents that has occurred in market societies is the result of egalitarian public policies—such as labor legislation and public education—designed to *mitigate* the impact of market practices. This is hardly surprising. A system in which rewards are proportionate not merely to talent and effort but to the resources one brings into competition, and in which social conditions or the lack of resources prevents or discourages many people from developing their talents, is not calculated to maximize either the development of talents or the benefits to society that such development may provide. Indeed, the reverse of the incentive argument may be more plausible: we develop our talents in response to *opportunities*, not incentives. They develop as the means for their development are available and as the opportunities to use them are perceived. More equal conditions could make these means available to many whom the market now passes over, could create opportunities for development now hostage to lack of resources or inadequate market demand, could offer incentives to more people. These incentives may indeed be smaller than those offered to the few by market society. But the experience of the social democracies of Western Europe indicates that this is less significant than is often believed.

Apart from the question of the development of talents, equality is said to deprive individuals of the results of their efforts. Suppose, we are often asked, A sacrifices to prepare himself for a career, works long hours, postpones gratifications, and finally accumulates some wealth. Should he not get to keep the proceeds of his effort? And if he should, does this not mean that, gradually, the A's in any society will be wealthier and, therefore, will skew egalitarian distribution?

The question is enough to make one despair of reasoned discourse. But that should not surprise us. Religions are built on symbols, the religion of inequality no less than the others. And religious symbols serve at least two purposes: they discourage us from asking whether they stand for anything real, and they allow us to suppose that what they do stand for is a practice exclusively our own. So raising the battle cry, "Reward effort," convinces the true believer that the market primarily rewards effort and that critics of the market system must naturally oppose this admirable practice.

The true believer is wrong on both counts. Effort is a virtue and, in market society, virtue is much praised and little rewarded. Effort may account for the success of isolated individuals, or for the progress of people from lower middle to middle class. (Perhaps that is why the members of these classes are its most passionate supporters. They have gained the most from expending effort—satisfying, if modest, increases in wealth and self-respect.) But it cannot account for the *significant* inequalities, nor for the *pattern* of inequality that is structured into a complex corporate society. These inequalities can only come from systemic causes; and in modern corporate society this means *from the positions and resources that give individuals the power to manipulate and control* social processes, the structure of reward, the laws governing social combination, and so forth. It was not effort that built the great enterprises of industrial society. It was the capacity to control resources and exercise power, combined with the generous support of government, which granted aid liberally and enforced the law desultorily. It is power, not effort, that sustains these enterprises today.

So even if egalitarians were disposed to ignore the claims of effort, they would not be much disturbed by a system that rewarded it. It skews the distribution of wealth by too little. The hardworking executive and the dedicated physician may make more money than their employees or patients. But it cannot be so much more as to distort social distributions of wealth in ways that systematically affect capacities to act. This distortion can take place only where people are enabled to act in combination, to associate in order to increase their power over a substantial part of the social environment. And it is the nature of the association, rather than the virtuous habits of its members, that is decisive. If it were not so, the medical researcher would be as well paid as the physician who profits by his discoveries, and the engineer would partner the corporate lawyer at golf.

The second count can be disposed of more easily. Egalitarians value effort. The problem, as they see it, is precisely that market society denies most people the opportunity to develop and exercise their best efforts. A society in which some people are born into environments of tension, violence, and poverty, and others into environments that equip them only for service on assembly lines, is a society that stunts ability and discourages effort. Egalitarians do not oppose rewarding effort; they favor it. What they oppose is giving special consideration to those whose efforts happen to be abetted by the possession of substantial resources or power. The conflict, as they see it, is not between those who want to reward effort and those who do not. It is between those who want to extend the opportunity to expend effort to all and those who, while protesting their fealty to effort, want to restrict that opportunity to the privileged.

There is, finally, the question whether social equality is undermined by the advantages that some families confer on their members and that others cannot or will not. Not all children will benefit from educational and cultural advantages such as those that may be passed on by concerned or well-educated parents, or from understanding and supportive nurturing, or, for that matter, from easy access to wealth and influence. While we may wish that these advantages could be conferred on all children, it is clear that they cannot be. How much of the resulting inequality must be corrected?

The answer to this question is determined by the meaning we give to equality. There are some who believe that equality entails identity of results, or who believe it requires that everyone have the same specific opportunities. I have argued that these views are wrong. Equality does not address the distribution of opportunities, resources, or positions. It addresses the question of our capacities to act. It requires that we be able to engage in moral action on generally equal terms with all others. If conditions are such that people's capacities to act are equal, and if they are generally able to influence each other's capacities, the demands of equality are met. Particular advantages that inhere in unique social relationships and that do not seriously or systematically affect these capacities are, therefore, irrelevant. Egalitarians may acknowledge, along with the rest of mankind, that there are those whose lives will be made happier, or better, or fuller, or richer, through no effort of their own. It would, of course, be splendid if they decided voluntarily to share their good fortune with others. But they cannot be required to do it in the name of equality.

Now it is unquestionably the case that certain advantages conferred on some people are purchased by withdrawing significant capacities to act from others, and by helping to create relations of domination. But it is worth noting that these consequences chiefly follow, not from family actions, but from the existence of systematically inegalitarian social practices in the first place. Opponents of equality like to cite family differences as a leading cause of inequality, just as they like to cite differences in personal qualities or effort. But the results of social inquiry do not support them. The chief inequalities (at least in contemporary society) are produced by deep institutional and structural forces. The process of developing progressively egalitarian policies must pretty clearly be aimed at these. Egalitarians should concern themselves with the inequalities that family-conferred advantages reinforce and build upon, rather than with the advantages themselves, because the diminution of institutional and structural inequalities will radically alter the sorts of advantages that can be conferred. The family may generally be left alone on the sensible ground that, absent its relationship to institutional and structural inequalities, the advantages it could confer would be random or too individualized to affect general capacities to act.

That this will result in minor inequalities surprises no one, egalitarians least of all. For equality is not a call to perfection but to action, and it therefore shares the uncertainty and ambiguity that characterize action. To believe that equality requires an absolutely even set of chances for everyone is, as I have said, to think along with equality's enemies (for whom the attempt to inject sense into the discussion is clearly fatal), or to conceive of it as describing a settled state of affairs. But equality is neither of these things; it is a process of constantly adjusting practices that constrain general capacities for action and reciprocity. It is no more remarkable that this process be required to tolerate incidental inequalities than that liberty be required to tolerate incidental private tyrannies.

8

CIVILITY

CIVILITY AND COMMUNITY

Civility can enter political discourse on any number of grounds. On the narrowest of these, it can stand merely for the imposition of orderly procedures on the conduct of social affairs. More broadly, it can stand for a variety of moral commitments, such as the need to eliminate violence and arbitrariness, to substitute some concept or other of civilization for barbarism. This substitution sometimes takes the form of using procedures of discourse as models for social processes. One thinks of a range of such suggestions, from Dewey's linking of community with communication, to Ernest Barker's notion of government by discussion, to Jürgen Habermas' usage of communicative rationality.[1] In Chapter 4, I rejected the use of discursive models of agreement as inappropriate. What Oakeshott called "the conversation of mankind" can, after all, be taken too literally. That conversation is, of course, sometimes conducted by talk; but most often it is an intercourse of action yielding ambiguous conventions and equivocal acquiescences. And it is hard to see why, in circumstances where their relevance is clearly hypothetical, the employment of discursive procedures to construct a model of civility is much of an improvement over rationalist methods.

I have sought to give civility a much wider sense by tying it to the idea of morality as a common enterprise. The creation of moral rules and the search for agreement lead us, as I argue in Chapter 4, to come to terms with the possibility of mutual contributions to moral enlightenment and, therefore, to seek out and strengthen intersubjective forms of enlightenment. Now clearly this does not prove that civility is a common enterprise. Quite the reverse: we give a communal meaning to civility precisely because it grows out of a conception of morality as a common enterprise. But the stress on intersubjectivity and agreement alone enlarges the scope of the concept of civility and gives it a moral dimension beyond that given it by philosophers such as Ortega and Oakeshott. This dimension already excludes certain forms of association, even before it is brought into concert with equality and freedom. For instance, the forms of association suggested by civility are inconsistent with forms of association conceived in exchange terms. A society structured according to the vision of a Nozick—or, indeed, of a Hayek or a Milton Friedman—could not be a civil society because its very underpinnings would serve to discourage civil relations.

The reason for this is not far to seek. Libertarian theories such as these depend on serial conceptions of freedom and, therefore, upon a willingness to see freedom and the individuals who exercise it as tied together only by (formal) voluntary arrangements. At best, non-exchange association is possible within families, but only because the family is—like the household in earlier times—pretty much a private institution by definition. The point is that no public association can even be imagined that is not formally voluntary. But these are the opposite of the arrangements needed to maximize intersubjectivity and agreement. Philip Green makes an apposite point about Friedman that is worth quoting:

> In a revealing passage in *Capitalism and Freedom,* Friedman suggests that if four friends were walking along the street and one of them spotted a twenty-dollar bill, not only should he not be coerced into the "generous" course of action (dividing the spoils) by the other three friends, but "the generous course of action is not clearly itself the 'right' one." In one brief paragraph he thus manages to de-moralize the notions of both friendship and generosity; refuses to confront the kind of life problem that the ethic of redistribution is based on in the real world; and fobs off the amorality of chance in place of a morality of effort.[2]

In short, to accept Friedman's argument we have to do more than take a particular view of freedom or the morality of exchange; we have to be willing to redefine the very passions of friendship and relegate moral questions that relate friendship to such acts as sharing to another sphere. But what sphere can that be? How can it not apply in the conditions Friedman specifies without converting friendship into an exchange relationship? And what effect can such a conversion have on civil life?

Titmuss rightly saw the need to differentiate economic policy from social policy in order to encourage "anonymous helpfulness" in society. Social practices and structures that do this are designed to reduce alienation, encourage altruism, create integration.[3] He understood that without these too much emphasis would inevitably be put on formal, contractual relationships, with society moving toward being a place of arms-length exchanges, a haven not for moral actors but for lawyers. Such a society barely distinguishes human association from exercises of power. The need, rather, is for associations "which derive from our own characters and are not contractual in nature," or, as Mill put it, that take account "of human feelings and . . . the filiation and connexion of feelings with one another."[4]

To conceive of civility in terms of intersubjectivity and agreement is, by itself, to remove self-interested conceptions of association from consideration. This does not occur because we place civility in a full communal context. It occurs because civility so understood implies the rejection of social systems rooted in a morality of hyper-individualism. A society founded on Nozick's principles could not be a civil society because it lacks any conception of human association that could conceivably encourage the intersubjective development of moral rules. It conceives of the other not as (partly) a fellow searcher for civilization but as a competitor for scarce goods. Now there are scarce goods and we sometimes ought to compete for them. But to make the terms of that competition the terms of human association is to trivialize the significance of those goods we can pursue by other means or in common. It is to do exactly what defenders of market theory say they do not do: to take economic man to be coterminous with the human being and to mistake the freedom of human beings for that of economic contractors. Not surprisingly, the social theories implicit in such a concept of association are overly formal and advance a vision of freedom that resists being extended to the powerless—who have too little of value to exchange—and describes nicely the choices capable of being made by the powerful or rich.

POLITICAL OBLIGATION

Civility implies obligations. But what sort of obligations does it imply? In Chapter 4, I argued that morality is a common enterprise in which we engage ourselves with other moral actors. This engagement creates a community of moral actors, membership in which is inseparable from our individual identities as moral actors. This identity is the totality of our moral identity—the only way we can be identified when we engage in moral action. And as this means that every moral claim must be put forward in the name of all moral actors, every moral claim is necessarily an explicit engagement with the community of moral actors.

Community, I concluded, is a moral concept manifested in the attainment of, or search for, equality. It is not to be thought of as a particular form of public authority or social organization. And if we do not identify community first of all with public authority, we cannot identify the member of the community first of all with the citizen of the state. More than that, the fact that this conception of community goes to the very heart of moral action means that the obligations owed by members to the community of moral actors transcend the obligations owed to a state. Our primary obligations run toward the set of moral relationships implied by the concept of community—that is, toward our fellows with whom we are engaged. Only after these obligations have been satisfied can we consider the obligations we might owe the state.

Suppose, however, I can be said to have agreed to obey the state on such-and-such conditions. Can we not say that I owe a moral obligation to do what I have promised to do? The answer is painfully obvious. We can only say this where we can establish a morally relevant justification for keeping promises in the first place. Obligations, of course, are not based merely on relationships between people, or between people and institutions, but on the particular moral implications of the actions said to create obligation. These implications are governed by the moral theory of which they are a part. The principles of this moral theory, which impose limits on our choices, must also impose limits on the promises we choose to make—which is to say, on the obligations we can rightly undertake. Now since the SP's only create the framework for moral choice, and since a great deal of moral choice is the product of agreement, it is certainly true that promises can create obligations. It is also true that the moral scope and status of those promises are governed by the SP's. That is, for a promise to have moral validity, it must be consistent with the boundary implications of the SP's. My promise to enslave another creates no obligation on my part, since that promise reflects a choice I have no right to make. Nor does it matter that another person is induced to rely on my promise. Promises are sometimes held to create obligations because they are designed to induce people to rely on them, often at considerable cost. But one cannot put forward as a moral validation of an obligation expectations that themselves have no moral justification.

If the SP's have any validity, they must govern all promises and, indeed, all other actions supposed to create obligations. No promise we make may rightly contravene our engagement with the community of moral actors. So the obligations we undertake toward states are clearly subordinate to the obligations we have toward the set of moral relationships known as community.

All of this, of course, assumes that we do in fact undertake obligations to a state. I have argued elsewhere that grounding authority in consent is deceptive and sometimes morally repulsive.[5] But even if it were not so, it lends itself to fraudulent usage. To adapt Berlin's critique of positive liberty, the uses to which the concept of consent have historically been put should not give us confidence in its liberating powers. For what does it mean to say that we have agreed to obey the state on such-and-such conditions? It means that once such an agreement is constructed—once it has been built by drawing implications from a wide range of ambiguous and often conflicting behavior—its conditional nature disappears. For who is to say that the conditions have or have not been fulfilled? The individual? Or the individual in concert with a reasonable number of her fellows? But the representatives of the state typically argue that these alternatives would undercut the reasons for constructing an agreement in the first place. To make the individual person, or a number of persons, the judge of the state's performance threatens the capacity of the state to carry on its functions, and that alternative is not secured to individuals by any state. Quite the reverse: state institutions, even in democracies, raise the cry of anarchy and subversion, and cite the need for order, in demanding that they, and they alone, be enabled to judge whether the conditions on which their authority is based have been met. They do so because the state needs to monopolize authority; and once it concedes to individuals the right to judge whether it has satisfied the basic conditions upon which its authority rests, it loses its character as a state. Even where, as in American constitutional law, individuals may challenge certain actions of government, it is the state itself—through the courts—that finally decides the issue. Nor does the Constitution contemplate a challenge to the legitimacy of the government itself. We cannot expect a court to rule that the government's action has vitiated its right to govern. Where an act of consent results, *de facto*, in a state characterized conventionally by the epithet "legitimate," the act of consent is, also *de facto*, a permanent act of submission. The conditional nature of consensually validated authority is a fiction, and a shabby one at that.

It may appear that my conception of obligation is inconsistent with my emphasis on agreement. But that is not so. Agreement plays a role in the making of moral rules only as part of a structured moral process. Nothing in this process suggests that these agreements constitute, or can be taken to create, a social contract. Indeed, it suggests the *reverse*. Our claims and actions create a relationship that is the primary and most basic source of obligation. Our obligations are directed toward each other as moral actors and, necessarily, toward the community of moral actors. As moral actors are constructs and the community of moral actors a conceptual device standing for a set of moral relationships, it is correct to say that our obligations are to a set of moral ideals—bare though this set is—and to a way of life characterized by them. The primary object of such obligation is not the state or any public authority but the body of our fellow moral actors.

The logic of membership in a community of moral actors includes the mutual support by members for each other's capacities for moral action. Social obligation grows quite naturally from this relationship and does not have to be further justified by the need to obey or to create an institution to protect ourselves from chaos, violence, or barbarism. This advantage seems to me important. For while it does not do away with our need to protect ourselves against chaos, violence, and barbarism, neither does it force us to obligate ourselves to a state to do this. Nor does it force us to ignore the plain fact that public authority and its laws can be forces of barbarism as well as civilization—indeed, that this is the more usual state of affairs. Ordinary theories of obligation frequently cause more confusion than necessary when taking account of this. If obligation means obligation to an institution of public authority (such as a state) and its laws, then we must distinguish rightful or "true" authority from wrongful or "apparent" authority, must safeguard the principle of lawfulness if we attack wrongful laws, must consider whether our obligation is or is not *prima facie*, and so forth. Most of all, we must acknowledge to be true what is often manifestly false: that the obedience-hungry state is chiefly an ally in the struggle for civilization. Such truths retain credibility only among those who identify civilization with indoor plumbing and tables of organization.

We may, for one reason or other, agree to obey the state, but the obligation created by that agreement is *secondary* and *prudential*, based on the belief that the organization of the community of moral actors into a particular authoritative institutional framework is, in the circumstances, the most practicable way of creating the stability necessary to attain civility and of satisfying other social aims. But while public authority may be a pre-condition of civility and, in certain circumstances, of the attainment of freedom and equality, it also tends to go beyond the requirements of civility and aggrandize power at the expense of people's freedom and equality. This contradictory role suggests that it is best to approach public authority prudently, lending it our allegiance where it acts within the boundaries created by the SP's and denying it where it does not. The obligations we have to each other and to the SP's take precedence over this prudential obligation. They deny that we have a *prima facie* obligation to obey the state. They give us a right to disobey the state where it requires things that are inconsistent with the SP's and their clear implications, or where it subverts or retards the rights upon which the realization of the community of moral actors depends. The nature of our obligations enables us to say that we have rights against the state (or against any institution upon which authority has devolved) without having to invoke hypothetical compacts or constructive agreements.

This raises the question of how to validate the concept of rights against the state. If we are to obey public authority when it acts within the boundaries created by the SP's and disobey it when it does not, a prudent regard for the role public authority plays in the creation of civility requires that we guard against disobedience undertaken frivolously or without due consideration of its effect on authority. This issue, however, is less central than partisans of order suppose. It is not irrelevant that the state seems less concerned than publicists or lawyers with the moral dilemmas of disobedience, that it is usually quite content to punish disobedients now and leave the moral verdict to history. States generally do not show much inclination to be hobbled by philosophers' doubts when their authority is at stake. They act to punish. And the knowledge that they do so, and that the officials who act in the state's name are legally obligated to do so and generally regard that obligation as politically necessary and morally desirable, is a significant inducement to sobriety. The real question usually concerns the need, not of disobedients, but of state institutions to discipline and restrain themselves—to ensure that they are not overzealous in converting political dissent into crime, moral disagreements into evidence of sin, or modest challenges to authority into threats to civilization. Upon what principle ought they to act?

Where a particular moral view or conception of a legal right is widely shared—shared, that is, by a substantial number of people, if less than a majority—political authority cannot impose a duty that contravenes that view with the same assurance as if that duty were generally approved. We do not possess moral truth; we seek agreement. And widespread disagreement, even where we believe it to be unjustifiable, must cause us to consider whether imposing that duty is appropriate. In addition, we regard (or ought to regard) disobedience based on a widely shared view as sober, rather than frivolous, and as reflecting deeply held beliefs, if not justifiable ones. This is not, of course, an argument in favor of recognizing the legitimacy of the disobedients' view. For it may be a view that contravenes the SP's or subverts the very idea of community. Or it may be that it defies reasonable standards of evidence and logic. But if we believe in community and agreement, we are bound to treat that view with respect and toleration, even if its advocates deny these to their opponents. And this means that, where people disobey a law that imposes on them a duty inconsistent with a widely shared view, and where that act is not itself a palpable violation of the SP's, the institutions judging them ought to act with restraint and tolerance. This does not preclude condemning an act of disobedience. It merely requires giving serious respect and consideration to the views of the disobedients if they are widely shared, and imposing on them sanctions consistent with that respect and consideration.

There may be instances where the rights of the community will be asserted by single individuals and rejected by the vast majority. The institutions charged with assessing disobedience are clearly within their rights if they recognize and vindicate that assertion. More likely, of course, they will not, and vindication, if it comes, will be by posterity.

DEMOCRACY

The idea that certain constraints are rightly placed on public authority is the most conventional and uncontroversial of conclusions. Its implications, however, are neither and raise surprisingly troublesome problems. For example, it seems obvious that the known system of government most consistent with my argument is democracy. At least I shall take it to be so, on the ground that democracy is more compatible with a structured agreement process than any other system. While democracy is a very complex concept, I want to think of it, at least initially, in its barest possible form. I shall take it to stand for a system in which majorities, either participating directly or through elected representatives, determine a society's public policies. I shall call this the democratic process. I realize that this process is bound to disappoint much of the time. It often distorts the expression and communication of beliefs, takes account of interests selectively, attends first of all to the wants of the rich and powerful, and applies only intermittently to economic and social forms of domination. Still, it is the best alternative around, and so we shall have to make do.

Few people deny that the democratic process is rightly subject to some constraints. The problem is that these constraints on majority action must be imposed somehow and we are never certain exactly how. The very logic of democracy is such that imposition of constraints on its actions may, in certain circumstances, conflict with the democratic nature of public authority. This problem does not disappear merely because the constraints derive from basic structuring principles of morality. Democracy was not derived from the SP's. It is consistent with a process of creating moral rules by structured agreements. But it is also a form of politics with a separate biography, with its own dynamic derived from other theories. If morality were less ambiguous and more certifiably rationalist, I could argue that democracy is *entailed* by a particular moral theory and is, therefore, subject to its particular vicissitudes. But I have forsworn such arguments.

Many democratic thinkers are prepared to assume that certain liberties and equalities are entwined in the method of majority rule or are entailed in the democratic process because they are needed to assure that the process works as intended. For instance, since the ability to vote on policies or to run for office is radically compromised where speech is restricted, freedom of speech must be part of the meaning of democracy. So far, so good.

It is even possible to justify, according to ordinary democratic theory, reliance on a non-representative institution such as a court to oversee majority decisions. So, in the conventional majority rule/minority rights version, it is acceptable for a populace to entrust the protection of certain rights to a court, provided those rights are given some sort of formal statement or represent values fundamental to the society and identified with its practices and traditions.

But the authority of such a court is clearly limited, and any attempt by it to stretch its authority or to depart from recognized tradition will be strongly opposed and will probably fail unless validated by the representative or participatory institutions. What happens, for example, if we come to believe that a particular right, which has been neither formally stated nor traditionally accepted, is vital to effective participation in defining the terms of agreement? What happens where the possibility of action depends not simply on the control of power, but on the attainment of equal capacities? What happens where a right concerns an action once slighted but now seen to be crucial to freedom, or a choice whose prior condemnation was suffused with social superstition? In short, what happens where the putative right is an implication, not from a fundamental societal tradition or constitutional norm, but from an SP? A court cannot vindicate it. And if the representative or participatory institutions will not, ought it to remain unvindicated?

There are those who argue that, while the protection of such claimed rights is important, democracy places ultimate responsibility for it in the hands of participatory or representative institutions. They may believe that, in the long run, freedom and equality will be best protected by sustaining the integrity of those institutions, rather than by compromising that integrity to attain particular results.[6] Or they may identify democracy wholly with participatory or representative practices and accept the intercession of a non-representative institution only in very narrow circumstances.

I think that this position, while substantial, is wrong. Its major flaw is that it compromises our attempt to justify the democratic process. How, except by appealing to something outside of that process, could we justify it? We could attempt to justify it on the ground that majority rule is self-evidently right, or agree with Barber that "democracy may exist entirely without moral foundations" but be "the form of interaction for people who cannot agree on absolutes."[7] But majority rule cannot be self-evidently right or self-justificatory for at least one reason: the obligations we owe to any public authority are secondary, overriden by the primary obligation we have to the community of moral actors. So if majority rule is right, it is right only as it is constrained by the principles that structure our obligations to that community—which is to say, by the SP's, or by any other set of principles that functions in the same way.

Barber's argument is not an adequate response. Our failure to agree on absolutes does not justify our dispensing with moral argument altogether. We need to decide, for instance, what democracy means. How can we decide this without at the same time setting out both reasons for preferring it and limits to the practices we call democratic? Again, we need to know why democracy is the most appropriate form of interaction for us. It is not immediately clear that this is so. Any type of interaction must be based on some form of antecedent understanding (such as agreement, habit, tradition, love, fear, and so on, or on some combination of these), even if that understanding is limited to an acceptance of "the autonomy of practice." But is the *worth* of any particular antecedent understanding not to be thought about? Is it conceivable that people who would be satisfied not to think about it could also be united by civic education and "made capable of common purpose and mutual action by virtue of their civic attitudes"?[8] Such people seem more likely to choose other forms of government—a market form, perhaps, or a guarded form of paternalism in which governance is entrusted to an enlightened and "scientific" elite. The assumption that people who cannot agree on absolutes would necessarily turn to democracy is not an inference from history but a covert moral judgment that tacitly serves as a foundational argument.

One might want to say that democracy should be defined in terms of a democratic process and that the values that limit the authority of that process should be considered, not properly part of the definition of democracy, but merely moral limits placed on it. But in order to have any impact on the political practice of a democracy, these limits would have to have some institutional or practical manifestation. In that case, they would still limit the actions of participants or representatives and we would have to say why and under what conditions this may be done. The practical problem of deciding how to impose limits on majorities in a democracy would remain. So this argument, even if it could be sustained, would be trivial. But it cannot be sustained. Even if we agree that majority rule can be justified without recourse to outside ideals, we would be unable to define the limits or boundaries of majority rule except by employing outside ideals. But then the ideals we appeal to to set those boundaries necessarily become part of the definition of democracy. Only where we show that majority rule is self-justifying and subject to no moral limits can we define democracy in terms of process alone.

COMMON ENDS

So no definition of democracy can be phrased in terms of the democratic process alone. It must be phrased also in terms of ideals. And these cannot simply be ideals instrumental to the democratic process, but must be those we invoke in order to justify that process. Democracy is, therefore, an amalgam of process and ideals, and public authority must act within the bounds created by those ideals or forfeit its title to be obeyed.

Now it is often the case that there is a large number of actions or policy choices, many inconsistent with each other, that exist within these bounds. Occasionally, however, circumstances arise where only certain policy choices can preserve the ideals that justify democracy. Majorities, therefore, have no right to pass over or reject these choices, for to do so would be to compromise the justification of their own authority. Such policy choices I call "common ends." By "common ends," I do not mean policy choices that represent the actual or putative preferences of vast majorities of people. Nor do I mean to imply that the boundaries created by the SP's can be so closed in all circumstances as to entail specific policies. It may be that the common end, in any particular case, cannot be identified with a single "right" policy choice, but only with a narrowed range of choices. But however we qualify it, the point is that the ordinary assumptions about democratic policymaking do not hold here. The authority of the majority to make policy is constricted, and in some cases its discretion wholly eliminated, by the ideals that justify democracy.

Common ends can also be identified with rights. I have not discussed rights up to now because I have not thought it appropriate to do so. I do not think it appropriate to begin a serious discussion of them now. But it may be necessary to say a few words about rights to clarify the problem of common ends. Briefly, there are times when it is necessary to translate the claims that a member of a moral community may make into rights. Rights are means (often, but not necessarily, conceived in legal terms) for guaranteeing that members be free and equal participants in the common enterprise of moral action and in the reduction of that enterprise to civil practice. In this view, rights cannot be determined *a priori*. They are necessarily products of an interplay between the SP's and contingencies. The contents of rights cannot be specified apart from a knowledge of the social practices and conditions that affect moral action. All we can know *a priori* is this: if the SP's are to be taken to be the assumptions upon which moral action is predicted, the SP's imply certain rights. They do so because we are able to say that, in the context of given social practices and conditions, we cannot be free and equal participants in the common enterprise without being guaranteed certain powers. The SP's also direct the way we take account of practices and conditions. That is, they form a moral framework for evaluating the importance and relevance of practices and conditions.

I shall call the rights that make the SP's realizable in practice—that guarantee that I can be a free and equal participant in the enterprise of morality—primary rights. That is, they are the rights upon which the security of all others depend. But I have secondary rights as well—rights that represent the actions implicated in the agreements made in a particular society. Secondary rights reflect actions whose scope and protection may be left to be governed by agreement. We may believe that a secure protection for every sort of promissory exchange does not appear to be implicated in the capacity to participate freely and equally in the moral enterprise, or to be the sort of protection whose restriction will affect the security of other rights. So a right to recover damages for breach of contract may be limited by the agreements governing the exchange of promises.

It would be wrong to assume that primary rights are somehow logically implicated in the SP's. Primary rights still state things about morality that can only be generalizations (perhaps tacit ones) from experience. What we may say is that certain generalizations reflect more persistently perceived attributes of social practices and conditions. So we might defend free speech as a primary right because we beleive that it is decisively implicated in free and equal participation in the moral enterprise. The conviction with which we hold this view is a function, not of some intrinsic truth, but of our experience with social practices and the persistence (as we perceive it) of the association of speech with participation. Similarly, if significant economic inequalities seem persistently to bear a casual relationship to diminished participation, we are entitled to see economic equality as a primary right. Finally—returning to the contract example—suppose we are warranted in believing that the abolition of all protection of promissory exchange persistently undercuts the security of social transactions in general and, with it, confidence in the idea of a common enterprise itself. Some form of protection for promissory exchanges may be a primary right because it is persistently related to the integrity of any common enterprise. (These three rights should be seen as examples of a larger category. As the list of primary rights changes with the practices and conditions that critically affect moral action, there may be more—or fewer—primary rights than I have listed here. Similarly, the range and content of these rights may change. But I shall not discuss these things because they are tangential to my argument.)

We can include those policy choices that appear to be indispensable means to the realization of primary rights in the category of common ends. Indeed, to be able to do so puts these choices in a decidedly advantageous position vis-à-vis others: the tie to rights gives them a more defined focus and makes general agreement on, or acceptance of, their special status more likely. But this advantage brings with it a substantial danger. It might be difficult to resist the temptation to concentrate entirely on such choices and thereby convert common ends *de facto* into legal concepts. And if the conversion of common ends into legal rights strengthens the ends so converted, it also narrows our understanding of common ends in general. The political context encourages us to deal with richer and more complex understandings of action and obligation than does the more formal, and constricted, legal context. Legal precepts are more easily hardened and, while not impervious to new interpretations of experience, are less affected by them. We need to resist identifying common ends with constitutional rights in order to protect the vitality of the SP's.

In determining common ends, we do not seek to harmonize people's wants, interests, or plans of life, as we might if we sought to determine common goods or public interests. We rather seek to identify practices inseparable from the justification of democracy itself. The fact that there may be no common goods or public interests in a society—the fact that no policy can harmonize the demands of importers and exporters or farmers and bankers—is at least irrelevant. Common ends do not stand for practices implicated in our identities as maximizers of utilities. They stand for practices implicated in our identities as moral actors in a democracy.

Now as participation is clearly a common end, it would be wrong to act in a way that would critically undercut it or radically reduce its value. But it is not uncommon for conflicts to arise between a process and the ideals that justify it. Consider, for instance, a majority's disenfranchisement of, or imposition of special liabilities on, a discrete social group, or the exemption of corporate governing power from ordinary democratic control, or the failure of a society to provide some of its citizens with the resources necessary to protect their rights. In cases like these, where the unimpeded operation of the participatory or representative process would produce results in conflict with the values that justify it, the moral standing of the process may be redeemed only by restricting its operation. It may be constrained by so much as is necessary to bring it back within its justified boundaries. The nature and extent of this constraint is, of course, a matter of judgment and prudence, and there are times when a balance must be struck that restricts the process only minimally. Nothing I have written presumes otherwise, or suggests that the democratic process may be trifled with at will. I merely suggest that, where it conflicts with another common end, a choice between them must be made and that choice may involve restricting the process.

I assume that no one expects to be able to specify, in advance, all of the circumstances in which this conflict may appear. The decision as to its existence and the nature of the resolution remain matters of judgment and cannot be reduced to mechanical or quantitative formulas. But if this sort of judgment is required, who is to make it? What institution or political body should be given the responsibility? Should it be taken away from the majority and its representative institutions and given to a non-representative institution, such as a supreme court or a council of state? If it is, will not such an institution—which now has the power to determine some critical policy issues and to limit the authority of the participatory or representative institutions—come to be the chief governing body of society? And does this not reduce the democratic process to relative insignificance? If, on the other hand, the responsibility for determining common ends is given to the majority or dominant coalition itself, is the idea of common ends as limits on majority action not fatally compromised? Are claims that the SP's have been violated to be judged by the institution that has purportedly violated them in the first place? If they are, then the limits imposed on the majority are nothing more than admonitions that it decide fairly and with care. But this reduces the SP's in practice to counsels of perfection, to pious hopes, which do not bind the majority's actions. Ironically, therefore, such a procedure gives to the majority a *de facto* authority greater than that rightly exercised by any political institution.

We can find a way out of this dilemma if we dispense with the fiction that an either/or decision is required. There seems to be no definitive solution. What we can seek, rather, is to foreclose certain alternatives and create the possibility of accommodating the conflicting demands. We can do this by imposing constraints on a majority or its representatives that, while serious, do not amount to a radical displacement of its authority. Suppose we decide that common ends be determined generally by the majority or its representative institutions. This clearly poses a problem. The power of representative and participatory institutions is justifiable precisely because it is problematical. To leave the decision of whether these institutions are living within their moral constraints to the institutions themselves is to make that power less problematical. It risks giving to these institutions a *de facto* authority to convert the secondary obligations they may rightly claim into primary obligations they cannot justify. So there arises a reason to empower an institution to supervise this process. Suppose that the decisions of the representative and participatory institutions are subject to constraint by a non-representative institution, such as a council of state or a supreme court, to which members of the community can appeal. It becomes the task of this council (as I shall now call it) to monitor the majority's determination of common ends and, where it thinks it appropriate, to replace that determination with its own. As the raison d'être of such an institution, and the prestige and sense of purpose of its members, will involve the exercise of such supervisory powers, it is unlikely to see itself as a rubber stamp for the representative or participatory institutions.

It is tempting to compare such a procedure with the intervention into the political process typical of American courts. But, as I have already indicated, such a comparison is misleading. American courts rely for their authority on the law of a constitution, itself, presumably, a product of the democratic process. Clearly, as they struggle to give meaning to such vague and ambiguous concepts as due process or equal protection of the laws, the judges must turn to moral, as opposed to narrowly legal, arguments. But the use of moral argument is at least guided and bounded by legal doctrines and traditions. This is not the case of the council I propose. Its decisions should be based on its conception of the implications of the SP's and, therefore, on moral arguments entirely unconnected with legal doctrine and freed from the restraints imposed by constitutional traditions. Does this not raise a clear possibility that the council will merely seek to impose its own moral preferences on society and will, if successful, become an organ of arbitrary power?

Of course it does. But society is not helpless in the face of such action. The council I speak of does not stand alone, out of contact with the rest of the political and social system, but is encased in an institutional structure. Such a structure limits its power in several ways. First, it forces the council to compete with representative and participatory institutions for a share of the enormous amount of ambiguous, and therefore contestable, space in the decision-making arena. Since the representative institutions are necessarily stronger than the council (having access to many more political resources), they can expect to limit the latter's intrusions into this space. Second, the strength of representative and participatory institutions allows them to influence heavily the pattern of informal power relations that develop between them and the council. Third, the power of appointment, which is ordinarily in the hands of representative institutions, allows them to shape, or at least influence, the ideological composition of the council. In addition, we may impose formal limits on the council's power, such as denying it the right to initiate actions or limiting the remedies it may propose. In the context of a reasonably vital representative system, such formal limitations could clearly help to constrain the council's activities. What may result is a council that has some authority to invoke the principles of community to constrain the democratic process, but whose authority is constrained by formal limitations and by its place in the political system.

In summary, in the reduction of the SP's to civil, and therefore democratic, practice, it becomes necessary to contemplate the disturbing appearance of common ends. Admittedly, common ends are sometimes dangerous notions, for their implementation involves creating institutional arrangements that seem to exemplify what is currently called elitist interference with democratic practice. Of course, since the premise of these arrangements is that institutions abuse power, not that certain learned people know better than ordinary folk what is best for them, and since the council is subject to institutional pressures more powerful than it can summon, the epithet "elitist" is somewhat inappropriate. Still, the fact that a select council is to monitor common ends cannot be taken lightly. It deserves serious and extended study. But my purpose in this section is more limited. It is to point out the inescapable need of common ends and to indicate that means consistent with a basic respect for the democratic process exist for their enforcement. A council's potential for emasculating the democratic process can be much exaggerated. Having said this, I think I have said all that is necessary and relevant here. Consideration of details, however important, will have to wait.

INSTITUTIONALIZING CONFLICT

The reason it will have to wait is that the concept of common ends presents a much more serious problem. It is axiomatic that the basic political and social practices of a society affect the behaviors and attitudes of its members. A common life, supported by declared common ends, may create a social atmosphere that improperly elevates the obligations owed to political society to first place. The existence of a council to monitor democratic institutions may prevent those institutions from arrogating unjustifiable power. But what is to prevent *the entire political system*—participatory institutions, representative institutions, and council together—from arrogating it? Clearly, one of the most prominent factors of modern life is the extent of the moral claims of the state. The state sees itself as the march of God on earth, and its claims are underwritten by the crude tribalism so frequently mistaken for national history and social morality. The idea of common ends may supply additional legitimation that could enable the state to magnify the obligations it claims we owe it. In addition, a social life marked by a reasonable degree of community—a common life—involves acting on a recognition of the commonness of the moral enterprise. I have argued that this does not require submerging the individual in a collectivity. But a high degree of commonality nevertheless requires the creation of social arrangements that reinforce it by, for example, eliminating informal inequalities or by supporting communal norms against individualistic ones. There are various ways to do this that stop well short of tyranny. We could seek to support strong communal norms by prosecuting criminally people who act in ways that are, in the common view, morally revolting.[9] A less severe method would be to create numerous public rituals and visible symbols of community, design educational practices that would support it, and so on. We could restrict competitive behavior and require certain forms of cooperation.

No one will have failed to notice that practices like these are, in varying degrees, present in every known society and are neither inventions of the left nor phantasms of the right. The development of conventional practices that reinforce existing political arrangements seems to be inevitable. This circumstance may not be altogether tragic: it is undeniable that a moderate amount of such reinforcement is perfectly tolerable, especially where it is only infrequently accompanied by strong sanctions. A morality of agreement tied to the requirements of civility does, after all, strengthen the claim of conventional values. But much depends on the details of its implementation. It is one thing for a society to make room for and encourage the development of certain kinds of attitudes and behaviors. The practice of toleration does not, as Hobhouse strenuously argued, require us to forfeit our social visions or to refrain from pressing for their realization through reasonable and democratic channels. But it is quite another thing to *require* allegiance to them, or to condition rewards on their professions. This alternative is closer to the sort of thing that Rousseau and Sir Patrick Devlin favor, although in much different degree. It is sometimes legitimate, but requires strong justification and careful limitation. These cannot be provided by recording the feelings of outrage Devlin writes about, nor by crude majoritarian consensus, but only by the sorts of arguments that justify imposing strict closures. Even so, we cannot ignore the tendency of compulsion, once institutionalized, to develop its own impetus and, bursting past justificatory restraints, to make unexpectedly strong claims upon us. How, then, can we guard against such unjustifiable looseness and institutional abuse?

One answer is not far to seek. Nothing prevents us from limiting such coercion in a way familiar to liberal theory—by imposing legal restraints on institutions. The external political and economic arrangements of the common life would profit from widespread attitudes favoring cooperation over competition. The state may certainly provide limited support for this cooperation. By limited support, I refer to social encouragements to cooperative behavior unaccompanied by sanctions or, at worst, accompanied by minimal sanctions. Beyond such limited support lies danger. To require people to support common arrangements by imposing severe sanctions on those who want to give them only limited support, or to condition people's life-chances on their affirmation of the values of cooperation, would be revolting. Therefore, we may agree to arrangements that concern only the externals of social organization. We could then set off, against the conventions and social norms that these external arrangements nourish, a system of legal protections against the grosser sort of sanctions that the state may impose. In short, we should try to structure the political and economic institutions of society in ways that make room for and even encourage cooperative behavior without requiring such behavior (except in limited and clearly justifiable circumstances), and trust that this will create social pressures favoring cooperation. And then, because we know that conventionalism often outruns its expected limits, we should create legal protections for dissenters and generally support practices that restrict the socializing impact of institutional arrangements. This will create a tension between the pressures of convention and the pressures of support for resistance to convention.

I want to make what I am arguing clear. I am not arguing that we need to reconcile the contradictory claims of the individual and the community or, by turning to a program of checks and balances or market practices, to create social equilibrium. The point is precisely the opposite. We should seek not to *resolve* the tension generated by the conflict between conventionalism and individuality, but to *preserve* it. We should seek to structure into the arrangements of the common life a conflict between the pressures of community on the one hand and the legal practices designed to constrain such pressures on the other. Rather than accept the statist and rationalist vision of equilibrium as the optimum condition of social order, we might consider the Nietzschean vision of conflict as the midwife of freedom. It is neither foolish nor inconsistent to establish institutions and then to create constraints on them. It is merely sound policy based on a realistic appraisal of institutional behavior.

CONFLICT AND REDEMPTION

This solution will undoubtedly appear to some to be a typical example of liberal hedging, and perhaps it is. But there are times when hedging reflects not a failure of nerve or commitment but a recognition of ambiguity. If this is one of those times, may it be because that ambiguity goes to the very heart of a justifiable common life? Does it suggest that there are significant conflicts between the justifiable claims of the community and those of its members?

I am afraid that it does. To some, that is a damaging admission, an acknowledgment of inconsistency in the very framework of the moral argument. And such an inconsistency is usually thought of as a crucial failure. What unsympathetic critic does not search for one to use as proof of incompetence, or, at best, as evidence of faulty theory? We are willing to acknowledge that conflicts occur in the *application* of moral principles or that, in their delineation, ambiguities may appear that lead to inconsistent results. But we see these possibilities as shortcomings of theory and products of human inadequacy. We seek to overcome them, reconcile the inconsistencies, resolve the conflicts. We may want to argue that the application of principles affects their meanings, so that we cannot think of principles apart from their applications. If we are realists, we will likely reject the possibility of harmonizing inconsistencies and seek, instead, to create accommodations in which each principle has been suitably modified, redefined, and made to fit with the others. But what we do not want to argue is that the principles do indeed conflict and that the conflict cannot, in any real sense, be resolved. That, as I have said, is tantamount to admitting a decisive deficiency in our thinking.

But if there is a deficiency in our thinking it is the imagination of consistency where there is none, the vision of a moral theory without conflicts, a philosophy without tears, and the consequent sanitizing of social thought. A sanitized theory is a naive theory, assuming that concepts that stand for actions can be separated from the actions they stand for—and therefore from the ambiguities attendant upon them—merely by being translated into another language (logic, mathematics). But ambiguity is inescapable and moral principles are ineluctably ambiguous.

The ambiguity of ideals leads us away from the pure moral principles we hope for, and from the unalloyed virtue we identify with golden rules and rational maxims. More than this, ambiguity is not simply something to be accepted as inevitable, but something to be valued in its own right. We should not be as aware of ambiguity as we are if it were not for the diversity of visions, intentions, experiences, that give moral life its vitality. The preservation of these things is the condition of freedom's existence as well as the source of its contradictions. We need to reject the possibility of resolving moral conflict, of creating moral equilibrium, not because it is utopian, but because, as Arendt warned, it is all too attainable, and because it promises the sterility that comes from reducing moral life to a single direction.

That reduction can take place in theory and, although it is far less deadly on this level than on the practical, it presents similar problems. The gradual divorce of economic theory from human action, which led to the perfectly functioning market constructions so prominent in economists' equations, also led to an inability to theorize about actual markets and, finally, to a view that exalts such inability as exemplifying the grand scientific virtue of elegance. Certain moral philosophies long ago ceased to test their conclusions against human intentions and actions, choosing to concentrate instead on topics fit for philosophers to analyze. But far from making particular philosophical projects possible—however abstract and sterile they might appear to be—the elimination of ambiguity subverts those projects and drives them into confusion. The most elegant economists, for example, disagree strongly among themselves, disappointing those who believed that unifying theories could emerge from discourse conducted at the most general and abstract level.

Although they may seem quixotic, such projects go forward less because of a sober, reasoned perception of the need for consistency in theory than because of a *passion* for consistency. Here, as everywhere, logic appears in philosophy as a supplicant, granted its status by the passions, as Hume believed. The passion for consistency is deeply ingrained in the western imagination, finding its most powerful modern expression in the philosophical revolution begun by the medieval scholastics, carried forward by the rationalists, and ultimately identified with science itself. In social theory, its most powerful expression was the social science of the eighteenth century. Much of the impetus for that science came from the desire to diminish the power of the state and transfer crucial social functions—particularly economic ones—to society. This desire fits closely with the general trend of secularizing society: clearly, Enlightenment liberals hoped that the secularization of society would lead to a general diminution of the esteem in which the state was held. Theretofore, church support for kings and the established orders had given them a sort of divine authority. The separation of church and state was supposed to eliminate the claim to divine sanction and make authority more matter of fact and down to earth. In the end, of course, the state usurped that sense of divinity and discovered that it could coopt God and his agents to its purposes as easily as the monarchs had to theirs. But many Enlightenment liberals did not suppose that this would happen. They thought, instead, that that secularization would lead to what we should now call the demythologizing of political authority.

It was at least unfortunate that the vehicle chosen for this demythologizing was science. For the social science of the eighteenth century was a science animated by the vision of equilibrium, a science that held out, as countless moral theories had held out before, a promise of redemption. By "redemption," I do not mean to indicate that the philosophers of the Enlightenment held out the possibility of creating a new human being, or freeing human beings from the temptation to sin. There were some, naturally, who felt this way, and critics of the Enlightenment like to think of them as typical. But if the salient ideas of an age are the ideas held by its leading thinkers, that contention is indefensible.

It is hard to say that Voltaire, Smith, Hume, Fielding, Burke, Gibbon, Montesquieu, held particularly generous or optimistic views about human nature. Indeed, the prevailing literary mood of the Enlightenment was the comic—a vision of human inadequacy. That mood contrasts vividly with the mood of the succeeding Romantic centuries, which is largely a tragic one built on a vision of human sinfulness. But sin and tragedy create the possibility of redemption, while a mood rooted in human inadequacy denies us such metaphysical comforts.

But while many of the great Enlightenment figures were less naive about human nature than their successors, they were caught up by the new romance of science, especially in its secular liberal guise. The genius of secular liberalism was that it dismissed the possibility of moral and metaphysical redemption while making social redemption a scientific possibility. It did this, as I have hinted, without descending—except sporadically—to optimism or naiveté. Hobbes's picture of the natural condition of mankind—from which so much of eighteenth-century social science ultimately flows—does not reveal a particularly bracing optimism. Voltaire's writings—the histories and satires especially—are not exactly catalogues of the benevolent virtues. While it is wrong to ignore Smith's (limited) sympathy for the poor and his ambivalence toward self-interest, it is not possible to think of him as a spokesman for altruism. Bentham dismissed compassion as old-womanish and natural rights as nonsense. The triumph of eighteenth-century liberalism was its capacity to *eliminate* the human factor altogether, to create a picture of society in the Newtonian image. Science, the ultimate representation of reality, made it possible for inadequate, even sinful humans to create an objectively "natural" mechanism that would neutralize the consequences of human inadequacy. This mechanism was a social system structured so that subjective human interests could be made to conflict with one another in such a way as to lead to an equilibrium of interests. Human wants and needs, if given appropriate room to express themselves, would inexorably drive people to mutually acceptable resolutions of conflict. In Smith's immortal image, an invisible hand worked to produce a social good out of individual self-seeking. But it is worth recalling, for a moment, in what that good consisted. It did not consist in equality, in providing realistic opportunities to rise to a statistically significant proportion of the poor, in legitimating the interests of the lower classes in fulfilling their ambitions. It consisted in equilibrium, defined, in effect, as a stable system characterized by less immoderate misery for the poor and opulence for the owners of productive property. If we accept this good as a good, it is clear beyond cavil that the social science of the eighteenth century worked brilliantly, if not as brilliantly as its promoters hoped, and certainly better than any competing social conception. It produced wealth greater than had ever been dreamt of, improved the well-being of the poor, revitalized the performance of national economies, and made it possible for us to create as well as perceive harmonies of interest. And it did this by working *as a mechanism*, leaving untouched the same human inadequacies that had, in the past, created misery, corruption, and ultimate failure. In politics, its most successful application was the American Constitution—the very model of a mechanical structure, so built that factional tensions and conflicts could be played off against each other until they could be mediated and resolved. This resolution would result from the rational—which is to say, the cool and disinterested—judgment of a public-spirited leadership. To place this leadership in the hands of a propertied and (it was hoped) aristocratic class was to make such judgment likely. It was to place it in the hands of those whose interests were precisely those of the mechanism itself and who could, therefore, be trusted with its maintenace.

This vision was, as nineteenth-century critics of liberalism saw, a vision of redemption. It was a vision of human beings rescued from their state of misery and placed in a social order at once rational, enlightened, progressive, harmonious. But such an order delivered what must seem to most people a state as close to utopian as they could imagine on earth. Christ, Dostoyevsky reminded us, only promised salvation after death; the liberal state promised it here and now, thus professing a power greater than God's. Dostoyevsky's criticism was, as almost everything about Dostoyevsky was, excessive. But he did catch onto a reaction or feeling that liberalism seemed to engender—a feeling that led to the widespread and smug faith in progress that animated Europe, that restored its morale and sustained its conquests, for a century.

The promise of social science is still the promise of equilibrium, of harmony, of the end of conflict. A generation ago, Lewis

Coser cautioned us, in a splendid little book,[10] of the futility of this promise and of the problems its realization would cause. That lesson remains largely unlearned. We still seek to resolve conflicts and, in the process of doing so, to articulate theories whose elements are symmetrical, imply transitive patterns of preference, or enable us to synthesize contradictions.

But if moral action and moral ideals are ambiguous, this vision is wrong-headed. It asks us to construct a social theory on an entirely chimerical evaluative foundation—to base policy recommendations on a set of assumptions that we cannot support. Instead, we need to understand just what a loose conception of rationality implies. In imposing boundaries on moral action, we accept the possibility that, within the range of acceptable choices created by these boundaries, lie alternatives that conflict. Ambiguity and doubt characterize moral action and moral judgment. But ambiguity and doubt cannot be thought of as merely formal or foundational postulates that we may ignore once we get our theory going. If we take ambiguity and doubt seriously, we need to accept the real possibility of conflicting implications. In his need to defy the mathematicians, e.e. cummings wrote, the poet must be willing to say that two plus two is five. The social theorist undoubtedly cannot take things so far. But we do need to see that moral argument may sometimes drive us in divergent directions and, if it does, we must be prepared to face this openly.

Ambiguity, doubt, and diversity make moral contradiction both probable and legitimate. Civility is the subjecting of human action to limits. But as those limits are not entailments of rational principles, but the ambiguous and sometimes conflicting implications of ambiguous ideals, civility is the reduction of ambiguity to social practice. A civil society will impose boundaries on this conflict. It may confine it, more or less, depending on the extent to which it can close those boundaries. But it cannot, and should not, eliminate it. Civility is politics without redemption.

NOTES AND INDEX

NOTES

CHAPTER 1. THE LIMITS OF RATIONALITY

1. In this discussion, as in others, I have benefited from the analyses of Alasdair MacIntyre, *After Virtue* (Notre Dame, Ind.: University of Notre Dame Press, 1981), esp. pp. 193–203. I hope it is clear, however, that my argument about characterization is addressed to a different set of problems.

2. Does this point rely on contingent evidence, unlike the keeping of promises, which can be established analytically? I deal with this below, page 19.

3. Bernard Williams, "The Idea of Equality," *Problems of the Self* (Cambridge, Eng.: Cambridge University Press, 1973), p. 232.

CHAPTER 2. MORALITY AS A TEMPER

1. Benjamin Barber's argument that democracy may not need justification suggests a possibility. *Strong Democracy* (Berkeley: University of California Press, 1984), p. 65.

2. Burton Zwiebach, *Civility and Disobedience* (Cambridge, Eng.: Cambridge University Press, 1975), pp. 41–44.

3. Thomas Nagel, "What Is It Like to Be a Bat?" *Mortal Questions* (Cambridge, Eng.: Cambridge University Press, 1979), pp. 166–67.

4. John Rawls, *A Theory of Justice* (Cambridge, Mass.: Harvard University Press, 1971), p. 143.

5. Peter Singer, "Rights and the Market," in John Arthur and William H.

Shaw, eds., *Justice and Economic Distribution* (Englewood Cliffs, N.J.: Prentice-Hall, 1978), pp. 212–15.

6. Rawls, *Theory of Justice*, p. 204.

7. Strong support for such a vision of morality comes from Bernard Williams, *Ethics and the Limits of Philosophy* (Cambridge, Mass.: Harvard University Press, 1985), chap. 9.

8. *Talmud*, Baba Mezia, 59b, quoted in Walter Kaufmann, *Critique of Religion and Philosophy* (New York: Harper & Brothers, 1958), pp. 238–39.

9. John Stuart Mill, *Utilitarianism, Liberty, and Representative Government* (New York: E. P. Dutton, 1951), p. 43.

CHAPTER 3. THE USE AND ABUSE OF COMMUNITY

1. Leon Duguit, *Theory of Objective Law Anterior to the State*, trans. Scott and Chamberlain (Boston: Boston Book Co., 1916); David G. Ritchie, *Natural Rights* (3d ed.; London: Allen & Unwin, 1916); George Homans, *The Human Group* (New York: Harcourt, Brace, 1950); Herbert Simon, *Administrative Behavior* (2d ed.; New York: Macmillan, 1956).

2. Sidney Webb, "Historic," in Bernard Shaw et al., *Fabian Essays in Socialism* (London: Allen & Unwin, 1950), p. 54.

3. Leonard T. Hobhouse, *The Elements of Social Justice* (London: Allen & Unwin, 1950), p. 39.

4. Leonard T. Hobhouse, *The Rational Good* (New York: Henry Holt, 1921), pp. 92–93, 124–25.

5. Hobhouse, *Elements*, pp. 40–41; on the issue of synthesis, see pp. 42–46.

6. William Connolly, review of MacIntyre, *After Virtue*, *Political Theory* 10 (May 1982): 318.

7. John Dewey, *The Public and Its Problems* (New York: Henry Holt, 1927), chaps. 5, 6; Benjamin Barber, *Strong Democracy* (Berkeley: University of California Press, 1984), pp. 267–81.

8. Alisdair MacIntyre, *After Virtue* (Notre Dame, Ind.: University of Notre Dame Press, 1981), pp. 244, 245.

9. F. A. Hayek, *Law, Legislation, and Liberty*, vol. 2: *The Mirage of Social Justice* (Chicago: University of Chicago Press, 1976), p. 2.

10. *Ibid.*, pp. 2, 1; cf. Hayek, *Studies in Philosophy, Politics, and Economics* (Chicago: University of Chicago Press, 1967), pp. 162–66.

11. The evidence on this point is too massive to summarize and the point itself is too well known to require extensive elaboration. The following studies on the effects of unemployment, worker migration, and workplace practices exemplify the argument. On the effects of unemployment and migration, see M. Harvey Brenner, "Estimating the Social Cost of National Economic Policy," U.S. Congress, Joint Economic Committee, *Achieving the Goals of the Full Employment Act of 1946*, 94th Cong., 2d Sess., 1976; Ralph Catalano and David Dooley, "Economic Predictors of Depressed Mood and Stressful Life Events in a Metro-

politan Community," *Journal of Health and Social Behavior* 18 (September 1977): 292–307; Barry Bluestone and Bennett Harrison, *The Deindustrialization of America* (New York: Basic Books, 1982), pp. 63–66, 101–3, and works cited therein. On conditions of work, see Martin Carnoy and Derek Shearer, *Economic Democracy* (White Plains, N.Y.: M. E. Sharpe, 1980), pp. 177–79; Carole Pateman, *Participation and Democratic Theory* (Cambridge, Eng.: Cambridge University Press, 1970), p. 53; Robert Blauner, *Alienation and Freedom* (Chicago: University of Chicago Press, 1964), *passim*. On the impact of the market, see Robert E. Lane, "Autonomy, Felicity, Futility: The Effects of the Market Economy on Political Personality," *Journal of Politics* 40 (February 1978): 19–27.

12. On this topic generally, see Jane J. Mansbridge, *Beyond Adversary Democracy* (Chicago: University of Chicago Press, 1983), and Samuel Bowles, David M. Gordon, and Thomas E. Weisskopf, *Beyond the Waste Land* (Garden City, N.Y.: Anchor Press/Doubleday, 1983), pp. 303–51. The literature on this topic is enormous and much of it is cited in these works.

13. This point was made by Dewey, *The Public and Its Problems*, p. 213. It has been restated by Peter Laslett, "The Face to Face Society," in Laslett, ed., *Philosophy, Politics, and Society* (Oxford: Basil Blackwell, 1956), and Mansbridge, *Beyond Adversary Democracy*, pp. 270–98.

14. Robert Paul Wolff, *In Defense of Anarchism* (New York: Harper & Row, 1970), pp. 78–82; Peter T. Manicas, *The Death of the State* (New York: G. P. Putnam's Sons, 1974), chap. 6. An earlier statement of Wolff's position on community is *The Poverty of Liberalism* (Boston: Beacon Press, 1968), pp. 180–93.

15. R. M. Titmuss, *The Gift Relationship* (New York: Pantheon, 1971), pp. 209, 212.

CHAPTER 4. MORAL RULES

1. Isaiah Berlin, "Equality," *Concepts and Categories* (New York: Viking, 1979), p. 84.
2. Abraham Edel, *Ethical Judgment* (New York: Free Press, 1955).

CHAPTER 5. STRUCTURING PRINCIPLES

1. Brian Barry, *The Liberal Theory of Justice* (Oxford: Oxford University Press, 1973), pp. 88–96.
2. Gregory Vlastos, "Justice and Equality," in Richard B. Brandt, ed., *Social Justice* (Englewood Cliffs, N.J.: Prentice-Hall, 1962), p. 43.
3. I am indebted to D. A. Lloyd-Thomas for this point, which is adapted from "Equality Within the Limits of Reason Alone," *Mind* 88 (October 1979): 549.

4. Ronald Dworkin, "What Is Equality? Part 2: Equality of Resources," *Philosophy and Public Affairs* 10 (Fall 1981): 283–345.

5. John Rawls, *A Theory of Justice* (Cambridge, Mass.: Harvard University Press, 1971), p. 544.

CHAPTER 6. FREEDOM

1. William E. Connolly, *The Terms of Political Discourse* (2d ed.; Princeton, N.J.: Princeton University Press, 1983), p. 143.

2. The *locus classicus* for the argument that not enabling one to act does not make him unfree is, of course, Felix Oppenheim, *Dimensions of Freedom* (New York: St. Martin's Press, 1961), pp. 68–72, 81–86. My argument is an attempt to deal with the problem generally, not to answer Oppenheim specifically.

3. Robert Nozick, *Anarchy, State, and Utopia* (New York: Basic Books, 1974). In the remainder of this discussion of Nozick, page references appear in parentheses in the text.

CHAPTER 7. EQUALITY

1. J. R. Pole, *The Pursuit of Equality in American History* (Berkeley: University of California Press, 1978), p. 6.

2. Ralph K. Winter, Jr., "Poverty, Economic Equality, and the Equal Protection Clause," in Philip B. Kurland, ed., *The Supreme Court Review—1972* (Chicago: University of Chicago Press, 1973), pp. 63, 66. Winter's admission that few people argue for an "absolutely equal distribution of income" (p. 63) might allow him to escape the charge of caricature, were it not for the fact that he sees it necessary to base his analysis on just such a manner of distribution.

3. R. H. Tawney's characterization is in *Equality* (4th ed., rev.; London: G. Bell & Sons, 1952), p. 92. Matthew Arnold's superb piece is "Equality," *Mixed Essays* (New York: Macmillan, 1903).

4. Examples, respectively, are Thomas Hobbes, *Leviathan* (Oxford: Basil Blackwell, 1957), chap. 13; Andrew Hacker, "Creating American Inequality," *New York Review of Books*, March 20, 1980, pp. 27–28; Gregory Vlastos, "Justice and Equality," in Richard B. Brendt, ed., *Social Justice* (Englewood Cliffs, N.J.: Prentice-Hall, 1962), pp. 48–53.

5. Morris Ginsberg, "Interchange Between Social Classes," *Economic Journal* 39 (December 1929): 565.

CHAPTER 8. CIVILITY

1. See, e.g., John Dewey, *The Public and Its Problems* (New York: Henry Holt, 1927), chaps. 5, 6; Ernest Barker, *Reflections on Government* (Oxford: Clarendon Press, 1942), esp. chap. 2; Jürgen Habermas, *The Theory of Commu-*

nicative Action, vol. 1, trans. Thomas McCarthy (Boston: Beacon Press, 1984), *passim*.

2. Philip Green, *The Pursuit of Inequality* (New York: Pantheon, 1981), p. 218. The quoted passage is from Milton Friedman, *Capitalism and Freedom* (Chicago: University of Chicago Press, 1962), p. 165.

3. R. M. Titmuss, *The Gift Relationship* (New York: Pantheon, 1971), p. 212, and chaps. 12 and 14 generally.

4. *Ibid.*, p. 212; John Stuart Mill, "Bentham," *Essays on Politics and Culture*, ed. Gertrude Himmelfarb (Garden City, N.Y.: Anchor Books/Doubleday, 1963), p. 102.

5. Burton Zwiebach, *Civility and Disobedience* (Cambridge, Eng.: Cambridge University Press, 1975), pp. 37–62.

6. The most persuasive recent statements of this view are by the late Alexander Bickel. See his *Morality of Consent* (New Haven, Conn.: Yale University Press, 1975) and *The Supreme Court and the Idea of Progress* (New York: Harper & Row, 1970). For other versions, see Justice Felix Frankfurter's concurring opinion in *Dennis v. United States*, 341 U.S. 494, 555–56 (1951), and his essay, "John Marshall and the Judicial Function," in Philip B. Kurland, ed., *Felix Frankfurter on the Supreme Court* (Cambridge, Mass.: Belknap Press, 1970), pp. 545–48; Learned Hand, *The Bill of Rights* (Cambridge, Mass.: Harvard University Press, 1958); Philip B. Kurland, *Politics, the Constitution, and the Warren Court* (Chicago: University of Chicago Press, 1970), chap. 5, esp. pp. 204–5.

7. Benjamin Barber, *Strong Democracy* (Berkeley: University of California Press, 1984), p. 65.

8. *Ibid.*, pp. 64, 117.

9. This position was given its most forceful statement by Sir Patrick Devlin, *The Enforcement of Morals* (Oxford: Oxford University Press, 1968), chap. 1.

10. Lewis Coser, *The Functions of Social Conflict* (New York: Free Press, 1956).

INDEX

Accommodation, 41; and common good, 60; and SP's, 124–25

Action, 3; and agreements, 101–3, 105; capacity of moral actors to engage in, 118; characterizing, 3–8; complexity of, 4; equality seen in terms of, 118–19, 132, 157–18, 162–13; freedom as tied to, 152; moral, as activity of equals, 117; and opportunity, 117–19; and power, 118–19

Agreement: ability to define the conditions of, 111; as action, 98–103, 105; creation of moral rules by, 92, 109; and elite influence, 100–10; and imposition, 94, 102–3; justification of, 92; limited requirements of, 110–11; and political obligation, 182–84; as requiring limited equality and freedom, 110–11

Altruism, 33, 179; in intimate communities, 80

Ambiguity, 3–8, 20, 203; and accommodation, 41; and equality, 164–65, 176; and freedom, 122–23; of ideals, 23–26, 42–45, 48–49, 199; introduced into ideals, 37; in law, 38–39; and moral rules, 85–87, 88; and rationality, 21, 43

Arendt, Hannah, 199

Aristotle, 42

Arnold, Matthew, 168

Art: and ambiguity of ideals, 43, 45–49; relation to referents, 16–17

Avant-garde, 47, 48

Baeck, Leo, 149

Barbarism, 95–96, 108, 109; defined, 94

Barber, Benjamin, 65, 187

Barker, Ernest, 177

Barry, Brian, 114

Bentham, Jeremy, 201

Berlin, Isaiah, 85, 121, 181

Briffault, Robert, 4

Burke, Edmund, 68, 201

Butler, Bishop Joseph, 30

Carlyle, Thomas, 47

Characterization, 3–8, 94–95; broad, 50, 51; and categorical laws, 7; and SP's, 107–8

Chelm, 41

Civility: and common ends, 189–95; and community, 177–80; and creativity, 109; defined, 94; and democracy, 185–95; and freedom, 6; as fundamental project of morality, 108; and hyper-individualism, 178–80; and maximization, 108, 110; and political obligation, 180–85; and rejection of redemption, 203; as SP, 108–10; threats to, 95; and toleration, 97; and toleration of conflict, 196–203

Closure, 87, 89–90, 106

Coherence, and rationality, 20, 21

Commanding intuitions, 51, 129

Common ends, 189–95; and rights, 189

Common enterprise, 103, 106; and agreement, 112; and moral claims, 125; morality as, 93, 103, 126, 131, 133, 177–78; and primary obligations, 180

Common good, 57–64

Common life, 83, 133; constraints on social arrangements of, 196–98; defined, 125, 134; delineation of SP's as delineation of, 125–26, 134

Community, 39, 58, 64; as basic element in moral theory, 83, 126, 133; and civility, 177–80; and communication, 65, 177; conservative theory of, 68–76; Dewey's vision of, 65; and equality, 125, 133–34; and freedom, 133–36; MacIntyre's vision of, 65; of moral actors, 125–26; and politics of intimacy, 76–81

Connolly, William, 64, 136

Conrad, Joseph, 16, 45

Consent: ambiguities of, 27–29; dangers of, 181–82

Conservatism: failure of theory of community, 71–76; theory of community, 68–70

Coser, Lewis, 202–3

cummings, e.e., 203

Democracy, 161; as amalgam of process and ideals, 189; and civility, 185–95; and common ends, 189–95; and council of state, 186–87, 192–95; as process of majority rule, 186, 187–88, 192

Devil's Disciple, The (Shaw), 47

Devlin, Patrick, 196

Dewey, John, 9, 64, 65, 110, 177

Dickens, Charles, 134

Disraeli, Benjamin, 34

Don Giovanni (Mozart), 46–48

Dostoyevsky, Fyodor, 202

Duguit, Léon, 58

Durkheim, Emile, 58

Dworkin, Ronald, 119

Edel, Abraham, 93

Elijah, 121

Elites, common interests of, 67

Entailment, 20

Equality: action as principal subject of, 118–19, 132, 134, 144, 157–58, 159, 162; ambiguities in, 164–65, 176; and common good, 63; of condition, 158–61; and development of individual talents, 171–73; and distribution of resources, 158, 159; and family-conferred advantages, 175–76; and freedom, 118–19, 132, 133, 134, 141–42, 154–55, 158, 171–72; of moral actors, 116–17; natural, 168–71; objections to, 165–76; as process of equalizing, 162–65; and reciprocity, 119–20, 125, 159; and rewards for effort, 173–75; social, 157–63; as SP, 110–20

Equilibrium, 164; dangers of, 199–200; preventing, 197–98; and social science, 200–203

Experience: common store of, 93; and rationality, 31; tacit reliance on by Kant, 19

Fielding, Henry, 201

Foucault, Michel, 64

Francis, St., 155

Freedom: and absence of restraint, 142–45; anticipated justifiability of, 137; as capacity to act, 120, 142, 143, 151–55; communal basis of, 36, 133, 145–47; as descriptive concept, 136–38; and equality, 118–19, 132, 133, 134, 141–42, 154–55, 158, 171–72; exercise of, and restraint of others, 119, 139–40, 141, 144, 148–49, 150–51; and individualism, 135, 136–40, 147–51; justification of, 121–23; lack of, distinguished from suppression of, 145; and membership, 132, 134–35, 140; and obligation to enable, 140–42, 145–47, 154–55; and reciprocity, 125, 139–47, 154–55; serial conception of, 139, 178; of speech, 39; as SP, 120–23

Freud, Sigmund, 110

Friedman, Milton, 178, 179

Gibbon, Edward, 201

Ginsberg, Morris, 172
Green, Philip, 178

Habermas, Jürgen, 177
Hegel, G. W. F., 9, 33, 40
History, relation of, to referents, 17–18
Hobbes, Thomas, 122
Hobhouse, Leonard T., 59–62, 63, 65, 196
Holmes, O. W., Jr., 53
Hume, David, 20, 29, 95, 200, 201

Ideals: ambiguity of, 23–26, 42–45, 48–49, 199; ambiguity introduced into, 37; and broad characterizations, 50; defined, 23; imperfectly developed, 50; as mood or temper, 50–52; shaped by practices, 29–36
Individualism, 39, 65; failure of, 66–68; and freedom, 135, 136–40; hyper-, and civility, 178–80
Inequality: basis of appeal of, 166; distinguished from difference, 169; religion of, 165, 166, 173
Intentions, 3; explored through action, 5
Interests, 31–35
Interpretation, 37–38
Intersubjectivity, 37, 178, 179
Intimate communities: and bonds of sympathy, 79–80; and formal procedures, 78–79; and reduction of altruism, 79–80; and toleration, 80–81

Justification, 26–29

Kant, Immanuel, 5, 6, 7, 19, 42, 95

Locke, John, 28, 29

MacIntyre, Alasdair, 46, 64, 65, 85
Man and Superman (Shaw), 47–48
Manicas, Peter T., 77
Mark, Gospel of, 49
Matthew, Gospel of, 49
Maximization principle. *See* Civility

Membership: in community of moral actors, 125–26; and freedom, 134–35
Mill, John Stuart, 47, 52, 59, 179
Moliere (Jean Baptiste Poquelin), 24
Montesquieu, Charles Secondat, Baron de, 201
Moral actor: defined, 116; as equal of all other moral actors, 116–19; as member, 125–26
Morality: as common enterprise, 93, 103, 126, 131, 133, 177–78; as indicative, 106, 121, 123, 126; purpose of, 94
Moral rules: and agreements, 90; and ambiguity, 85–87, 88; as boundary-markers, 86–90; closure of, 87, 89–90, 106; and experience, 93; imposition of, 90–91, 103; as precepts, 85–86
Mozart, Wolfgang Amadeus, 46, 47, 48

Nagel, Thomas, 31
Newton, Isaac, 109, 201
Nietzsche, Friedrich, 47, 58, 85
Nisbet, Robert, 68
Nozick, Robert, 83, 147–51, 178, 179

Oakeshott, Michael, 177, 178
Objectivity, 37–38
Opportunity: to define the conditions of agreement, 119–20; equality of, 160; relation to moral action, 117–19
Ortega y Gasset, José, 172, 178

Pareto optimality, 62
Patriarchy, 36
Paul, St., 121
Plato, 9
Pole, J. R., 165
Political obligation, 180–85; community as primary object of, 182–83; and disobedience, 184–85; state as secondary object of, 183–84

216 *Index*

Power: to act, 118; relation to moral action, 119
Process: democratic, 186, 187–88, 192; equality defined in terms of, 163–65

Rationality, 3–21, 113–14; and ambiguity, 21, 42; and creativity, 52, 53; and envy, 33; exclusively valid conception of, 8–11; and experience, 31; and interests, 31–35; loose version, 19–21, 106–8; as reconstructive argument, 19–21, 51–53; Weberian conception of, 9
Rational person: as male, 35–36; properties of, 31–32
Rawls, John, 15, 30–36, 52, 62, 100, 114, 115, 131, 141
Reciprocity. *See* Freedom
Redemption, 200–203; civility as rejection of, 201–2; 203 and Enlightenment social science, 201–2
Referents: and art, 16–17; defined, 11; function of, 12–14; and history, 17–18; modifying effects of, 16–19; store of, 17; and universality, 14–15
Restraint: as causal concept in analysis of freedom, 142–45; and intentions, 144; poverty as, 143–44
Rights: and common ends, 189; defined, 190; primary and secondary, 190–91; against state, 184–85; vested, 147
Ritchie, D. G., 58
Rousseau, Jean Jacques, 63, 196
Russell, Bertrand, 9

Sartre, Jean Paul, 20, 121

Seriality, 139, 178
Shaw, Bernard, 37, 46, 47, 48, 101
Singer, Peter, 32
Smith, Adam, 201
Social science: Enlightenment version of, 200–201; and equilibrium, 200–203; and redemption, 201–2
Structuring principles (SP's), 105–26, 129–31, 181, 184, 185, 186, 187, 189, 190, 191, 194; accommodations among, 124–25; and common life, 125–26, 134; differentiated from categorical principles, 107; political character of, 131–32, 134; priorities among, 123–25; relation to experience, 107–8. *See also* Civility; Equality; Freedom

Tawney, R. H., 141, 165, 168
Temper, moral ideals as, 50–52; relation to moral rules, 87–90, 107, 124
Titmuss, Richard M., 79–80, 179
Toqueville, Alexis de, 40
Torah, 49
Traditions, as elite interests, 71–72, 74–75

Universality, 14–16; of SP's, 107–8
Utilitarianism (Mill), 52

Vlastos, Gregory, 114–15
Voltaire (François Marie Arouet), 201

Webb, Sidney, 59
Weber, Max, 9
Williams, Bernard, 15
Winter, Ralph K., Jr., 167, 168
Wolff, Robert Paul, 77